PHILIP SCHLESINGER

Putting 'reality' together

BBC news

CONSTABLE
London

First published in Great Britain 1978
by Constable and Company Limited
10 Orange Street London WC2H 7EG
Hardback ISBN 0 09 462040 7
Paperback ISBN 0 09 462050 4

Copyright © 1978 by Philip Schlesinger

Set in Monotype Times
Printed in Great Britain by The Anchor Press Ltd
and bound by Wm Brendon & Son Ltd
both of Tiptree, Essex

IN MEMORY OF MY FATHER

'Ne hagyd magad . . .'

Acknowledgements

My acquaintance with this book first began some time ago, in late 1971. If our relationship has been a little longer and less harmonious than first envisaged, I can only reflect that while life makes strange bedfellows, eventually, for one reason or another, someone *does* get out of bed. Parting with this particular paramour is a sweetness unmixed with sorrow. During the course of our relationship many others, one way or another, became involved, and sustained us through difficult times. I should like to thank them.

First there are those who allowed me to scrutinize their activities and to pursue them with questions: the newsmen of the BBC. They were most co-operative. Permission for access to the BBC's national news operation came from Mr Desmond Taylor, the Editor of News and Current Affairs. In the News Departments my work was made much easier by the Editors: Mr Derrick Amoore and later Mr Andrew Todd at Television Centre, and Mr Peter Woon at Broadcasting House. I am especially grateful to Mr Gerard Slessenger and Mr Stan Taylor for bearing the brunt of my importunings. Many others in BBC News gave me generous help, but are not named here for reasons of confidentiality. I am particularly obliged to those who read, and commented on, an earlier draft of this book.

This book began its life as a PhD thesis at the LSE, and I thank Michael Burrage and Ernest Gellner for supervising it through that stage. (My research while at the LSE was supported by the Social Science Research Council.) Especial thanks go to John Downing, a sustaining friend and acute critic throughout the time of writing; to Philip Elliott for his meticulous and stimulating critical assaults on successive drafts; and to Jeremy Tunstall for his general encouragement and extensive commentaries on earlier versions. I should also like to thank those others who were so generous with their time and help, particularly at an early stage of the work: Jay Blumler, David Cram, Gregory Clegg, Ian Jarvie, Gladys Lang, Kurt Lang, Robert Peck and Malcolm Warner.

There are two members of my family without whose indispensable support this book would never have seen the light of day. My brother

Ernest gave me true fraternal aid in the shape of a home and the facilities for work when I was unemployed. My wife Sharon some-how managed to accept my long-standing and curious passion for writing this book with tolerance and humour; but no words are adequate to thank her.

It goes without saying, however, that the guilt of authorship is mine alone.

P.S.

May 1977

Contents

	Acknowledgements	7
1	Introduction	11
2	The formation of BBC news	14
3	The production of radio and television news	47
4	A stop-watch culture	83
5	The missing link: 'professionalism' and the audience	106
6	The mediation of control (1): the editorial system	135
7	The mediation of control (2): corporate ideology	163
8	The reporting of Northern Ireland	205
9	The limits of change	244
	Notes and references	273
	Bibliography	285
	Index	293

1

Introduction

Every day millions of people watch or listen to the news broadcast by the BBC. But how is that news actually put together in the BBC's newsrooms? And how does the way in which it is assembled result in a specific version of reality?

These questions are the starting-point of this book, which examines the practices and ideology which lie behind the making of the news by Britain's most prominent broadcasting organization.

Based as it is on extensive inside observation of the BBC's radio and television news departments, this study is the first such full-length analysis of how they construct those daily pictures of reality we receive. An enquiry into the nature of the BBC's news organization cannot, in some measure, avoid being a study of the BBC itself, of aspects of its organizational style and milieu, its corporate ideology, and its view of the place it occupies in contemporary British society. Probably, there are few British organizations which arouse such interest, both at home and abroad, as the BBC. It is an 'institution', and its sheer size and cultural and political weight ensure that it is rarely out of the public eye.

The fieldwork for this book was conducted in the national newsrooms at Broadcasting House and Television Centre in London. As a sociologist I was trying to grasp how the world looks from the point of view of those being studied. The amount of access permitted by the BBC afforded a genuine opportunity for an immersion in the newsman's world-view, and the possibility of experiencing the atmosphere of a politically exposed organization which lays some stress on the need for ideological self-control on the part of its personnel. Such extended opportunities for direct observation in British broadcasting organizations have been rare.[1] I hope that my having seen the 'inside' will to some extent meet the criticism put forward by many newsmen during fieldwork, and by journalistic critics of media sociology, that sociologists' analyses are incorrect because they are ill-informed and 'don't know what it's really like'.[2]

To arrive at a sociological analysis, however, one must go beyond immersion. One must become disengaged and reconstruct the data gathered in terms of a number of themes deriving from a sociological perspective.

These themes are crystallized in the chapters which follow, and this book may be read as an answer to the following questions:

How did BBC news develop, and how was its growth affected by the state and by competition in the media industries? And how have these continued to affect it?

What sort of work processes have to be gone through before a news bulletin hits the air? And is such news really the product of accidents of space and time or is it rather the result of heavily routinized activity?

What sort of effect does the journalistic obsession with being up-to-date have on the news, and what are its origins?

Are the BBC's journalists producing news for an audience they actually know – or are they producing news according to their own 'professional' intuitions?

How does a vast organization such as the BBC manage to control the way in which its newsmen produce stories? And are those newsmen really as free from control as they think?

Is the BBC's news really 'impartial'? And can it realistically claim that it is, in view of its position in British society and its relationship to the state?

Why did the BBC have to reject explicitly its customary policy of 'impartiality' in its coverage of the Northern Ireland crisis, and how has this subsequently affected its news?

Can 'the news' easily be changed (assuming that change is desired) or are the present structures of news broadcasting so constricting that there is little room for manoeuvre?

As this book will show, the answers from an outside sociologist diverge from those given by the BBC's journalists. I have viewed the BBC's claim to 'impartiality' more sceptically than BBC newsmen will like. But their own view of the claim is not simply a matter of preference but one of necessity. They *could not* reject the central tenet which legitimizes their activity because it plays an indispensable role in their belief-system. This limits their own evaluation of what they do. Similarly, it would be difficult for BBC-men to accept the argument pursued here concerning their record over Northern Ireland, as it throws doubt on the justifiability of the BBC's claim to have acted independently of the state.

Two methods were used in gathering most of the evidence to support the arguments developed here.[3] Direct observation took place on three different occasions. Such separate pieces of fieldwork allowed a check on earlier perceptions of the news operation and the longer term development of particular lines of investigation. The first observations were made during 1972–73 when some forty days in all were spent inside the radio and television newsrooms. These were supplemented by further days in 1974. This first phase consisted of separate two- and three-day stints during which a picture of the overall organization was pieced together, and some of the main themes of this book were first identified. The later phases were more concentrated, and once familiar with the basic procedures and ideas, I was able to investigate and develop the analysis more closely. During August and September 1975 I spent three weeks at Radio News. And in July and August 1976 I spent a similar period at Television News. Going in on successive occasions helped to establish long-term contacts, and to develop both a sense of change and of continuity.

The other method I used was the interview. During the first phase of access I interviewed ninety-five members of the BBC's news staff. They occupied positions at every level of the hierarchy, and worked in all sectors of the news operation: reporting, editing, producing and technical support. About half of these interviews were 'formal', the rest were loosely structured discussions around a number of recurring points. Each interview or discussion lasted an hour. During the later two phases thirty more interviews were conducted, and extensive discussions held with twelve journalists, who had been particularly good informants, and with whom I had maintained contact throughout much of my research.

In all, therefore, the chapters which follow are based on detailed interviews with more than 120 of the BBC's news staff, and ninety full days' observation (totalling some 1,260 hours) spread over four years.

2

The formation of BBC news

An historical sketch of the development of broadcast news in Britain may be guided by a number of straightforward propositions. Until the Second World War, the BBC's news broadcasting was exceedingly limited in its time and resources. Its growth before and after that year was occasioned by two major crises. The first, the General Strike of 1926, was a national crisis. The second was international: namely, Britain's involvement in the Second World War. The War created a special link between the BBC, a key national institution and, the British people and, indeed, peoples on the European Continent under German occupation. Central to this link was the role played by news. A particular, and to a certain extent, enduring idea of the 'BBC's news' was developed in the national culture. During the War, as during the General Strike, the BBC became an instrument of state information policy. Its key role, on both occasions, provided the opportunity for breaking the trammels imposed by press and news agency interests which saw broadcast news as a worrying competitor.

Commercial and political forces, therefore, interacted to shape the growth of broadcast news. The impact of the economic sphere is especially clear from events after the War when major changes in the form and content of news flowed directly from the creation of the commercial television network which broke the BBC's monopoly. This anyway took place in the context of the rise of television to cultural pre-eminence. The history of broadcast news mainly becomes the history of television news, and the impact on news production of commercial and televisual values.

ORIGINS, 1922–26

To consider the origins of BBC News from the vantage-point of the present is to realize how considerable are the changes of the past fifty-five years, but also to note considerable continuity. The BBC began its organizational life as a commercial company, set up by a combine of six radio manufacturers. It was no ordinary company, being a monopoly licensed by the Post Office, and its revenue was derived from the original ten-shilling licence fee payable to the

Post Office by those who bought BBC-marked wireless sets, and received its broadcasts.[1] Monopoly was the British solution to the 'chaos of the ether' characterizing the United States, with its proliferation of commercial companies. British broadcasting began within a framework of state-regulation, although not one of direct state-ownership.

From the outset the broadcasting of news posed tricky problems for the new British Broadcasting Company. Press interests in Britain (and in America and Sweden, for example[2]) saw broadcasting as a directly competitive medium. Accordingly, they sought to limit the likely impact of that competition by imposing restrictions. So, the broadcasting of news was limited to between 7 p.m. and 1 a.m., a restriction known as the 'seven o'clock rule'. The BBC's first news bulletins, moreover, were not produced by its own staff, but rather sent over the wires by a consortium of news agencies, and formally attributed to them.[3]

This latter arrangement was of the utmost importance in influencing broadcast news as a cultural form. Broadcasting began by incorporating wholesale press definitions of news value, as the earliest broadcast news was agency-produced. News agency values are based on a specific conception of 'objective reporting' which developed in the late nineteenth century, and which, as Carey has pointed out, was 'grounded in a purely commercial motive: the need of the mass newspaper to serve the politically heterogeneous audiences without alienating any significant segment of [them]'. This strategy was 'subtly raised into a canon of professional competence and an ideology of professional responsibility'.[4]

An interesting affinity exists between the news agency values of 'impartiality', 'accuracy' and 'factuality'[5] and those characterizing today's public service news broadcasting. Both, by claiming to produce unsullied information, based upon a multiplicity of sources, appeal to the same Western liberal doctrine of truth. While agencies developed these notions as part of their economic logic, broadcasting, as we shall see, developed them as part of its political logic.

Furthermore, the press's conception of news as daily intelligence was straightaway embodied in the early broadcast product. The fact that immediacy and topicality were limited by the agreement did not mean that they would not eventually be striven for, as natural extensions of this approach to news.

The first public hearings on the development of broadcasting also played their role in structuring a 'neutral' news approach into BBC output. The Sykes Committee, which reported in 1923, and was the first of what has become a continuing series of reviews of broadcasting policy and practice, noted the official desire for 'uncoloured news' from the BBC.[6] At the hearings the press representatives reaffirmed their view that the BBC should not collect news, and that the proper arrangement required the content of the news to be dictated by the experts – the newspapers and agencies. There was considerable resistance to the BBC's broadcasting of key events such as the King's Speech, the Boat Race, and racing and football results. The press and agencies argued there was a need to restrict the potentially unfair competition of a monopoly.[7]

The BBC's Managing-Director, John Reith, continued in his efforts to build up news and outside broadcasts. By March 1924, the BBC still had to live with the seven o'clock rule. However, some restrictions on the broadcasting of ceremonies, speeches, and official functions were removed, a move towards the Sykes Committee's recommendation that news and special events broadcasting should be gradually extended. Asa Briggs, historian of the BBC, has summed up the position in the early years as follows: 'It was not until January 1927 – in the first month of the new Corporation – that the BBC was given freedom to arrange early news bulletins, running-commentaries, and eye-witness accounts.'[8]

The event which produced this significant shift, leading to a brief waiving of the agreement with the press and news agencies, was the General Strike of 1926. Maurice Gorham has rightly judged it the 'greatest landmark in the early history of British radio'.[9] It was the first of a series of critical junctures affecting the development of news. The General Strike, which naturally affected the production and distribution of newspapers, thrust radio news broadcasting into a position of prominence, and created the opportunity for regular and extensive outputs outside the hours decreed by the newspaper publishers.

Here is not the place for a detailed review of these events, and full accounts are to be found elsewhere.[10] However, a few comments concerning the historical evidence are essential. The virtual absence of other major means of communication meant that the BBC's news service assumed especial importance in the information policy of the state. There has been some dispute over whether, as the official BBC myth has it, the organization retained its 'independence' and produced 'impartial' news, during the Strike. Or, whether, on the other hand, critics who argue that it was subordinated to the needs of the state are right.

Briggs, in his detailed account of news policy during the Strike, argues that the BBC 'retained a precarious measure of independence'.[11] Much hangs on what is meant by 'independence'. For Briggs, it would seem to mean that no clear-cut state take-over of the BBC occurred at the hands of the Baldwin Government. In this sense, 'independence' is simply a *formal* matter. There is ample evidence, produced by Briggs himself, and also in the Diary of the Managing-Director, Reith, that the BBC simply did as the government asked.

For example, the government refused to permit the BBC to allow Ramsay MacDonald, the Leader of the Opposition Labour Party, to broadcast during the Strike. Nor, indeed, were any other trade union or Labour Party leaders allowed to do so, despite their requests. Reith noted, as well he might, 'they will not say we are to a certain extent controlled and they make me take the onus of turning people down'.[12] Yet another speaker rejected by Reith at the Government's request was the Archbishop of Canterbury, who wished to put a conciliatory message to both coal-owners and miners, the main parties to the dispute. There were, in addition, 'editorials' broadcast during the Strike, which made appeals for calm, and for a brief while after its conclusion pushed the line that the miners, who remained on strike after the capitulation of the TUC, ought to settle.

Tracey, in a recent re-examination of the Strike, has argued that 'Basic decisions on content were in effect being made by the Deputy Chief Civil Commissioner, Davidson [the government official who liaised with the BBC], rather than by Reith.'[13] Certainly, links between the BBC and elements of the government during the emergency occasioned by the Strike were very close, to the extent of sharing offices at the Admiralty Building, as well as jointly formulating news policy.

In effect, the BBC's personnel were mobilized, with the Company itself being declared an 'essential service' by the government 'so that no member of the staff could volunteer for other duties'.[14]

But the connection between the BBC and the state went further than the discernible organizational links. There was also an ideological consonance between the views of Reith and those of the 'moderate' members of Baldwin's Cabinet. Reith, like the government, took the view that the Strike was a threat to the Constitution. The BBC's position was set out in a famous memorandum signed by its Chairman, Lord Gainford:

> As the government are sure they are right both on the facts of the dispute and on the constitutional issues, any steps which we may take to communicate the truth dispassionately should be to the advantage of the government.[15]

This view was expressed even more succinctly in the celebrated Reithian syllogism, found in a memorandum to Davidson during the Strike:

Assuming the BBC is for the people, and that the Government is for the people, it follows that the BBC must be for the Government in this crisis too.[16]

It was quite consonant with this position for a directive to have been sent from London to all station directors asking that 'nothing calculated to extend the area of the strike should be broadcast'.[17] Clearly, this partial definition of the truth aligned the BBC directly with the established capitalist order against the strike, which was perceived as a disruptive and potentially insurrectionary phenomenon. The Strike was, therefore, a critical juncture for the BBC: it was henceforth to be defined as 'an organization within the constitution', and given that constraint, 'impartiality' was permissible.[18]

Some crucial points need to be considered. First, the BBC was mobilized to act as an instrument of state information policy. But this mobilization took place in a manner designed to maintain the BBC's credibility. Thus, it produced 'factual' news, but this was linked, as Tracey has argued, to a clear-cut propaganda end – namely, the defeat of the Strike. Even Briggs, who is sympathetic to the BBC, admits that there was a 'natural bias' in the BBC's approach to the government's version of events.[19] In all probability, this was due less to a lack of sympathy with working-class goals and methods, than to a recognition of the structural necessities which held the BBC in thraldom to the possessors of state power.

A second major point is the myth of independence which has been fostered about the BBC, and remains extraordinarily persuasive. The government had the powers necessary to commandeer the BBC. It did not do so. Rather, a subtle relationship evolved which was far from the crude take-over advocated by Winston Churchill. Instead, the BBC was politicized by making it into an emergency service, and incorporating its top echelons into the government information-machine, run by Davidson. There was nothing so crude as planting a censor in the makeshift newsroom. It simply was not necessary as Reith and his staff knew what had to be done, and moreover, fully accepted its propriety. This strategic use of the BBC supports the view that it was seen by Baldwin and Davidson as having a distinctive part to play in the ideological division of labour. Whereas the *British Gazette* run by Churchill was a blatant propaganda sheet with little credibility among the working-class, the BBC, despite its anti-labour bias, was listened to, and widely thought credible. To sustain its formal independence was therefore exceedingly shrewd, because its content was anyway closely controlled.

Thirdly, the role played by the BBC in the General Strike assured its news of a prominent place in the national culture, and not least the political culture. The Strike caused the press agreement to be waived, and five news bulletins were broadcast daily. The BBC now had to devise its own news bulletin, in the absence of the news agencies'. After a shaky start, a form was created which has definite points of continuity with today's bulletins: 'The regular news bulletins included special messages and announcements, official notices, full reports of parliamentary proceedings, [an] "appreciation of the situation", and a weather report, as well as news items.'[20] The Strike stimulated the setting up of a News Section for the first time which 'dealt chiefly with topical talks and special news items from government offices',[21] and gave the BBC its first opportunity to actually *collect* news itself.

SLOW GROWTH, 1927–39

In 1927, the BBC, having shown its importance and reliability as a national institution during a time of crisis, became suitably dignified as one of the first public corporations in Britain. It was henceforth to operate under a Royal Charter, essentially an enabling document, and a Licence from the Post Office.

This change had been foreshadowed by the Crawford Committee, which reviewed the state of play in broadcasting during 1926, and recommended that the BBC should become a public corporation, and cease to be a public company. A key document which had already specified this view of the BBC's place in British society was Reith's book, *Broadcast Over Britain*, published in 1924. By then, as Briggs has remarked, Reith was managing the BBC as though it were a public corporation, rather than a commercial monopoly. He was guided by several key principles in his approach to broadcasting: that it was not to be governed by the profit-motive; that it should come under 'unified control' in one institution; that it should produce material of a high standard in line with a view of what the public needed, rather than what it wanted.[22]

Reith's views about broadcasting constituted a coherent 'mass media ideology',[23] one which Raymond Williams has labelled 'paternalism': 'a control directed towards the development of the majority in ways thought desirable by the minority'.[24] It has been aptly commented by Scannell and Cardiff that Reith's conception of the role of broadcasting implied 'not simply a monopoly in a business sense, but a cultural dictatorship with the BBC as arbiter of tastes and definer of standards'.[25] Reith's paternalism implied a highly centralized view of broadcasting, one in which 'the brute force of monopoly', as he was later to call it, assured the maintenance of a tradition of public service, the exercise of a sense of moral obligation, and assured finances.

'Reithianism', the shorthand phrase for this complex of ideas, has been linked to ideas of public service in the Christian ethic. It has also been seen as embodying 'widely shared cultural assumptions', most notably those held in the élitist/aristocratic 'tradition' identified by Raymond Williams in his book *Culture and Society*.[26] The broadcasting monopoly was devised before Reith came on the scene. He was permitted, however, together with the pioneers of British broadcasting, to inform it with a particular set of purposes. As many have observed, the BBC is an extraordinary organization. Appropriately enough, in Reith, it has its own larger-than-life culture-hero, whose person is invested with a mighty creation myth.[27] But Reith was a man of his time, and whatever his personal role in the development of the BBC, cognate ideas of public ownership were then *au courant* across the political spectrum in Britain.[28]

The relevance of this for the development of news was that news, like broadcasting in general, was seen as part of a service for the nation, and its form and content were substantially influenced by this. The General Strike had defined the limits of 'impartiality' by crystallizing the BBC's status as an 'organization within the constitution'. Reithianism as a mass media ideology reinforced this stance. For the BBC's public service mission was based on the assumption that there was a 'national community', and that just as the BBC had identified itself with the constitution and assumed an ostensibly supra-factional role in the Strike, so was it to identify itself with the nation and assume a role as broker of the 'best' in the national culture.[29] A memorandum on news policy written in 1926 embodies some of this thinking, arguing that the news ought to be 'what those in control of the BBC think listeners *should* hear (a responsibility greater than any that has arisen since Adam's fateful choice)'.[30] It also placed a stress on accuracy as against sensationalism.

With the new corporate status of the BBC came a revision of the agreement with the national and provincial presses and the four main news agencies. During January and February 1927, an agreement was negotiated permitting the BBC to broadcast its first news bulletin at 6.30 p.m. each day rather than 7 p.m., and restricting it to no more than 400 eye-witness descriptions of events per year. News, however, still had to come from the agencies.[31] There was at this time an embryonic news staff of only two sub-editors, enlarged to three by the end of 1927.

A slight advance for the BBC occurred with the next agreement between the press and agencies in February 1930, which made a 6 p.m. news bulletin possible. By then, the editorial staff consisted of two editors and two sub-editors, and the BBC's newsmen began to receive news agency tape directly, rather than just a pre-edited bulletin.[32] Broadcast news was still a very passive operation which simply filtered agency material, and did not have its own news-gatherers. A BBC document, *Review of the Year 1930*, gives us a sense of the prevailing, rather genteel and amateurish approach: 'When there was not sufficient news judged worthy of being broadcast, no attempt was made to fill the gap, and the announcer simply said "there is no news tonight".'[33]

The small News Section did not have a settled organizational place until 1934. From December 1929 until 1932 it was separated from the Talks Department, its original home, and then linked once more. Not until 1934 did News become a Department in its own right. Before this yet another press agreement had been signed in 1932 which permitted the BBC to put out at any time news of unforeseen events which were especially important.[34]

Developments during the 1930s were rather slow. A significant, but short-lived experiment took place in the summer of 1933 when the first radio 'news reels' were broadcast for several months. These had a style and content recognizable in today's news magazine programmes:

> News and comment were welded into a continuous fifty-minute programme, with switch-overs to Manchester and Paris, gramophone and Blattnerphone excerpts, including Denis McCulloch talking about the anniversary of the Somme and a lawn-tennis commentary earlier in the day.[35]

Such reportage was not revived again until 1940, when the war made it a regular feature.

Reith actively supported the growth of news, and the first major changes of the 1930s were the appointment of John Coatman, a professor from the London School of Economics, and two journalists from the newspaper world to the new News Department.[36] One of those appointed in the mid-1930s was Richard Dimbleby, who was later the doyen of current affairs reporters. He showed astonishing prescience about the potential of radio news, gaining an entrée into BBC News some time after sending Coatman a gentlemanly critique of existing news practice, including suggestions which subsequently became standard news practice: the use of reporters, eye-witness accounts and interviews, recordings, and the 'enlivening of news by the infusion of the human element'.[37] The news controllers were very slow to respond, a possible reason being concern about the use of staff reporters who would have to take direct responsibility for the output.[38] The two reporters, or 'news observers' as they were called, of the 1930s, had to plead for money to follow up stories, and those they did cover were mainly of the human interest kind.

Slight developments in news practice continued throughout the 1930s. 'News talks' were used in the bulletins, generally being commentaries on foreign affairs. There was however no team of foreign correspondents, nor any regular extended news programme. While the technology for on-the-spot reporting did exist, it was relatively little used. There were two mobile recording vans, but the 'news observers' were expected to pursue 'actualities' outside their normal working hours.[39] Dimbleby, together with his colleagues David Howarth and Charles Gardner, was very active in establishing the practice of on-the-spot reporting. Two notable occasions were the coverage of the Fenland Floods of 1937, and the fire at Crystal Palace in November 1936, the latter being the first breakthrough – by Dimbleby – for this kind of reporting.[40]

At Crystal Palace, Dimbleby pioneered the use of the telephone system as an outside broadcast link with the news studio. By 1938, the use of on-the-spot reporting for BBC News was firmly established, and for example, Neville Chamberlain's arrival at Heston airport with his famous piece of paper and hopes of 'Peace in our time' was covered. By 1939, just before the War, Dimbleby and Howarth had begun using 'an ordinary car with recording gear on the back seat' which was far less unwieldy than earlier reporting equipment.[41] It was with this that they were later sent to France to report on the British Expeditionary Force.

During the 1927–39 period, there was a further enquiry into broadcasting, by the Ullswater Committee which reported in 1935. In the BBC's evidence, it was argued that greater freedom was needed in news broadcasting, with an increase in staff and fewer restrictions on hours.[42] The restrictions were not lifted until the outbreak of war. News was, however, a 'fixed point' in the broadcasting schedules, although its scope was severely limited. As Paulu has observed: 'News broadcasting was slow to develop in the United Kingdom: it took fifteen years and a world war to put day-round bulletins on the BBC.'[43] The September 1938 Munich Crisis was the first opportunity since the General Strike for the BBC to put day-time bulletins on the air. Just prior to this, the BBC made a further agreement with the press and agency interests which confirmed existing restrictions on news broadcasting, but eased limits on outside broadcasting.[44]

During the 1930s, too, the controversy in political reporting was extended. A further point was the development of Empire and Overseas broadcasting in response to the likelihood of war, a growth which foreshadows the eventual centrality of news in programming during and after the War.

'Controversy' is a theme more properly examined in relation to 'talks' rather than news. We find early on in the history of British broadcasting the rudiments of a distinction which was to become fully institutionalized in the 1950s, in Britain and elsewhere – namely, that between 'news' and 'current affairs'. Talks were the rough equivalent of today's current affairs programmes, and then, as now, posed special problems of control, given sensitivities in the political (and the religious) domain. As early as 1923 the Sykes Committee had recommended that 'given guarantees of equality and fair treatment, a moderate amount of controversy should be allowed'.[45] After the BBC had proved its trustworthiness to the state in its coverage of the Strike, the ban on 'controversy' concerning matters of politics, industry and religion was withdrawn in March 1928, although it was stressed that there should be no 'editorializing'.

The emergence of even a carefully bounded approach to 'controversy' put the BBC more firmly in the centre of the social and political stage. The organization responded to the need for vigilance by setting up a 'controversy committee' of top executives in 1928.[46] Such institutionalized caution has persisted since then, as will be seen in Chapter 6.

An immediate outcome of the move into more adventurous broadcasting was the transmission of the Chancellor of the Exchequer's defence of his Budget in 1928, and then again in 1930 and 1931. The first party political broadcasts in a general election came in 1929. The political parties retained a large measure of control over who appeared at the microphone, and effectively kept out political mavericks such as Winston Churchill, the undoubted effect being more prominent coverage for those speaking for the consensus on Indian independence and re-armament. The now seemingly inevitable row over the allocation of time to the parties was a notable feature of the elections of 1931 and 1935.

We also find at this time the first major controversy over the personal 'bias' of BBC personnel. Vernon Bartlett, the BBC's foreign affairs commentator, was accused of being pro-German on account of talks given in 1933 and 1934, in which he argued that, for example, Germany had been justified in leaving the League of Nations. After strong parliamentary and Foreign Office pressure made his position untenable, Bartlett left the BBC for the *News Chronicle*.[47]

1934 has been identified as a turning-point by John Coatman, the BBC's first editor of News. He has argued that with the expansion of news, which he saw as stimulated by important political developments on the European Continent – notably the rise of fascism – 'a new player of the first importance had stepped on to the political stage'.[48] Barnouw makes a similar analysis of the growth of news broadcasting in the US networks in the mid-1930s: 'News broadcasting grew: it had to. As Hitler mobilized and Mussolini moved troops into Somaliland, and rumblings came from Spain, the networks resumed newsgathering. Slowly they grew into news media. Half reluctantly they had met a challenge and moved forward.'[49]

Unlike the national press, the BBC had no staff coverage of the Spanish Civil War – until it virtually ended, at which time Dimbleby was sent to the Franco-Spanish frontier as an observer. According to one account, there was Foreign Office pressure to be cautious and the News Department tried to steer a middle course between the Republican and Nationalist sides: 'the word "rebels" (to describe Franco's forces) was replaced by the more respectable-sounding "insurgents".' Foreign Office pressure became so intense at one point that the Foreign News Editor protested to the Director-General. He was dismissed for this, and retained only because of support from the News Department.[50]

Non-domestic broadcasting expanded in direct response to developments abroad. The BBC initiated Empire broadcasting without government support, and there is no doubt that it began to develop these services in relation to a clear-cut political purpose: the safeguarding of the 'national interest'. Briggs has commented: 'The sense of imperial interest was enlivened in the mid-1930s by fear that the unity of empire was being threatened not so much by the natural development of movements towards self-government inside it as by the machinations of other great powers.'[51] News and topical talks programming were the obvious forms chosen to 'counteract the subversive propaganda of all foreign stations' as the BBC put it in its submission to the Ullswater Committee in 1935. In 1934, when the domestic news service was set up, an Empire News Department, with an Editor and three sub-editors, was also created.[52] By 1937, the British government was alert to the need to build up this operation and 'invited' the BBC to begin foreign-language broadcasts, the first of these, the Arabic Service, being inaugurated in January 1938. This kind of activity proliferated during the War. A monitoring service was first set up in 1935 by the Foreign Office, as part of its intelligence gathering, and this was later more fully developed by the BBC. The initiative taken in this area demonstrates quite clearly that the BBC perceived itself as an 'organization within the constitution' which ought to act in the national interest.

As early as 1934, serious consideration was being given to what the BBC should do in the event of war. The question of the BBC's formal independence then arose: ought it to liaise with the government, or ought it to be entirely taken over?[53] Reith outlined the BBC's desired wartime role:

> It is essential that the responsibility and reliability of the BBC's News Service should be established beyond doubt, even though in practice accuracy did not amount to more than the nearest approach to absolute truth permitted by the overriding war conditions including censorship.[54]

Such stress on the formal autonomy of the BBC echoes the lessons of the General Strike. It also shows considerable foresight concerning the wartime propaganda pay-off having a broadcasting organ which while manifestly constrained by the state is not transparently a 'creature of the executive'. The BBC had learned, and indeed was teaching, *raison d'état*.

1938 was the prelude to yet a further critical juncture for the BBC's news service, a further forced pace of change. The Munich Crisis of September 1938 produced a rapid growth of news bulletins to European countries in French, Italian and German. These subsequently became a permanent feature of the output. Briggs has pertinently observed that the BBC found a 'double role' during the crsis: 'first for the home audience to give orders and maintain morale; and second for the world – to spread reliable news and views'. During the run-up to 1939, the basic lines of war broadcasting policy were worked out. The government initially wanted to control the content of bulletins in German. The arrangement which emerged between the BBC and the Foreign Secretary was 'regular but informal contact with the Foreign Office' rather than 'direct Foreign Office control' of the BBC's output. This subtle approach was later embodied in the wartime censorship policy, one which was 'indirect, informal and voluntary, based on liaison with the Press Division of the Ministry of Information'.[55]

Crucially, the grasp of the press over the development of news broadcasting largely disappeared with the national emergency induced by the entry into total war. By 1939, plans were in train to run a twenty-four-hour service of news bulletins. We can see that the leap forward which BBC news made was induced by external factors – a crisis for Britain as nation-state and imperial power. Pre-war crises had similarly affected news reporting in the US networks: coverage of Munich aroused great interest and news henceforth attracted a good deal of sponsorship, making it commerically viable.[56]

Adoption of the news approach outlined in the mid-1930s made the BBC's news service credible on the Continent and elsewhere, and therefore a potent weapon in the 'war of words' which accompanied physical combat. It was once again outlined in 1939, by R. T. Clark, the Home Services News Editor:

> It seems to me that the only way to strengthen the morale of the people whose morale is worth strengthening is to tell them the truth and nothing but the truth, even if the truth is horrible. After all, what is horrible is a matter of taste or conviction, and depression is as often as not caused, not by the news itself, but by the peculiar conditions, physical or otherwise, in which the recipient hears it.[57]

THE WAR YEARS, 1939–45

The BBC was a key part of Britain's war effort, and in its general programming it aimed to support this. There were close institutional links with the state, and as Briggs has noted: 'The whole apparatus of government, greatly extended as it was, impinged more or less directly' on the BBC.[58]

Views differ concerning the precise nature of the BBC's freedom for manoeuvre. Coatman, for one, considers that 'during the war the BBC passed under the control of the government, and became part of the latter's information service'.[59] Gorham, while not questioning the BBC's explicit absorption into the political domain during the war, differs: 'Responsible work in the BBC was classed as work of national importance. Security regulations were extended to its premises, and it was treated in many ways like a government department, although it retained a great measure of its independence throughout.'[60] Briggs too inclines to the latter view, suggesting that despite extensive constraints, the BBC managed to retain 'every substantial measure of independence'.[61]

While it is true that the BBC's constitutional position as a public corporation remained unaltered (although in the earlier part of the war the Board of Governors was reduced from seven to two in the interests of 'streamlining') to focus on the Corporation's formal status is not especially illuminating. The really significant index of the BBC's position lies in the network of personal and institutional links between it and the government, and such propaganda bodies as the Political Warfare Executive. Of particular importance was the fact that 'In most of its activities the BBC was "officially guided" by the Ministry of Information.'[62] The complexities of these connections and the BBC's ups and downs in official eyes are charted in admirable detail in Briggs's history, and need not be repeated here. A reading of Briggs's account leads one to conclude that, in general, from the point of view of the control of 'sensitive' material, it mattered little whether the BBC was officially controlled or formally independent.

It would be mistaken to assume that this meant that the BBC slavishly adhered to every policy directive it received. It did not, and anyway often received contradictory advice from different quarters. There were frictions and disagreements with military leaders over the reporting of specific stories – notably coverage of the campaign in North Africa, and at various points during the opening of the Second Front. Moreover, the BBC was subjected to periodic governmental criticism of its news coverage and other programming, especially earlier on in the war. And there were one or two occasions on which a 'take-over' was threatened.

Having said this, however, it is clear that there was no need for coercive control, apart from censorship applied in the interests of security, which was anyway extended to the press. The BBC saw itself as part of the war effort, and hence the question of its pulling in a very different direction from that deemed officially desirable did not arise. A clear statement of its general position was given in 1940 by F. W. Ogilvie (Director-General from 1938 to 1942) who thought that the BBC 'ought to diffuse with reasonable freedom views which did not conflict with the national interest, but which were very far from being those of the Government itself'.[63] So far as news itself was specifically concerned, A. P. Ryan, the top wartime news executive, and a special adviser to the BBC, thought that the corporation should supplement the army, navy and air force as 'a fourth arm in this war'.[64]

While the BBC retained its formal independence, therefore, its approach was conditioned by the idea of working for the national interest. In one particular respect, the BBC's formal independence was exceedingly important. It was a potent propaganda weapon which provided legitimacy for the BBC's overseas broadcasts, and was a favourable point of contrast with the German approach. News was a particularly important part of the effort to represent and gain acceptance of the British version of events on the international stage.

The war, as will be seen, forced the pace of change in news programming, as news came to be seen as of central importance in combating German propaganda, both nationally, and internationally – especially in occupied Europe. Changes in news, however, should be seen against the wider background of the reshaping of broadcasting's output to meet new social requirements. Scannell and

Cardiff have argued that the formation of a 'new and genuine consensus, widely shared by all sections of society, that egalitarianism and community feeling should be the principles that informed social life' had considerable effects on wartime broadcasting.[65] It was this consensus which was to return the post-war Labour government, and to support the extension of the welfare state. The ethos of wartime broadcasting shifted from Reithianism, with its insistence on a uniform National Programme, to a policy later called 'generic' broadcasting. The first move in this direction came in 1940 when the Forces' Programme was created. This was a network based on the recognition that a populist and entertaining approach was needed. The Forces' Programme became the dominant network attracting an audience half as large again as that for the alternative more 'serious' Home Service. Such populism, both in form and content, was of some importance in reshaping the news, as the war progressed.

The BBC entered the war with a limited news output and a small staff. In 1939 the News Department had fifteen members and the six o'clock rule imposed by the press agreements held until September 1939.[66] There was no foreign news service and there were no foreign correspondents. On the first day of war the BBC broadcast a bulletin at noon, giving the details of Chamberlain's declaration of war, followed with a further bulletin at 1 p.m. This began the BBC's entry, at last, into regular daytime news broadcasting.

Yet the role of broadcast news was not instantly and clearly established; instead, 'there was confusion in the newly-founded Ministry of Information, suspicion in Press circles of the BBC entering into serious competition with the newspapers "to their detriment", and an inadequate sense within the BBC itself of the key importance of news as a major wartime service'.[67]

It was an inauspicious start, but as the Corporation's wartime importance became established the arguments of the press and news agencies, which had successfully inhibited the development of news broadcasting since the 'twenties, at last lost their potency. Cries of 'unfair competition' did not disappear, but became manifestly less significant during a total war in which the expansion of radio news was plainly in the national interest, particularly in countering Nazi propaganda. The press, however, did try to stay developments. In September 1939, for example, the BBC's news bulletins were reduced in number by the Minister of Information in response, partly, to protests from the press, and partly to a general feeling that there were too many. Even at the end of 1939, the BBC was still struggling to put 'war correspondence' on the air as quickly as it wanted, rather than wait until the following day.[68] The press were to continue protesting as they did in 1942, for example, when the BBC broke a news embargo (after it had already been broken by the American CBS network). Later, in 1944, when the BBC's war reporters began to scoop the press, this too produced recriminations. In general, though, the war emergency put an end to broadcasting's inhibition by the press.

From the modest beginnings of its 1939 establishment, BBC news was to grow by fits and starts to become an entire BBC Division by 1942. Changes precipitated by the war were extensive. Briggs has summarized them as 'a remarkable achievement in News technique both in the domestic and even more in the overseas News services of the BBC – collecting information through war reporters; increasing the range of outside "contacts"; introducing recorded insets into News programmes; experimenting with special News programmes; associating comment with fact; above all gaining an advanced sense of professionalism'.[69] The war accelerated the pace of innovation, fostering new forms and techniques, many of which were subsequently incorporated into the news programming of the post-war period. The creation of a hunger for news in a national emergency had similar effects in the USA where, by 1940, more Americans were relying on radio news than on newspapers for reports of the *blitzkrieg*. As Barnouw notes, the war promoted the expansion of a 'world wide news system' and the growth of foreign postings for US radio correspondents.[70]

By 1940 the newsroom had evolved a system of shift-working to meet increased output, and newsroom staff rose to eighteen in number, shortly thereafter increasing to 23. In addition to this four BBC newsmen were seconded to the Ministry of Information.[71] The audience for news had undergone a striking growth by 1940, with four out of six people in Britain regularly listening to BBC bulletins. The Nine O'Clock News became an 'institution' which attracted an audience of between 43 and 50 per cent of the population during the course of the war.[72]

Given the news' centrality, it is not surprising that the role of the BBC's newsreaders assumed great prominence. As Gorham has put it, 'The well-known voices of the newsreaders and announcers became symbols of reality in a topsy-turvy world.'[73] On 7 June 1940, newsreaders, who had hitherto been anonymous, began to be named. The rationale for this change derived entirely from considerations of national security. As an internal document pointed out: 'The aim is not to publicize the announcers, but to ensure that listeners get aquainted with their voices, *so that there may be no confusion in times of emergency*.'[74]

The idea that newsreaders should for the first time be identifiable individuals (although at the same time 'corporate voices') is taken for granted today. But in the 1940s it ran counter to the BBC's traditional policy on announcing, one which severely disparaged individualism.

Significantly, therefore, arguments of national security rather than any intended 'humanizing' of the news brought about the change, although it was widely welcomed by the public. Given its relation to security policy, news announcing undoubtedly engaged interest at the highest political level, as is evident from a letter to the BBC's Director-General from the Minister of Information, Brendan Bracken, written in 1943. In this Bracken suggested that now the danger of invasion was over there was no need to give the news-reader's name: 'I think the time has come when you can safely disregard the precaution. It is much better that all BBC bulletins should be spoken by an anonymous announcer.'[75] The BBC declined to return to anonymity just then, but reverted to it in May 1945 just before VE Day. This was one of a number of unimaginative decisions, which, it will be seen, adversely affected the post-war development of BBC news. Newsreaders became national celebrities (much as today) and their appearances were closely attended to by politicians, critics, and the general public, and as such they were an important bridge between the Corporation and its audience.[76]

The war stimulated significant developments in techniques of radio news reporting and presentation. Until 1939, virtually all 'news' was conveyed in the bulletin form, a monologue recitation by anonymous announcers, although occasionally on-the-spot reports and 'news talks' were included. There was virtually no news-gathering. The first major break with this style came with the news programme format of *Radio Newsreel*, produced by the Overseas Service in July 1940. This was 'a programme *about* the news of the day' using radio despatches. Briggs describes it as 'deliberately designed to suggest "immediacy", seeking "radiogenic stories", and "sequences", and relying on slick continuity'.[77] This formula later dominated post-war news features and current affairs programmes, and *Radio Newsreel* was broadcast on the new post-war Light Programme (the peacetime extension of the Forces' Programme) from 1945 until the restructuring of radio in 1970, and is still broadcast on the BBC's World Service.

The move to more vivid forms of radio reporting was, however, a slow drift rather than a sharp shift. Before the war, the BBC had taken tentative steps forward in technique and content. At the beginning of the campaign in France, in 1939, it had one 'news observer' abroad, Richard Dimbleby, who was stationed with the

British Expeditionary Force. There was no policy for war correspondence, however, and while in the first months of war, there were 'front-line despatches' from France, these played a minor role in the output, and there was a reluctance to use 'actuality' material (sounds and voices), such as the sound of gunfire from the Maginot Line. By 1940, the BBC had increased its reporting team to four 'observers' in different theatres of war, but tended not to see how their reports could be used quite differently from the routine material of the news agencies.[78]

As the war began to turn in the Allies' favour, the BBC began to be more adventurous in its news coverage. 1942 saw the first serious moves to expand radio war reporting. 'Actuality' now came into favour and the use of reporters' despatches was encouraged by the Controller of News, A. P. Ryan, and by the Director of Outside Broadcasts, Michael Standing. There was an increased investment in manpower, and the number of reporters covering the British campaign in the Middle East rose from one in 1942 to five in 1943. Voice reports and recordings were used much more in news programmes – although not in the news bulletins where they were thought inappropriate.[79]

In general, a more populist approach was now fostered. This policy change was the product of the desire in various quarters inside the BBC, the War Office and the Ministry of Information to develop a form of vivid reporting which would involve the civilian audience in the British military campaign. The models for the new approach were existing German and US programmes. The BBC, moreover, began to compete overtly with the press for stories, and its directorate was concerned about US military successes overshadowing British ones because of inadequate reporting.

In January 1943, the first reports of air raids on Germany were broadcast. And shortly after, in March 1943, BBC reporters took part in non-broadcast reporting of secret army exercises, during the first trial attempt at covering an unfolding military campaign. The reports proved satisfactory to the War Office, and in May 1943 steps were instituted to set up the BBC's War Reporting Unit 'which had the responsibility for getting active service war material in any theatre of war . . .'.[80] The unit developed its technique by reporting mock military invasion exercises and its members underwent special training in military knowledge and survival techniques, and how to stay inside the limits of military censorship. The needs of rapid campaign reporting stimulated technical innovation too. BBC engineers developed a new recording device, smaller and lighter than earlier models, and 'news traffic' facilities were set up in anticipation of a flood of reports on the progress of the invasion of Europe. The

BBC was now geared to speedy coverage, and competition with the press was an openly acknowledged goal.

The new approach to wartime radio journalism found its vehicle in *War Report*, a programme first transmitted when the Second Front opened in June 1944 with the D-Day landings. The BBC now had a substantial corps of war correspondents (no longer 'observers'): nineteen men covered the Western Front, six, Italy and North Africa, with others stationed in the Far East, Middle East, Ceylon, India, the USSR, the USA and the Pacific.[81] *War Report* was a highly successful programme, which commanded audiences of between 10 and 15 million listeners. It ran immediately after the Nine O'Clock News each night, being produced until just before VE Day in May 1945.

The creation of *War Report*, and the general expansion of news output in the later part of the war, were consequent upon organizational change, namely, the setting up of the News Division in September 1942, an act demonstrating the increased importance of news. Right at the beginning of the war, BBC News had come under fire from the Foreign Office because there was no central control over home and overseas bulletins. A year later, in 1940, the BBC had elaborated a policy of 'consistency' for all broadcasts.[82]

The unification of virtually all news outlets in 1942 under A. P. Ryan's controllership was a further move towards applying a uniform policy to news. Ryan, who had significant political contacts in his other role as Home Policy Adviser to the BBC, wanted to simplify the flow of 'guidance' to the news producers, and for the BBC to rely solely on policy directives from the Ministry of Information, as opposed to going to all the Services and the Foreign Office for clearance. During early 1942 regular news policy meetings began, and the setting up of the News Division later in the year created, for the first time, an organizational basis for developing the team of news correspondents the following year.[83] This change in organizational structure marked the new prominence of news – one to be enhanced with post-war developments in television.

THE POST-WAR PERIOD

The first crucial feature in the development of broadcast news after the Second World War is the growth of television news, and its eventual supercession of radio news by 1960, to become the dominant information source for the public in this, as in other developed capitalist states. The second is the breaking of the BBC's broadcasting monopoly, by the creation of a rival television system, and a move into what has been termed 'commercial democracy' in the form and content of programming. This latter structural change sharply accelerated the shift away from Reithian and neo-Reithian conceptions of broadcasting, and induced a continuing 'battle of the ratings', the inevitable concomitant of which is a conception of the audience as a mass market. These contributed to the 'news explosion' of the 1950s and 1960s, when new forms of news programming were developed, and television and radio journalism became a substantial and prominent part of broadcasting's output.

The BBC's radio news was exceedingly well-established by the end of the war, and had an international reputation for probity. The BBC's news policy, however, was somewhat unimaginative and conservative. The War Reporting Unit, which had proved very successful, was broken up, with the consequent loss of some able journalists.[84] With its innovative phase now ended, BBC News was to pursue a decidedly élitist conception of news until challenged by commercial television in 1955. Lord Simon of Wythenshawe, the BBC's Chairman in the late 1940s and early 1950s, wrote of the Corporation's most relevant 'news public' as a 'serious' one, 'such as the readers of the quality press'. He drew a distinction between 'these standards and those of much of the popular press'.[85] In this conception, Simon expressly defined the key audience addressed by the news as the 'three million' comprising Britain's 'élite', who were identified as university and grammar-school educated readers of *The Times* and the (then) *Manchester Guardian*. Nonetheless, the 'majority' also found a place in Simon's conception of the audience, for news was seen as 'undoubtedly the most important and effective broadcasting from the point of view of the information and education of a majority of the population'.[86]

The notion of a stratified audience expressed above relates to the BBC's post-war restructuring of broadcasting. The success of the Forces' programme during the war had stimulated a new approach, known as 'generic' broadcasting. Central to this policy was the idea that programming should be organized in three networks aiming at different types of listener with differing levels of taste and cultural accomplishment. In effect, broadcasting openly recognized the existence of a class structure. Programming was streamed into three networks: the Light Programme, the Home Service and the Third Programme.

This structure had first been proposed by William Haley, the Director-General, in 1944 and was 'neo-Reithian' in conception. In 1946, Haley described the relationships between the three networks as resting on a concept of 'the community as a broadly based cultural pyramid slowly aspiring upward . . .':

B

Each programme at any moment must be ahead of its public but not so much ahead as to lose their confidence. The listener must be led from good to better by curiosity, liking and a growth of understanding. As the standards of education and culture of the community rise so should the programme pyramid rise as a whole.[87]

This tortuous metaphor summarizes a policy which continued the Reithian one of giving the public 'something better than it now thinks it likes'. While continuing to stress the BBC's leading role in the national culture, it also recognized that social stratification entails there is no homogeneous national audience. Still, as Henry Fairlie has pointed out: 'The element which is common to both Reith's and Haley's attitude is their belief that culture is something which can be transmitted to the mass of a population by a curriculum of humane studies.'[88] This was not to prove the best formula for withstanding the onslaught of commercial television.

News, as Simon's formulation makes clear, was seen in a rather Reithian way as an important means of instruction in a democracy. It was to make no populist compromises. As an earnest of its serious intention to educate the public in the work of the central political institution the BBC began to broadcast *Today in Parliament* in October 1945.

This section of the narrative will be less concerned with radio news, for the post-war period is characterized by the rise of television as the pre-eminent medium. While in 1950 only 10 per cent of households in Britain possessed a television receiver, by 1963, only 10 per cent did not.

The BBC's audience research shows that the audience for broadcast news shifted from radio to television in the late 1950s. While a report published in 1957 showed that radio bulletins were still attracting the largest single news audiences, a further piece of research in 1962 indicated that television news had 'assumed the role previously played by Sound radio news'. By then, the main concern of the study was to compare BBC Television News with its commercial competitor, and a survey of 'News on Sound' was added only as an afterthought. Five years previously, it had been television which ranked low in priority.[89] This points us forward to a time when the BBC's long-standing monopoly was already broken and it had entered a duopolistic market structure, and a new pattern of broadcasting.

Suez

Since the war there have been two crises of especial importance
concerning the BBC's independence from the state. The first concerns
the coverage of the Suez invasion in 1956, the second, the coverage
of Northern Ireland, particularly in 1971–72. As the latter is the
subject of Chapter 8, only Suez will be dealt with here.

The BBC's handling of the Suez crisis, is seen inside the BBC, and
outside, as evidence of its independence from the state. The other
examples cited do not command general assent. During the Strike
of 1926, as during the war, the BBC became an integral part of the
state's information machinery. Over Northern Ireland, as will be
seen, a revision of the orthodox view of BBC independence is needed.
Suez, however, stands out as an occasion when the BBC quite clearly
did resist government intervention, and this has been of great
importance for the corporate image.

But what precisely did it resist? There are two major views: the
more dramatic avers a take-over was imminent; the more down to
earth argues the BBC faced severe pressure.

The main source for the 'threatened take-over' account is Harman
Grisewood, who during the crisis was near the top of the BBC's
editorial hierarchy. He has argued that the then prime minister,
Eden, threatened a 'revival of wartime measures' and intended to
introduce a special instrument enabling the government to take over
the BBC. Eden objected to the broadcasting of dissenting views on
the invasion of Egypt, and defined the situation as a wartime one.
The Labour opposition denounced the adventure, and claimed the
right of reply to Eden's ministerial broadcast.

The BBC's Board of Governors decided to broadcast the opposition's dissenting view on both the home and external services. The
decision, says Grisewood, was 'tantamount to a refusal to Eden to
recognize his insistence that Britain was at war in the sense that
Britain as a nation went to war in 1914 or 1939. Neither the BBC nor
the nation consented in this interpretation of the action in Egypt.'[90]
One might contrast this broadcasting of opposing views to the
BBC's refusal to give the TUC, Archbishop of Canterbury and Ramsay
MacDonald access to the microphone in 1926. Thus far, Grisewood's
account is not disputed. However, MacKenzie has argued that talk
of a threatened government take-over is erroneous. First, the
government did not need special powers, as the charter enabled it
to instruct the BBC to omit certain views – although that would have
been an important precedent. Secondly, as no take-over was actually
planned, to talk of resisting one is to deal in mythology. 'On the
other hand', MacKenzie says,

There was real and severe pressure put on the BBC in other ways. This took several forms: attempts to impose pro-government speakers and curtail critics of the Suez policy; rows over the Opposition's right to reply to Ministerial broadcasts; the planting of Foreign Office liaison officers at Bush House; threats of financial cuts in the Overseas Services; and Parliamentary measures designed to clip the BBC's wings.[91]

Without doubt, this constituted a considerable assault by the government. The BBC was able to resist it because there was an extensive constituency in the country which did not agree with the Suez adventure, and moreover, the social order in Britain was not under threat. This contrasts strikingly with the war, which was a national emergency which permitted no fundamental conflict over overall war aims, and in which the security of the state was at risk.

The rise of TV news

Television broadcasting resumed after the war in June 1946 by covering the Victory Parade with outside broadcasting units. While the BBC had established the world's first regular television service in 1936, it was closed down in 1939. There had been no pre-war television news output although by agreement with the Movietone and Gaumont-British Film Companies, the BBC had screened two newsreels a week. After the war, the film industry would not re-establish this arrangement for fear of competition.[92]

Since the BBC could not use commercial cinema newsreels, it decided to produce its own television newsreel, which was first broadcast in January 1948. It was produced by the newsreel division of the Television Film Department, based at Alexandra Palace and in no manner connected with News Division at Broadcasting House. Harold Cox, sometime Newsreel Manager, has described how the newsreel team worked, and their values. There was a strong emphasis on pictures for their own sake and on drama. The newsreel covered stories such as rescues at sea, rail crashes, fires and earthquakes, in line with a filming policy of telling the audience 'where, how and sometimes, why'. The newsreel stressed 'actuality': 'wherever possible, newsreel stories are shot with what is called "live sound", that is speech or background noises recorded on the spot'. The key figure was the newsreel cameraman, who acted as reporter. Cox drew a distinction between the 'newsreel' form, and that of the 'news bulletin', considering the latter to stress news values as much as pictorial values. Recognizable aspects of the current professional ideology of television newsmen were the emphasis on pictures, immediacy, drama, and the unpredictability of events.[93]

In July 1954, the Newsreel came at last under the control of the News Division, which had, until then, produced only radio news bulletins. The production became known as *News and Newsreel*, and began to have five editions a week, with a 'composite weekend edition'.[94] Until then the only News Division output on television had been, since 1946, a *sound-only* ten-minute bulletin transmitted from Broadcasting House, which was read over the BBC symbol just before the end of transmission.[96] To judge from the rather fragmentary evidence available, this was hardly compelling viewing. An early audience research report indicates that perhaps 20 per cent of audience each night would listen to the news on television, but that 50 per cent switched off as a matter of course before it came on.[97]

The News Division was under very cautious leadership. The then Editor, News, Tahu Hole, has been described as 'a man of rigid views on the sanctity of news and the importance of keeping it undefiled by such things as persons'. There was, in addition, some opposition from radio reporters to the introduction of new television techniques.[98] Television news languished therefore under the dominance of radio news values and production ideas. It was not for nothing that News Division was known as 'the Kremlin of the BBC'.[99]

An idea of the approach to style and content in the radio news of the early 'fifties – and this informed television production – is provided by Paulu, who writes of the 'impersonal, sober, and quiet manner' of the newsreader (a reflection of the revived policy of anonymous newsreading, which, in radio, was to last until 1963). The style of BBC news was like 'a foreign office communiqué': 'Human interest and accident stories never take precedence over or crowd out significant developments. BBC news programmes never become entertainment broadcasts; "shows" are never built around "personalities" . . . .' Paulu, whose point of contrast was American radio news, stressed the 'hard' and 'heavy' news content of the BBC broadcasts:

In the main, programs are devoted to international and foreign events – including much news from the United States, especially if it relates to the United Kingdom; news of the British Commonwealth; home, political, and industrial events; significant developments in literature, the arts, science, and other fields of learning; and the activities of the royal family (though the BBC does not report, while still in the gossip stage, such things as Edward VIII's abdication or Princess Margaret's romance with Peter Townsend).[100]

Paulu's observations suggest a somewhat stuffy set of ideas about good taste and rather middle-class news values. There was, for example, a tendency to eschew the reporting of crimes and accidents, a lack of humorous or 'light' stories, and an absence of colourful adjectives. Of especial importance, Paulu found, was an emphasis on 'accuracy': 'In editing primary attention is given to being strictly accurate. There is no hurry to be first, to "scoop" the newspapers or anyone else. When facts are indisputable they are broadcast, not before.'[101] This policy expresses a sense of continuity with the agency origins of broadcast news, of caution, and trying not to offend any significant group which might retaliate.

An instance of the policy that 'the BBC does not have scoops' has been given by Douglas Stuart. When he was BBC correspondent in India, he, together with the Associated Press correspondent, had a 'world beat' story of the Dalai Lama's coronation and escape from Tibet. This was only reluctantly accepted by London for 'during the time of Tahu Hole's editorship of the BBC, "beats" by BBC correspondents were frowned on. It was essential to have your story confirmed by at least one agency.' On another occasion, Stuart's up-to-the-minute report of the nationalization of the Suez canal by Nasser's government was 'spiked' and not used until the following day.[102]

It was against this unpromising background that television news struggled to its feet. *News and Newsreel* was certainly shaped by journalistic judgements. Paulu describes it as 'definitely fast, many national events being on the screen a few minutes after they occur. The items selected are more serious than those in the average theater newsreel, news values taking precedence over the pictorial appeal of the beauty contest and the human interest story.'[103] The 'news values' in question were specifically BBC ones, and the 'running order' of the news was dictated by Broadcasting House. *News and Newsreel* was a 20-minute programme, summarizing 'the main news of the day, followed by a newsreel of the latest pictures of current events at home and abroad'.[104]

Again, the available audience research suggests that *News and Newsreel* left much to be desired and 'revealed a very strong feeling that there would have to be some drastic revision before the present TV news presentation could be considered to have made some worthwhile advance'. Many of the audience thought the old Newsreel had been superior, and there was dissatisfaction with the 'copious use of stills' which was likened to 'an old-fashioned lantern show'.[105]

In September 1955, BBC Television News bulletins finally superseded the newsreels which were hived off, appearing less and less frequently, until they disappeared altogether in February 1957. The new Television News was still, as Hood has sharply observed, 'a radio bulletin with some illustrations, read to camera'.[106] Certainly, the hold of Broadcasting House was strong. Hole, the Editor, News, symbolizes the conservative mood, though he was not alone responsible for it. Pursuing the traditional approach to radio newsreading, he held out against any personalization of newsreaders. There was little concern then with whether the newsreaders were telegenic, and it was insisted that the television news 'running order' should be identical to that of the sound bulletins: there were no concessions, therefore, to 'picture value'.

The early days of television news were characterized by amateurism and frustration. Newsreaders first appeared in vision in September 1955, and behind the scenes were teething problems among new staff learning to write to film and put bulletins together. Stuart has noted that 'Radio staff were hastily given a short training course and then sent over to Alexandra Palace (the TV News base) to put out a nightly television bulletin'.[107] One veteran television newsman interviewed during my fieldwork gave an evocative account of the time:

It progressed from being a radio team working in TV to being a medium of our own. When it first started there were two genuine TV-men on the team. Most of the rest from radio had been newspaper journalists. It was not a medium then: it was just a way of putting the news across. The earlier bulletins were terribly hamfisted, very dull and very wordy. We weren't using picture value, and we were writing reports as though it was for radio where the pictures were incidental. There were primitive gadgets for stills and maps. For instance for the stills there was a machine like the Great Wheel in Vienna: when a still went on the screen you could often see the operator's hands.

Teething problems were, of course, by no means restricted to BBC television news. Robin Day has described the hectic background to the creation of ITN, and Erik Barnouw, in his history of American broadcasting notes how:

Television news at the start of 1953 was an unpromising child. It was the schizophrenic offspring of the theater newsreel and the radio newscast, and was confused as to its role and future course.[108]

The conventional forms of television news programmes are now taken for granted and widely diffused. In the early to mid 'fifties when the same problems of constructing this new cultural form were faced on both sides of the Atlantic, the borrowings from other media and conventions were very similar.

The take-over of the newsreel by the News Division in July 1954 was no accident for it coincided with the passage of the Television Act. This Act ended twenty-seven years of broadcasting monopoly, and the first commercial television broadcast took place in late September 1955. By the end of 1961, 95 per cent of the population could be reached by the stations of the Independent Television Authority, the body constitutionally responsible for commercial television's programming, and the BBC had suffered a crisis in the 'battle of the ratings'.

The details of the shift from monopoly to duopoly in broadcasting need not detain us. It is however worth noting H. H. Wilson's speculation in his definitive book on the subject, that 'the introduction of commercial television symbolizes a change within the Conservative Party [elements of which had been instrumental in bringing about the change], which in turn reflects and expresses forces which are shaping British society. In simplest form this is described as the decline of the aristocratic values and the substitution of commercial standards.'[109]

This interpretation has received some support from other writers. Burrage for instance has argued that in post-war Britain the 'legitimation of the majority' had to be sought for programme content, as the élite which had formerly supported the Reithian approach became an inadequate social base. He considers the dismantling of the Reithian approach 'may justly be called a process of democratization, that is to say, the criterion for determining programme content has increasingly been popular taste rather than some notion of cultural or moral standards'.[110] This concept of democratization should more correctly be called 'commercialization', namely, the marketing of cultural products in a manner which is most likely to yield profits, or maintain high audiences.[111]

The move towards a broadcasting duopoly, with commercial television financed by advertising, had striking effects on the BBC. The changes in news production were just one instance of a more wholesale transformation of neo-Reithianism.

The News Division was caught unprepared. Hood has written of how its 'upper echelons manifested an almost pathological fear of the new medium. It was, they felt, not serious. They saw themselves as supplying (in sound) the equivalent of *The Times* or *Daily Telegraph*; to use pictures was to descend to the level of the popular press.'[112] This recalls exactly Lord Simon's remarks, cited above. BBC News was hopelessly up-market.

As Robin Day indicates, the new commercial network station, Independent Television News (ITN) set out to challenge the BBC's nostrums:

> As one of ITN's original newscasters, my job was to break with the BBC tradition of announcer-read national news. The ITN newscaster was to use his own knowledge and personal style. He was also to be a reporter going out to gather news with the camera crews.[113]

For the first time personality was injected into news presentation. ITN showed that it could remain within the understood conventions of impartiality and still mediate the news in a more populist manner. Day has also noted the explicit audience-grabbing intention at ITN: 'as the newscaster became known to viewers, his professional grasp of his material, and his lively interest in it would make the news more authoritative and *entertaining*'.[114] In the pursuit of authority, ITN was entering the BBC's traditional stamping-ground. But by aiming to be entertaining, commercial television news was rejecting the BBC notion of news as a solemn ritual. The idea of news as entertainment was mediated through the news *programme*, rather than the newsreel or bulletin. The programme was constructed around the 'newscasters' (this term was an American import) and 'other distinctive ITN characteristics were vivid "action" film with natural sound, warm human interest stories, an incisive interviewing style, a robust news sense, and (revolutionary development!) humour.'[115]

This was a move towards populism in both the form and content of news – the 'programme', action, drama, human interest, jokes. It was also a decided shift down-market from *The Times/Manchester Guardian* conception outlined only a few years earlier by Lord Simon. This reference to newspaper categories is by no means fortuitous, for Day's book makes it clear that ITN's news was seen as filling a specific place in the media culture, one which took 'a middle road between the BBC and the popular press in the order and arrangement of news'.[116]

While the BBC's television news remained for some years dominated by radio and newsreel values, ITN set out very rapidly to utilize the media values of *television*, to create, as Day puts it, its 'own set of news values': 'We quickly learned how television affects the selection and arrangement of news. The fact of yesterday's air disaster may no longer be top news tonight – but the *first* film of the scene may well merit first place in this evening's television news.' Like the BBC's news, ITN's was seen as the 'front page' of the organization's output, and in developing its appeal there were attempts to use good visual lead stories to hold the audience's attention, and the development of what is now a common feature of both news services, the 'light tail-piece'.[117]

The development of a successful, slick, audience-grabbing news production formula had a considerable impact on the BBC's television news. But Hugh Greene, later to be the BBC's most outstanding Director-General since Reith, when commenting (in 1958) on the challenge of ITN preferred to think that autonomous development would have created an equivalent service at the BBC:

> Perhaps competitition has in some ways been a spur. For instance, it might be claimed that our television news programmes have benefited from the stimulus of competition in the method of their presentation – but one cannot be sure that they would not have attained today's standing even without competition.[118]

In fact one can be reasonably sure they would not have. There was little in the entire record of BBC News's development which suggested that extensive change would have come about without external stimulus. Previous bouts of innovation had largely been forced by crises in the political domain. Now there was pressure from the sphere of economics, which raised the basic question of the BBC's survival. Moreover, Greene's comment ignores the effects of ITN on the *content* of news; it was not only presentational *forms* which changed. Burton Paulu, who might be expected to be a less partial commentator than Day, and who is notably admiring of the BBC as an institution in his writing, observed some five years after the creation of ITN that 'the principal example of how competition has improved the BBC' was the change in news production. He went on to say: 'primary emphasis is still given to items of long-term value, but there now is coverage of human interest stories which previously were ignored or minimized'.[119]

Other developments

The conservatism of News Division had important consequences for other developments in broadcasting journalism in the BBC. In the early 'fifties, two subsequently prominent figures in British television journalism began to develop the concepts now associated with the 'current affairs' programme. Grace Wyndham-Goldie who was then a producer in the Television Talks Department 'had developed the radio "talk" into the "illustrated talk", by using pictures, prints, photographs, and films to accompany the arguments of her speakers'. This was a didactic and analytical programme in form and content. Meanwhile, in 1950, Richard Dimbleby, after an outstanding career as a radio reporter, began to work out ideas for covering 'the big and vital field of topical but non-immediate news'. In a memorandum of that year to the Head of the BBC Film Department, he distinguished between the 'immediate news' of the newsreel, the 'permanent news' of the documentary and 'current news', for which no form as yet existed.[120] This latter category came to be known as 'current affairs'.

The first major BBC programme of this type was *Panorama*, launched in 1955 and still running today. It moved quite rapidly into areas of controversy, with its coverage of political and social stories, and of international affairs. The programme built up the role of its anchorman, Dimbleby, and by comparison with earlier practice, allowed its reporters considerable leeway in putting a personal stamp on their stories. Another feature of 'current affairs' reporting was on-location filming. All this was taking place when News Division had, a year before, only just accepted that it ought to be running *News and Newsreel* in order to compete with the forthcoming commercial television news. There was still little imaginative use of the potential of televised news, and it is small wonder that in a short period of time 'an artificial wedge' was 'driven between "news" (controlled by BBC Radio) and "current affairs" (created by BBC Television)'.[121]

The 1950s were to see a 'news explosion' which continued into the 1960s. As Smith has pointed out, this involved 'the invention of a series of technical and creative methods', among which were new styles of interviewing, some investigative journalism, the introduction of 16 mm film and new cameras, new attitudes towards film editing and processing, developments in electronic news-gathering, miniaturization, the use of satellites.[122] Much of this 'news explosion' occurred not in the field of 'news' but rather in 'current affairs'. In addition to more weighty programmes, such as *Panorama*, another current affairs model was the 'news magazine' the archetype of which was the *Tonight* programme of the late 1950s. This was an exceedingly successful and influential formula, which, it has been pointed out, greatly assisted the BBC's case when it submitted evidence to the Pilkington Committee on Broadcasting in 1960. Indeed, this 'miscellanized' news programming, as Tracey has labelled it, with its formula of human interest, pop politics, and personalities has, together with the news bulletin come to be the dominant form, overshadowing more weighty current affairs programmes.[123]

Radio journalism was also affected by the 'news explosion'.

BBC Radio News itself did not undergo really substantial changes until 1970 (see Chapter 9). In October 1957, however, in an obvious populist move, news summaries were broadcast for the first time on the Light Programme. Despite declining audiences, changes in radio news scheduling could still arouse passions, as in 1960, when the Nine O'Clock News was axed to clear the Home Service schedules for plays and concerts, and this aroused a storm of protest from letter-writers to *The Times* and the like, who still regarded it as a national institution.[124] The more significant changes were to come in radio 'current affairs', with the creation of the news magazine *Today* in 1957, the news analysis programme *Ten O'Clock* in 1960 and *The World at One*, with its emphasis on the testing political interview, in the mid-'sixties. Such news programmes evolved new styles of reporting, and radio journalism expanded into new areas of news interest. By the late 'sixties, there had been a general move towards more 'tabloid formats' and personality presenters. This set the stage for the creation, by 1970, of a news and current affairs dominated channel when radio programming was next restructured.

A later development of the 1960s which showed the well-established commercial success of television news was the adoption of the American 'big news' formula. This was first taken up by ITN in 1967 with its programme *News At Ten*, which follows the American style of personality anchormen, on-the-spot reports, specialist reporters, and short film stories. The extended news programme was later adopted by the BBC on its main channel in the early 1970s with the creation of the *Nine O'Clock News* as direct competitor to ITN.[125]

By about 1960, therefore, a pattern of national network television news broadcasting had formed which in its essentials remains unchanged today. Not only had television news attracted large audiences, but it was also costing considerable sums to produce. The annual cost of production in each service in the early 'sixties has been estimated as £1 million.[126] By the mid 'sixties, Norman Swallow could write – in a vein which was not then likely to be questioned – that 'news and current affairs is today almost certainly television's main programme function, just as for a long time it has been its principal social obligation'.[127] Broadcast journalism has assumed a commanding position in the schedules, and increasingly in the 1960s became the object of scrutiny by politicians, pressure groups, and media sociologists. The subsequent disintegration of consensus politics in the 1960s, and widespread concern with 'violence' and 'law and order', have ensured that the broadcasting media's representations of the national news have become increasingly discussed.

It is clear that the introduction of commercial television, and the need to fight it on its own terms in order to keep audience figures high – the *ultima ratio* of such broadcasting – brought about a considerable change in the BBC's news approach. While it has retained Reithian overtones it has had to move down-market. Paulu, writing at the beginning of the 'sixties, considered there to be 'few content differences between the two services'.[128] The convergence of ITN and BBC Television News toward a 'common form' was also noted in 1965 in a special survey of broadcasting carried out by *The Times.* This quoted Geoffrey Cox, then Editor of ITN as saying 'We are aiming to be a popular newspaper of high intellectual content', and Desmond Taylor, then Deputy Editor of BBC Television News, who similarly observed 'We are trying to find a level somewhere between the popular and more serious newspapers'.[129]

More recently, a detailed content analysis of British television news has substantiated the view that in most respects, apart from variations of style, the news outputs of the BBC and ITN are essentially the same.[130]

CONCLUSION   *Condense*

The formation of BBC News, both as a cultural product and as an organizational structure, has been a somewhat uneven process. Most of the impetus for change has derived from factors external to the BBC, rooted in the politics and economics of British society. The BBC was faced with a series of crises – the General Strike, the Second World War, the advent of commercial television – which successively promoted innovation in the scope, form and content of news. It is now a ubiquitous product. But the story of its growth to present-day prominence is certainly not one of steady expansion. Rather it is disjointed, with periods of relative equilibrium interspersed by innovative bursts.

The two major leaps forward prior to the creation of commercial television were induced by national crises threatening the integrity of the state. The General Strike, so it was argued, constituted an internal threat. And fascist aggression undoubtedly represented an international one. The economic arguments advanced for restricting the scope of BBC news by the press and the news agencies gave way before such political necessities. The expansion in broadcast news occasioned by these crises coincided with the interests of the BBC, which established itself thereby as, first, a prominent national source of information, and then as an organization of international repute.

Crises in the political domain forced the BBC to confront the structural limits of its independence. During the Strike it first assumed its continuing character as an 'organization within the constitution'. But it is important to counterpose the constraints on its 'impartiality' in 1926 to the room for manoeuvre the BBC evidently had during Suez. This later crisis showed that given a dispute about whether national security was really at stake, and a powerful body of support to argue that it was not, the BBC had adequate scope to define its constitutional responsibilities in a way which ran counter to the definition produced by the incumbent government. Such variation in the corporation's room for manoeuvre means that it is simplistic to argue that it is either entirely independent, or, alternatively, a straightforwardly subordinate apparatus of the state. The BBC does not occupy a static position in British society. The relevance of this point will be clear in Chapter 8, where the BBC's approach to the Northern Ireland crisis is analysed.

It is also pertinent at this point to note that the political sensitivity of broadcast news has powerfully inhibited any redefinition of its scope. Thus, historically, it has retained its identity as an 'objective', 'impartial', 'neutral' product. This version of appropriate journalistic practice derives directly from its news agency origins. The national news is not legitimized as an *interpretation* of reality, but rather as a straightforwardly factual presentation of it. The basic framework which has defined news for the past 55 years has not been transcended, but rather has been supplemented by 'current affairs', an institutionally separate creature, explicitly licensed to deal in values and interpretation. While its origins are somewhat contingent, the expansion of current affairs broadcasting in radio and television, fuelled by the 'news explosion', indicates that its separation from news has been a helpful solution to broadcasters concerned about the credibility of the news output. Currently, as will be seen in Chapter 9, this legitimation is under critical pressure.

Lastly, it is clear that the creation of commercial television, and the consequent redefinition of broadcasting's terms of reference forced the BBC to abandon neo-Reithianism, and to move downmarket. Broadcast news is now a popular peak-time form. Such prominence is an essential part of present-day production, and it is to the organization and activity of the newsroom that we now turn.

3

The production of
radio and television news

Entrenched in newsmen's mythology about their work is the belief that news is somehow the product of a *lack* of organization. News, rather than being seen as the imposition of order upon the chaos of multifarious, often unrelated events and issues, is seen as a kind of recurring accident.

It is not surprising, therefore, that newsmen who had read an earlier draft of this study expressed astonishment that it was actually possible to depict a system at work, operating with a determinate set of routines. This view is summed up in the comment of one newsman: 'It's surprising to find there's a grand design.'

This chapter presents an account of the routine practices of the two London-based, national newsrooms of BBC News. These are located at Broadcasting House (radio), and Television Centre (TV). Together, the radio and television news departments constitute the News Division. It is important to show that such production systems can be accurately described, particularly in view of one recent, and regrettable, sociological failure to do so.[1] To present a yellow press pastiche as sound sociology is simply to give a hostage to fortune. It arouses understandable ire among newsmen, who are often, at best, dubious about sociologists telling them anything worth knowing about journalism.

The routines of production have definite consequences in structuring news. To delineate their main features goes some way towards providing a rational understanding of an important form of work. The news we receive on any given day is not as unpredictable as much journalistic mythology would have us believe. Rather, the doings of the world are tamed to meet the needs of a production system in many respects bureaucratically organized.

A related point is that the production of broadcast news, as presently constituted, is a *reactive* form of reportage. Broadly speaking, BBC newsmen wait for things to happen, and then register their occurrence. To some extent this results from the BBC doctrine that news refrains from investigation and elaborated interpretation. (This ideology is shared elsewhere, as Golding and Elliott point out.)[2] Organization and ideology are in fact mutually reinforcing.

1976

THE NEWSDAY CYCLE: AN OVERVIEW

News is produced in daily cycles known as 'newsdays'. Each newsday is divided by a number of transmission times for which bulletins and programmes have to be prepared. These transmission times constitute a series of deadlines towards which the entire production machine is oriented.

Production at Television Centre is organized to service two channels, BBC-1 and BBC-2. On BBC-1, the main outlet, there are three major programmes: at 1.45 p.m. (15 minutes), 5.40 p.m. (15 minutes) and 9.00 p.m. (25 minutes). On BBC-2, there are two broadcasts: at 7.30 p.m. (10 minutes) and at about 11.00 p.m. (usually 15 minutes). At Broadcasting House, radio news is produced for four channels. On Radios 1 and 2, one and two-minute news summaries are broadcast between 6.00 a.m. and 12 midnight, with a five-minute summary at the latter time. Radio 3 broadcasts five-minute summaries at 7.00 a.m., 8.00 a.m., 9.00 a.m., 1.00 p.m. and 6.00 p.m. Radio 4 is the BBC's main news and current affairs vehicle. The longest news bulletins are broadcast at 7.00 a.m. (10 minutes), 8.00 a.m. (10 minutes), 1.00 p.m. (10 minutes), 6.00 p.m. (15 minutes), 10.00 p.m. and 11.30 p.m. (15 minutes and 20 minutes respectively). There is also a regular series of five-minute news summaries between 9.00 a.m. and 5.00 p.m.[3]

Production in the newsrooms for these outputs is handled by a number of distinct work groups, organized mainly on the 'desk' principle; these are represented in figures 3.1 and 3.2. At Television Centre there are two production teams. One team largely concentrates on producing news for BBC-1's main news programme, the *Nine O'Clock News*. The other team produces most of the remaining outputs.

At Broadcasting House, all outputs for Radios 1, 2 and 3 are produced on the 'summaries desk'. The major production effort is concentrated on the 'bulletins desk' which produces all the Radio 4 outputs. These, like the *Nine O'Clock News* on BBC-1, are regarded as the 'flagship' productions.

Production, therefore, is organized in relation to particular cycles, and is based on a division of labour within each newsroom.

CONTROLLING PRODUCTION

A central theme of this study is how the production of news is controlled. There are two separate mechanisms through which day-to-day and minute-to-minute control of production is exercised.

On a day-to-day basis, control is exercised through the daily editorial conferences which start each newsday in each of the News Departments. These are known as the 'morning meetings'. As the two News Departments are organizationally separate, the meetings are also an important means of control at the Divisional level since they are linked each weekday by a radio circuit, over which discussion of mutual problems takes place and news judgements are exchanged.[4]

Each weekday morning senior newsmen in the Radio and Television News Departments meet to discuss the previous day's coverage and to work out coverage for the coming day. At Radio News the meeting begins at 9.15 a.m., at the conclusion of the night shift. Television's conference begins later at about 9.45 a.m. These meetings are chaired by the Departmental Editors, or their deputies. The Editors are the executive and managerial heads of the News Departments, and have access to policy decisions made at the highest levels in the BBC. They are joined at the meetings by senior editorial staff from the newsroom, planners of news coverage, and such specialist correspondents as are available, the major purpose being as informed a discussion as possible of the news in prospect. The Deputy Editor, Radio News described the 'morning meeting' this way:

> We take a brief look back, and also forward, and ask: 'what should we lead with?' We try to plan the coverage for the day. Sometimes we look back and decide we led with the wrong thing, and have a brief discussion.

Certain features of the meetings can be distinguished. First, there is a retrospective discussion. At Radio News, where there has been overnight coverage, the chairman asks the night editor whether he has had problems, and often makes observations about the previous day's output. For example, on one occasion in 1972 at Radio News, one newsroom man was singled out for praise for having obtained early details on the burning-down of the British Embassy in Dublin. On the negative side, outside complaints were relayed by the meeting's chairman about the BBC 'overplaying' coverage of the funerals of the thirteen people killed by British troops in Londonderry on 'Bloody Sunday'. One newsman said: 'Friend of mine thought it was the Coronation'. After joining in the laughter, the chairman made the editorial point: 'To be serious that is the danger'. This is sufficient to indicate that the conferences are a forum for appraising performances and transmitting editorial judgements. I will return to these points shortly.

Next, the morning meetings begin to address a definite agenda. This is the News Diary,[5] a document which lists home and foreign news stories which are thought to be newsworthy. Each service has its own diary. They are separately compiled overnight at Radio News, and in the late evening at Television News. The diary gives information on the availability of reporting staff at home and abroad; it lists the times at which circuits are available for feeding in reports from home and foreign correspondents, and reporters in various parts of the British Isles. The Television News diary contains a lot of detail about the arrival times of film from abroad, satellites and Eurovision link-ups.

The diaries have two distinct sections: Home and Foreign. In both services, home news stories, which are generally far more numerous than foreign stories, are considered first. I will give some indications of the way in which stories are assessed, by considering typical examples which cropped up during fieldwork.

Guidance

The morning meeting is an opportunity for the editors to push the handling of news in particular directions. On one occasion in September 1975, the Editor, Radio News, wanted to know why a speech by Mrs Margaret Thatcher, Leader of the Opposition, had not been reported. She was then on a tour of the USA. The editor of the day in charge of the newsroom said that he thought it had been 'platitudinous', that he was 'amazed the papers ran it', and that it had said nothing new, being 'well-acknowledged Tory philosophy'. The Editor was unimpressed, and observed that you had to take account of where and when the speech was made, and that it would have an effect on the Tory party. He thought Mrs Thatcher 'ought to be watched'. She was, and her speeches were reported in subsequent coverage. The following day the Editor noted 'Thatcher got her run for money'. My impression was that he was responding to outside pressures.

News angles

There is sometimes a discussion of the particular construction to put on a story. When, in July 1976, the Chancellor of the Exchequer announced further cuts in government expenditure, it was decided at Television News to deal with the story 'along Budget lines'. Thus, at the outset of the day it was essentially decided that the cuts would be the main story, and a detailed discussion about appropriate contributions from the specialist political, economics and industrial correspondents ensued.

Another example occurred when there was a discussion of an official report on 'Privacy' to be published that day. The editor of the day and the home affairs correspondent, within whose brief the story came, agreed that the theme of the radio report should be 'the public interest'. The story was seen as both attractive and significant, having 'James Bond aspects' concerning electronic bugging and snooping, and dealt with such practices as members of the public being given covert credit ratings.

Assessing the strength of pressure groups

During the 1976 Olympics, a group called the South African Non-racial Olympic Committee (SANROC) claimed credit for bringing about a boycott of the Games by African states in protest against Apartheid. There were reports about SANROC in the morning papers, and at Television News it was discussed whether to interview members of the group. The Editor said: 'Their actual strength of influence isn't that much'. This was a clear instruction to treat them with circumspection. In discussion with the Editor, Radio News, over the sound link with Broadcasting House there was quite spontaneous agreement that 'We shouldn't overplay that'.

Deployment and logistics

At this early stage of the newsday there is much concern with the deployment of reporting resources. News organizations have limited manpower and can cover only those stories they think the most newsworthy. These arrangements are especially complex in television news, where there is a pre-eminent concern with 'logistics', with what is often described as 'the mechanics of the thing, getting the stuff in'. Because television has a more complex technology than radio, the morning meeting at Television Centre brings in people with technical expertise (such as film editors, graphics assistants and studio directors) as well as journalists. Discussion of 'satellite times' and 'picture lines' abounds, with talk of technique dominating far more than the substantive news judgements which actuate the quest for pictures. A senior news executive compared the problems of television coverage with those of radio:

TV at its optimum working method uses much more complex
equipment, it is also larger, more cumbersome and more obtrusive.
The newspaper reporter is indistinguishable from the general
public apart from his notebook and pencil. The radio reporter is
also a single man with his own equipment. But the TV reporter
will need a crew (cameraman, sound recordist, lighting man). To
do the job effectively you need a certain amount of physical movement over varying distances in order to get the picture on the
air. Compare this with radio: you can get a totally effective
report through provided you can get to a phone anywhere in the
world.

The news diaries contain detail of deployments which have already
been made. The central problem is that of ensuring that reports are
available to meet the transmission times.

Problem stories

Some stories pose particular problems. One noteworthy category
was civil disturbance, and coverage of Northern Ireland was pre-
eminent here. An example comes from a meeting in September 1975.
There was a discussion of the Press Association's (PA) reporting
of a murder in South Armagh. The PA interpretation differed from
the BBC's Belfast newsroom's. The message from the Deputy Editor,
Radio News, was: 'We've got to generally watch the thing: we've
still got to check PA on sensitive political stories involving Protestant
and Catholic areas. Straight court cases can be accepted on PA but
we've got to check killings and casualty figures so they're consistent
with (BBC) Belfast output. There're people listening to our news
immediately after the local Ulster BBC.'
    A different example comes from the retrospective discussion of a
shooting incident in Leicester. The story, compiled by BBC Radio
Leicester was a vivid account with 'actuality' of the shooting and
struggle. The question was, should it have been run so fully, since a
man had been arrested. The BBC's lawyers had given conflicting
advice and the story had been run. The overnight editor's defence
was that the man who had done the shooting was not named. The
editor said: 'If we're going to disregard the lawyer's advice, I'd
better know about it.'
    The meetings last for about 20 minutes to half an hour. They
provide a forum for the exercise of editorial control before the locus
of decision-making shifts to the 'shopfloor' level of newsroom
practice. Editorial attitudes emerge during the course of running

through 'diary stories'; where they do not, it is because they are taken for granted.

The link-up

Although the Radio News and Television News departments are autonomous units within the BBC, they have radio, telephonic and teleprinter links, and the contact which takes place before the new day's main coverage is particularly significant. The chairmen of the respective meetings discuss one another's diaries over the sound link at 10.00 a.m. An extensive degree of shared understanding is clearly demonstrated when the chairman at Radio News can run through a list such as this which remains unquestioned and unexplicated. It is rather like swopping headlines: 'Lots of industrials: TUC, CBI, Docks Board, Chobham offer, BUA including redundancies. Race relations – decline in discrimination. Radio news trial special. Provisional IRA truce. Foreigners: New York Primary; Kissinger in Peking. Not much else.' TV News: 'We didn't find anything.'

Where coverage is routine, in the sense that it does not present politically, morally or legally sensitive material – and in most cases this is so – discussion is quite minimal. Occasionally, one service has the edge over the other. For example, Radio News had information about the visit of a government minister from Pakistan in connection with recent racial conflict in Britain. The link between the two services is a way of making sure that the BBC speaks with one voice – a long-established goal – and of co-ordinating logistical demands. Sometimes, Radio will pass on sound recordings to Television, and vice-versa.

There are two major mechanisms for controlling production at the newsroom level. The first is the morning meeting, which works out unwritten guidelines for treatment on a pragmatic day-to-day basis, and the second the editorial structure inside the newsroom.

To follow the routines of production through the newsday from the perspectives of those at the centre of editorial decision-making, it is essential to begin with the structure of the newsroom, and then to consider its relationships to the news-gathering operation.

The BBC's editorial system vests maximum responsibility in editors and producers at the level of production. At the centre of newsroom operations, with overall responsibility for the production of bulletins on any given day is the editor of the day. In Television News, there are two editors of the day, one supervising the work of each of the desks. In Radio News, where there is a 24-hour cycle, an editor of

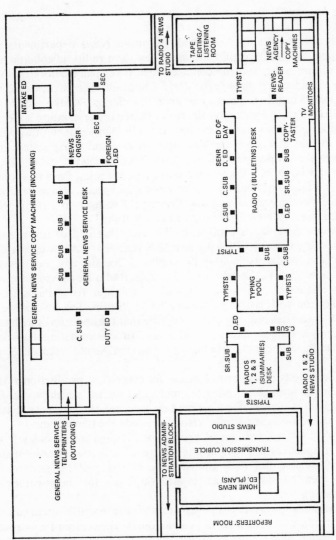

Figure 3.1: The Radio Newsroom

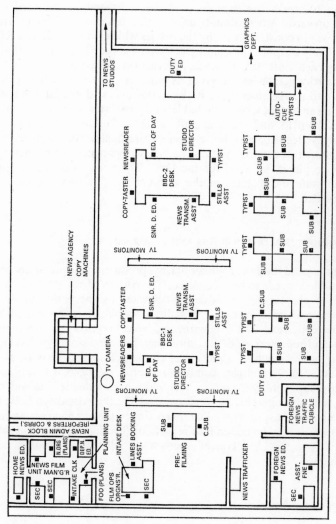

Figure 3.2: The Television Newsroom

the day is responsible for each shift, one from 9.00 a.m. to 10.30 p.m., the other until 9.00 a.m. the following day.

Editorial autonomy is certainly stressed in the BBC's corporate ideology. But the scope of individual decision-making, although not subject to crude directives from above, *is* limited by the need to 'refer upwards' where doubts arise. Also, newsroom decisions are made within constraints set by the diaries which list the bulk of each day's likely output. The guiding principle behind the system is that, during each shift one (in Radio) or two (in Television) senior and trustworthy personnel are given as complete an overview of newsroom and news-gathering activities as possible, with the intention of securing an output which is 'reliable' in the BBC's terms. For reporters out in the field, and editorial staff inside the building, the editor of the day is a legitimate authority figure with a final say on the duration and content of reports. Within the News Department he is seen, as someone put it, as 'God for the Day'. The gods rotate according to the mundane dictates of the shift-system. But they are always represented.[6]

THE PRODUCTION OF BULLETINS AND PROGRAMMES

To understand the daily routines of news production the pre-eminence of deadlines needs to be recognized. The pattern of work falls into a series of phases, each of which is delimited by the period of time between transmission times. A radio news bulletin is composed of written copy read by the newsreader, 'voice' reports by correspondents and reporters, and 'actuality' (i.e., recorded sound of 'events' taking place – such as, shooting or rioting). Televised news is, as a product, a more complex combination of elements. It is composed of scripts spoken by the newsreader which are written to film, video-tape, still photographs, maps, diagrams and other visual symbols; it contains 'on the spot' or studio reports from reporters and correspondents which may be edited film reports or 'live inserts'. In what follows I give an 'ideal typical' account of bulletin (or programme) production.

Planning the bulletin

At about 10.30 a.m. with the deliberations of the 'morning meeting' behind him, the editor of the day takes his place at the Radio 4 desk, or at one of the two output desks in the television newsroom and confronts the main problems of constructing a bulletin. Let us assume we are considering the processes leading to the production of lunchtime bulletins on Radio 4 and on BBC-1. The central and recurrent concern is with the *selection, ordering* and *treatment* of news stories. Together with his chief subordinate, the senior duty editor, the editor of the day must assess the stories likely to be used for the next bulletin.

When the news diary has been discussed, the morning papers have been read, news agency copy sifted through and 'tip-offs' have been received from the BBC's correspondents, the two senior editors are able to draw up a 'provisional running order'. The running order is a list of news items which seems to the editors to make good sense in production terms. In general, they broadly agree on their judgements, and where they do not, the editor of the day has the last word.

The day's production does not begin with a blank sheet. By that time of the morning, coverage of several stories, both home and foreign, is already in train. For example, 'Routine Industrials', Northern Ireland Coverage, Ministerial Press Conferences, Court Coverage and the like are the kinds of diary story which would automatically be covered. Similarly, the arrival time of a film story from abroad is generally known a day in advance. The running order is expected to change as the morning wears on and new stories 'break'. The keystone of the bulletin is the 'lead', which is equivalent to the main front-page story in a newspaper. When the editors have found a story which they think is sufficiently newsworthy to head the bulletin, they have a yardstick against which to judge the newsworthiness of others.

In Television News, unlike Radio, it is standard practice for editors of the day to have a 'running-in day'. Before a two-day shift at the desk, they spend a day in familiarizing themselves in detail with proposed coverage worked out in planning meetings which they have attended; requests are made to the News Intake section, which pre-plans coverage to 'set-up' any other stories thought likely to be worth carrying. This extra involvement stems from the overweening concern with the complexities of logistics, and the greater organizational size of television news, which has bred a need for more formality in planning than radio. For instance, to obtain a film report on the drought in Western Europe in 1976 required several days' advance planning, whereas a radio 'round-up' could be easily arranged.

Sub-editing, or writing stories

A news bulletin is the product of a number of interlocking skills. The main journalistic division of labour is between news-gathering (reporting) and news-processing (editing). In the newsrooms in summer, 1975, there were thirty-six editorial staff in all at Radio News and some sixty at Television News. Each section of the bulletin is allocated to a sub-editor (or sub) who works under the detailed control of the senior duty editor. In Radio, the sub-editor is responsible for supervising the editing of audio tape and writing copy for the newsreader. In Television, the sub-editor (more often called a script-writer) supervises the editing of newsfilm and videotape (vt) and selects graphics. In both News Departments, the technical function of editing film, videotape, or sound tape is carried out by specialized staff. The subs also liaise with reporters and correspondents covering particular stories. From this synoptic account, one can see how the lines of control stretch out from the desk, down from the editor of the day, via the sub-editorial staff through to the technical and reporting arms of the news operation.

The bulletin as collective product

A news bulletin is a collectively-assembled product, dependent upon the orchestration of a number of discrete skills. Once stories have been assigned, a series of parallel selection processes is set in train. These are woven together in the hour before the bulletin goes out over the air, and sometimes not finalized until transmission itself has begun.

The sub-editing processes

When a sub-editor is given responsibility for various stories, he, in effect, controls a segment of bulletin time. This time-slot is 'filled' in various ways. According to current conventions of news production the main forms are these: written copy spoken by the newsreader, 'voice' or visual reports from reporters, edited voices or film of interviewees or eye-witnesses, graphics, 'actuality' sound and footage. Sub-editors have to 'package' these forms into the relevant mix under guidelines set out by the editor of the day. Copy-editing and script-writing is common to both radio and television production. Television news, however, largely obeys a visual imperative, and the knitting together of a segment of a television bulletin demands the ability to marry words and pictures.

The detailed control of the sub-editing process lies in the hands of the senior duty editor. The role was described by one newsman in this way:

All the copy goes to him. He makes suggestions about change and development. He keeps the subs supplied with up-to-date copy; he's the central clearing agency; he has to make sure that everyone knows what's happening – for example, changes in the running order.

All written copy passes through the senior duty editor's tray. In Radio News, he also listens to tape-recordings and gives editorial instructions. Such detailed supervision is also common at Television News, where the editors of the day oversee most major stories, going with the sub-editors into the cutting-rooms and videotape suites to supervise the selection of shots. On one occasion in Radio News, the editor of the day took over a story from the chief sub-editor; it was about an Orange Order parade in Northern Ireland. A further illustration comes from this observation recorded in my field notes:

> There was a filmed interview from Scotland with Jimmy Reid (shipbuilding workers' leader) and a representative of the US company which was buying up the bankrupt shipyard. Both the Editors of the Day agreed that a shot of the two men shaking hands would make a 'good headline shot': it represented a mixture of programme considerations and the guts of the story as seen by them. Editor, BBC-1: 'That could be an "out". I want it simple, quick, easy as possible. Where should we put the handshake?' (the Editor cut out the sub's discretion). 'We'll have one minute-forty of the interview in. It probably gives the flavour of what he thinks. Forty-five seconds of thingy with a good handshake in between.'

The sub-editing process in television is complicated by the fact that so much of the work has to be done by technical editors under the direction of the newsroom journalists. The technical dimension in radio news production (editing audiotapes) is simpler because reports or 'actuality inserts' can be directly slotted into the newsreader's script. In television production sound and visuals have to be related.

The updating process

The concept of news presupposes a notion of change, and so 'updating' is integral to the entire production process. It involves accommodating 'new facts' in stories kept in the running order, and replacing entire stories by 'new' ones in line with the newsman's law of the survival of the newsworthiest.

While most news stories eventually broadcast can be predicted each morning, some cannot. The earlier they 'break' before the bulletin is due to go out over the air, the greater the chance for editors to arrange coverage. There are various ways in which they can become aware of these new stories, or of developments in, and ramifications of, the old. The BBC itself contains various sources which feed into the news-producing system. The BBC Monitoring Service at Caversham Park is often the first source to hear of sudden developments abroad – the death of President Nasser was first learned of in this way. BBC newsrooms around the United Kingdom can send messages on the teleprinters to the London newsrooms – news of murders or fires, for example. Correspondents and reporters covering stories may telephone in with reassessments of their importance. In addition to all of these, by the time the first running order is revised at about 12 noon, the early editions of the London evening papers are available and are carrying stories which might influence the editor of the day's final judgement.

Apart from these sources there are the news agencies, without whose services no news organization could function adequately. On the foreign side the BBC subscribes to Reuter, Agence France Presse, Associated Press and United Press International, and Tass. At home, although the BBC takes news from various agencies, the dominant source is the Press Association together with the BBC's general news service (see Appendix). Clearly a considerable sifting process has to take place.

Much of this, in both News Departments, is done by the 'copy taster' who has to make the flow of agency tape manageable for the senior duty editor. He is strategically seated next to the two senior desk editors. One copy taster with a touch of hyperbole described his job this way:

> All the news in the world comes into this tray. I read it and discard 90 per cent. 10 per cent isn't an arbitrary figure, you know: what's worthy of consideration I offer.

The passing-on of 10 per cent of the copy acts both as a goal and as a standard: it is considered important not to overburden the senior duty editor, and the copy taster measures his efficiency by how well he is keeping the flow down.

The copy taster deals with the flow of news agency copy alone. In Television News, where the visual aspects of news are of key importance, there is a separate pictures desk, at which incoming news agency stills are sorted and catalogued by a specialist stills assistant.

Much of the selection of copy takes place within the framework of expectations about newsworthy stories which is embodied in the news prospects and the running order; in addition, the copy taster orients himself to the selection of news stories by having heard the most recent morning bulletins and having glanced through the most recent newspapers. Efficiency in selection is judged in terms of 'experience' – the development of a 'news sense' through time.

The updating process gives a dynamic structure to the production of bulletins. The editor of the day and the senior duty editor have to take account of a constant flow of information, and make changes in the sub-editing process which will accommodate it. Reporting is also affected as new requests may go out to reporters already working on stories. The role of the copy taster is particularly important when it comes to changes of fact in stories in the immediate period before the bulletin is transmitted. He knows which subs are working on particular stories and can directly inform them himself of changes, or pass messages through the senior duty editor. The updating process allows immediacy and accuracy to be maintained right up to transmission time.[7]

There are two other important sources of regular updating in both the News Departments. Incoming reports and film are channelled through the home and foreign 'intake' desks (discussed below), and these units keep up a continuing flow of messages to the output desks about how the day's coverage is shaping up.

The hour before transmission

By 12 noon at Radio, and 1.00 p.m. at Television, the senior duty editor, after consulting the editor of the day, will have drawn up a revised running order which expresses the basic intended shape of the lunchtime bulletin; this new order is revisable in the light of any significant changes in existing stories, or the appearance of new ones which seem to have greater 'news value'. At this point there is still a good deal of flexibility in terms of arranging for fresh reports and making changes in emphasis. There is a built-in expectation of change.

The sub-editing process reaches its peak during the pre-transmission hour. By then many of the scripts for the newsreader have been written and much of the tape-editing finished. Several stories remain to be completed, however, and the updating process is continuous. At about this time, in Television News, the newsreader comes into the newsroom and begins to run through the available scripts, waiting to familiarize himself with the rest as they begin to pour in during the next half hour. In Radio News, where there are far more outputs, the newsreader tends to spend the entire day in the newsroom.

Scripts go first to the senior duty editor who makes any editorial corrections he sees fit, querying the use of language and grammar, and paying particular attention to the formulation of issues, descriptions of people and of organizations. The scripts then pass to the editor of the day who makes any further alterations he thinks are necessary before passing them on to the newsreader.

The editor of the day has a fairly precise knowledge of the duration of the available material at this point as he has added up the running times of the individual news items. As bulletins are normally slightly 'overset' (have too many stories for the available time slot) he needs to have his priorities clearly in mind so that he knows which stories he will eventually 'drop' (leave out of the bulletin). This decision is deferred until the last possible moment in case there are shifts in the relative news value of particular stories.

The editors, while compiling the running order, decide which stories merit 'headlines'. These tend to be written, however, only in the last ten or fifteen minutes before transmission. Again, as with decisions about what to drop, the editors prefer to leave their options open about the final priorities and significances accorded various news items until the last possible moment. The headlines are written by either the editor of the day, the senior duty editor or the chief sub.

In Radio News, about two minutes before the start of the news bulletin the senior editors rush to the news studio to supervise its presentation.

At Television Centre, there is a striking difference in the run-up to transmission. Whereas the newsreader's run-through in Radio News is simply an informal reading of available scripts, and a familiarization with where tape-recorded inserts come in the sequence of items, at Television News there is a full-scale rehearsal. This derives directly from the greater technological complexity: so much more can go wrong. The programmes we see certainly are live, but they are far less spontaneous than they seem.

Half an hour before the bulletin is due to be transmitted, there is a studio rehearsal on the basis of the existing script and visual content. The studio director assigned to the output desk works through the anticipated sequence. He tests the range of visual sources which are fed into the bulletin to see if they are in working order. For example, newsfilm has to be laced into reels for the telecine machines (a device which converts film into electronic pictures), but these have to be in a sequence which follows the script. The director has to make sure that 'live' sources – for example, an outside broadcast unit, or the BBC television studio at Westminster – are in working order. Camera movements are practised to see if they fit into the split-second timing of the script. The newsreader is alerted to the cues he might expect. This kind of preparation means that the possibility of making major changes in the running order is circumscribed. As one editor of the day observed:

> The bulletin is changeable while on the air, but you have to balance the desirability of last-minute change against practicability. You can't drop and change with absolute freedom. There mayn't be time for me to run through the story. There are technical limitations – it's not sure you can get everything in time.

Despite the rehearsal, there is still a last-minute rush from the newsroom by the editor of the day and the senior duty editor to the news studio in order to supervise the transmission.

Transmission

A news bulletin, although a collective product, displays the characteristics of a unified one. The role of the newsreader as 'anchorman' in presenting the series of items which comprises a bulletin is a crucial one. He opens, intersperses, and concludes the sequence with his own voice, and, in television, his presence in vision.

There is, again, a striking contrast between a radio news broadcast and one of television news. Both are tense occasions because it is always expected that the existing order of news items, will, in one way or another, be upset. The contrast lies in the differing physical arrangements made for transmission. In Radio News, these are quite simple: the senior duty editor sits in the news studio next to the newsreader and passes late or changed news items to him. By contrast, television transmissions are directed from a studio, the production decisions taken by the editor of the day being executed through a studio director. There is a more complex interplay of roles due to the greater formality of organization.

During the television news transmission, the newsreader sits in a studio, separated from the gallery where direction takes place by a glass partition. He has an earpiece through which he receives instructions from the studio director. The editor of the day cannot, as in a radio transmission, wander in and alter the running order: the very existence of the camera in the studio rules out such easy behaviour. While in a radio transmission the production is handled by only two technical officers who monitor the quality and sequence of tape-recordings, the television gallery contains a large number of personnel whose activities are harmonized by the studio director: the vision mixer, engineers, cameramen, sound and lighting technicians.

Nevertheless, the editor of the day retains the power to decide last-minute changes of content. Throughout the transmission he and the senior duty editor are obsessed with the timing, and terse instructions follow to the director: 'Drop 14 Dublin; first words 14 slightly changed. 63 docks out; we don't want docks.' As in Radio News, though less directly because of the intervening organizational and technological complexity, the editor of the day exercises control over the detail of the bulletin's content. During the last minutes of the pre-transmission period and during the transmission itself the need for control expresses itself in terms of a fixation with duration:

> The sheer pressure of time takes over. If you want to drop one minute fifty-four seconds then you look for a story of that size, and out it goes. You'd only keep it if it was really important – and sometimes not even then.
>
> (Senior duty editor, Television News)

Changes occur at this late stage, both in Radio and in Television News, because bulletins are routinely 'overset'; this occurs because editors like to leave their final selection to the last possible moment. For example, two minutes before one lunchtime radio bulletin, the police rang the newsroom and asked for some information to be left out of a murder story. A teenage girl had been stabbed to death, and they did not want the murder method to be disclosed while they were still conducting enquiries. The editor of the day agreed to the request, but this meant that alternative arrangements had to be made, literally at the last moment. The newsreader's script had already been written and a reporter had recorded a 'voice piece'. Two minutes into the bulletin, the editor decided not to use the pre-recorded report, and ask the reporter to go into the studio 'live' with the amended story. In the event he did not have the time to do this, and so the newsreader read a brief piece of scripted copy written in the newsroom. A more usual reason for changing the running order is the occurrence of a 'late newsbreak'. On one occasion for example nineteen minutes through the *Nine O'Clock News*, news of an aircrash in Paris came into the gallery and was duly included in the bulletin. If an important 'newsbreak' occurs, and it is difficult to alter the running order, the story is accommodated by using phrases such as 'We've just heard that . . .' or 'Some late news . . .' at some convenient moment in the sequence.

Briefings and post-mortems

A quite distinct feature of work at Television Centre is the formal briefing. Each output desk has its own news conferences at various points of the day which bring together the editorial staff and the studio director and his assistant. The central purpose of these meetings is to decide the running order and the presentation of content for the next bulletin. The following extract from my field notes captures the flavour of one such occasion:

Editor of the day: 'All right – Docks is the lead. We should have an interview. Have they finished the mass meeting?'

Chief sub: 'Yes.'

Editor of the day: 'Then we'll assume we have an interview . . . Rail: let's do industrial disputes. Harland and Wolff – we've established that there's library film. A still and film for vision . . . Shall we go abroad now? Hijack? Vietnam? Leave space for that Belfast vt. There's the Eurovision, so we mightn't need a still. Vietnam: vision, map, vt. We might get film for the 9 o'clock. us Primaries: vt., stills, wiping. The mine?'

Senior duty editor: 'We've got a nice still.'

General news
  service
  announcement: 'Vietnam talks suspended.'

Editor of the day: 'Possible vision.'

The meeting is dominated by the editor of the day who basically states the stories to be covered, and having determined their order and visual treatment after quite minimal consultation with his colleagues, he dictates the running order to the senior duty editor. The basic programme concept is therefore set out by the editor of the day who consults available staff concerning likely production or technical problems. Orders are placed with the graphics department, lines are booked, and the sub-editors given some guidelines on how to handle their individual stories. The meeting lasts between twenty minutes and half an hour.

These last few pages have given an ideal typical account of how a single radio or television news bulletin is produced. The editorial practice of the newsrooms is supervised by the dominant figure of the editor of the day. But this is not a form of editorial control which is in the least sense individualistic; rather, it is intended to ensure

C

consistency, and corporate safety. On any given newsday, the practices outlined here are repeated in relation to each of the various output times.

NEWS INTAKE: AN OVERVIEW

The newsday begins with a structure of expectations about what is likely to make news. But the production process itself represents only one element of the behind-the-scenes activities of the News Department. Extensive logistical arrangements have to be made for news-gathering to meet the deadlines posed by the output times. 'News Intake' is the branch of the operation which makes these arrangements. It falls into two sections. One for 'Home News' which is under the supervision of the News Editor, and the other for 'Foreign News' which falls under the aegis of the Foreign News Editor. There is a further relevant division of labour. For both types of news there is both a daily function and also an advanced planning function.

Daily Intake

Home News
The intermediary between the newsroom and the reporting staff (including the specialist home correspondents) 'out on the road' is called the news organizer. Working under the instructions of the editor of the day he acts as a channel between the output desk and the reporting staff. The specific visual needs of television have created an additional intake role. The news organizer works together with a film operations organizer who is responsible for deploying camera crews in line with the news organizer's instructions, and seeing that they are provided with the requisite facilities: cameras, lighting and sound equipment, vehicles and so forth. The television intake function was described as 'similar to the news editor on a newspaper: here it's getting the film in'.

The intake desks produce the news diary (mentioned at the beginning of this chapter), act as the logistical focus for incoming reports, and give briefings and updatings to the output desks.

Discussion at the morning meeting centres mainly on information contained in the news diary. In Radio News this document is compiled for distribution at 8.00 a.m. by the news organizer on the overnight shift on the basis of various sources: there are BBC advanced planning documents (dealt with below) from which stories relevant to the day are selected; the Press Association diary sent over the wires during the night; the various PR hand-outs from government departments and other institutions and groups; the morning papers which may provide a story which merits following up. At Television News, where the news operation ceases by midnight, the diary is prepared in the later hours of the evening, and additions made the following morning.

The typical diary stories are those staples of reporting: news conferences, demonstrations, meetings between unions and employers, the publication of government reports, House of Commons business, Royal comings and goings, sport and so on. A specific feature of the television diary is its reference to the visual treatment of stories required – whether, for example film should be shot 'mute' (silently) or with combined sound and picture. The time at which visual material becomes available is of clear importance for planning the running order, and the later bulletins are planned on the assumption that most stories will be 'in' by then.

This brings us to the logistical aspect of intake. The news organizer has to see that reports which have been 'ordered' are fed into the newsroom in good time for editing to take place. This means that there has to be constant radio or telephone contact with reporters and crews to keep the editor of the day informed of any likely problems. For example, one weekday afternoon, the news organizer in Radio had arranged for a report from Aldershot about people charged with bombing the military barracks there. The report was needed for the 6 o'clock bulletin. The outside broadcast unit had failed to turn up and the reporter was asking for advice. The news organizer bemoaned this: 'All your best plans go up shit creek.' He told the editor of the day who was furious. At 5.15 p.m. the news organizer spoke to the reporter by telephone: 'If something hasn't come up by 5.35 you'll have to do a phone piece. Do a phone piece now, and an update later.' The news organizer therefore 'fixed' an alternative channel of communication for the reporter. By 5.35 that proved unnecessary as the engineer had arrived.

This example shows how the intake desk provides a picture of news-gathering for the editor of the day, and how crucial it is for keeping the scheduling of items in line with deadlines.

Apart from executing decisions about deployment the intake desk keeps the reporting staff alerted to developments in stories they are working on, passing on the latest agency material. Instructions from the editor of the day about the treatment of stories are also relayed through the desk.

Foreign News

The intake function for foreign news is handled by the Foreign News Department, whose 'representative' in the newsroom is the foreign duty editor. Broadly speaking his role is similar to that of the news organizer. Just as home news reports have to be co-ordinated and scheduled to meet the output times so do the reports of the BBC's foreign correspondents. The Foreign News Department produces that part of the news diary which deals with overseas coverage. Routine discussions are held between the foreign desk and correspondents in the field. The foreign duty editor sends out requests for stories to correspondents if asked by the editor of the day. As often as not, correspondents 'offer' stories which they think are worth following. Discussions with correspondents relay news judgements from London, establish arrival times for film and videotape inputs coming via Eurovision or communication satellites. In the case of radio, reports are compiled to meet specific circuits booked in advance.

The foreign duty editor is the foreign correspondent's main regular point of contact 'at home'. The correspondent is thought of as an expert interpreter of events in his particular 'patch', and briefings are based on the assumption that he knows how to tell his story for a domestic audience in Britain. One foreign duty editor described the briefing process this way:

> The story comes up, and we tell him what the main lines are. In the case of a highly trained correspondent, I say 'Do one minute for the next bulletin' and he'll do it. Or he may state a particular interest in his story. We give light guidance: we don't say 'We want such and such a line'; we leave it to the chap on the spot – he's immersed in the story, and we're guided by that. We still exercise the editorial function.

In Television News, one of the foreign duty editor's routine tasks is to sit in on the daily Eurovision newsfilm exchanges. At this exchange each Eurovision member offers available film to the international network and accepts newsworthy offers from others. There are three Eurovision exchanges each day, one at 12 noon, one at 5.00 p.m. and one at 6.55 p.m. Central European Time. The foreign duty editor makes his offers in line with the programme requirements of the editors of the day. Exchanges are costly. A Eurovision item may be taken unilaterally (by one television station alone) or multilaterally (shared by a number of stations). A unilateral item cost £170 for up to three minutes' duration in 1975, and in 1976 the same amount of time cost £186. The BBC originates considerably more items than it receives: during 1974 there were 1,434 'origins' to 922 'receptions'. Together with ITN, BBC News plays a predominant role in Eurovision exchanges.[8]

Foreign intake is also in constant touch with Visnews, an international newsfilm agency partly owned by the BBC, which supplies it with a great deal of film. Television News also has access to radio despatches sent to Broadcasting House and the BBC's External Services at Bush House. When Television News has no film for a story, because it was too costly to cover, or its crew has not yet arrived, it frequently uses a radio correspondent's despatch together with a still photograph in the bulletin.

Quite often, complex arrangements have to be made for the collection of film and videotape. For example, on one occasion Television News was taking film of fighting in Vietnam via satellite from the CBS network. (Such satellite links are very expensive. Material sent unilaterally by satellite from the USA to Britain in 1976 cost $1,760 for up to ten minutes, plus the cost of American facilities involved in the transmission.) The cost of this particular 'multilateral' was shared with other Eurovision members, who did not want the spoken commentary, which was in English. The foreign duty editor had the commentary sent by a sound circuit via Hong Kong; it arrived separately from the pictures.

In Radio News, the foreign duty editor tends to be a specialist, often a retired correspondent. It is common practice to call on him for a 'voice' report when there is not yet a correspondent in the field.

Overall, the role of the foreign and home intake desks is very similar: both are channels for organizing deployment through which reports flow in and instructions out.

Future planning

Home News

The day before the news diaries are drawn up in Radio and Television News, an earlier document called the advanced diary is compiled, by the Home News Editor (Planning) in Radio News, and by the News Organizer (Planning) in Television News. These intake editors arrange the deployment of reporters and the collection of recorded material one day ahead. It is estimated that 95 per cent of these advanced diary arrangements are embodied in the following day's diary, and that some 70 per cent on average are finally used, in some way or other, in the production of bulletins. Most news is not spontaneous, or unanticipated.

The advanced diaries are compiled from a number of standard

sources, already mentioned, notably newspapers, PR hand-outs, and the news agencies. Sometimes tip-offs come in from outside contacts cultivated by the BBC or people seeking publicity for some event. An additional source of a routine kind is the BBC's Future Events Unit, which acts as a clearing house for publicity hand-outs, distributing a regular list to the various news and current affairs teams. The planners at Broadcasting House and Television Centre exchange documents regularly.

The advanced diaries list events and their times of occurrence. Where the story is certain to be newsworthy – for example, a full meeting of the TUC General Council at a time of industrial crisis – the planners arrange for a correspondent or reporter to cover it: such arrangements can be, and are, altered in the light of the following day's news developments. This pre-planning of coverage is known as 'fixing'. A television news organizer gave a good description of how it works:

> The big problem is with government departments – trying to get coverage. If a Minister is speaking we particularly want to know if it's related to a crisis. The Secretary for Trade and Industry is talking at a packaging exhibition. I expect he'll have something to say. I'll phone his department and find out what he's doing, what his programme is. You can't find out what it's all about even on the morning, sometimes. It's all right if it's print or radio, but in TV you have to set it up. Some departments aren't interested in TV's needs; they're living in the days of archaic Victoriana. You just can't light every politician without knowing it's worth while: there are the expenses of allocating a crew let alone the film footage.

One is given a sense of the overall predictability of such events. At present, it is far easier to send a radio car to them than to deploy a large television 'OB' unit – although the coming shift to a more lightweight and compact television news-gathering technology in Britain should change this a good deal.

Every Thursday, at Television News, a Home News Futures meeting is held, which is attended by the Editor and Deputy Editor of Television News, the Home News Editor and his deputy, the five assistant editors who take it in turn to act as editor of the day, and the news organizer (planning). The agenda on this occasion is compiled by News Intake, and is called the Weekly Futures List. This list is divided into six distinct categories which indicate stable expectations of what is likely to make news: Ulster; Political; Industrial and Economic; General; Sport; Others.

The Home News Editor runs through the futures list for the next seven days and tries to 'sell' the stories to the output editors. Discussion at the meeting is a mixture of news judgement and logistical talk, although by comparison with foreign news coverage the technicalities of home 'fixing' tend to be less of a problem. The list contains details of advanced arrangements made with the BBC's regional newsrooms for sending pictures over video circuits for recording in London. Indeed, as in all television news discussions, the 'picture merit' of proposed stories is a highly salient factor. The 'hard' news – political and industrial/economic stories – is not as a rule seen as having great visual interest, as many such stories include 'arrival shots' of politicians and other national leaders, or take the form of interviews included in a correspondent's report. These therefore tend to be discussed in terms of their 'straight news value' and implications, although a pictorial angle is sought wherever possible. For example, at one meeting when Dr Caetano, then Portuguese Prime Minister, was expected in London on an official visit, the Editor noted the possibility of 'interesting' footage: 'Rent-a-demo will turn up.'

Foreign news

There are similar foreign futures meetings held both at Radio News (on Tuesdays) and Television News (on Thursdays). Each is attended by the Editor and Deputy Editor of the Department, the Foreign News Editors from both radio and television services, the Diplomatic Correspondent, the foreign duty editors, the output editors, and a representative of the External Services News. The futures list is run through by the Foreign News Editor of the Department in question. It consists of a list of potential stories for transmission within the next month. The list is divided into continents and sub-continents, and within each of these sections are listed stories being pursued or as of likely interest. The Foreign News Editor (Television) described the meeting as a way 'for us to estimate the interest among the editors of the day – we wouldn't do anything without that'. Foreign news coverage – especially in television – is very expensive.

The total budget for television news in 1976 was around £3 million. The amount set aside for foreign news was £$\frac{1}{2}$ million, a figure which included Eurovision and satellite costs, teams sent abroad, and four permanent staff foreign correspondents. In 1974, the foreign budget for radio news was about £290,000. Radio has far more foreign staff postings (see Figure 3.4) and the bulk of the money is spent on these. Another indication of costs in this area is the communications budget for both radio and television news. In 1974 the total came to £130,000 which was spent on circuits, cables, 'stringers' and so on.[9]

The underlying cost constraint, which is not very apparent at the level of newsroom routines, emerges in discussion at futures meetings: 'We estimate the news interest, and then whether it makes economic sense.' (Foreign News Editor). Concern about costs was particularly apparent during my concluding fieldwork of 1976. There was a palpable anxiety about the overall budget which had not been there in 1972. But this was hardly surprising after more than two years of exceedingly high inflation. The Editor, Television News said in an interview that there was now a tendency to leave out 'the worthy rather than the important story. For example coverage of the European Parliament. Though we've promised ourselves that we'll try to put it in later on.' In the newsroom it was said that people now thought far harder about using satellites, and sending crews on 'spot' news stories. Such financial constraints are of crucial importance in news coverage, and make agency material of greater importance as a stand-by.

The discussion at foreign futures meetings is a mixture of logistical and evaluative talk. Some stories are rejected as 'not interesting' on various grounds. For example, at one Television News meeting a proposed story about the South of France being ruined by property developers was rejected as 'the usual thing'. Another rejected proposal was that of:

> A Kurdish journalist [who] has asked if we would be interested in sending a reporter and camera team to look at the situation there. The prospect of further fighting is very real as the Kurds are becoming increasingly dissatisfied with the failure of Baghdad to honour the agreement on autonomy . . .

It was immediately asked if this was 'propaganda'. Who was the journalist acting for? Was the struggle coming to 'anything'? The Foreign News Editor noted that it had 'not been looked at for some years'. The Editor said: 'I want something definitive – I'm not grabbed by it as background.' In response to the suggestion that the News Department ought perhaps to make a 'special' of it, the Editor said he thought they ought to wait, and in the meantime try to 'sell' the idea to the current affairs programmes *Midweek* or *Panorama*.

Certain stories may be stockpiled for use when a 'peg' presents itself. At a foreign futures meeting in Radio News in May 1974, one story seen as of particular significance was the likely resignation of President Nixon over the Watergate scandal. The futures notes read:

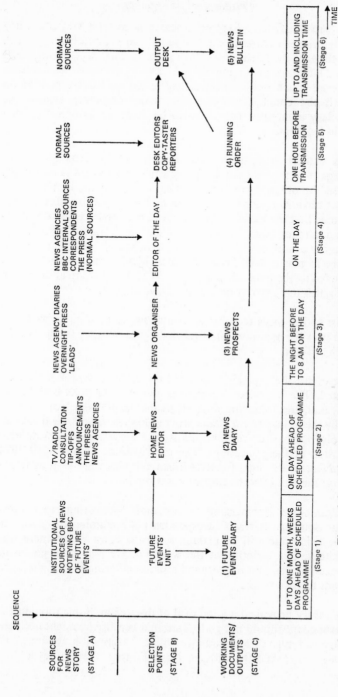

Figure 3.3: Planning and selection leading to the construction of a news bulletin

The crisis is expected to reach a peak time around May 21st when the televised hearings of the House judiciary committee begin . . . it is thought the hearings will take place on Tuesdays, Wednesdays and Thursdays beginning at 1430 BST . . . Given the mass of material which has been unearthed in the last twelve months on which the committee will focus, many observers believe the judiciary committee hearings will be more sensational than the Ervin hearings.

This extract encapsulates the duality of concerns at futures meetings. On the one hand a story's newsworthiness is evaluated. And on the other, there is a practical concern with its timing, as this has obvious relevance for planning the output. The futures list also noted that the Radio newsroom and a correspondent in Washington had 'already begun to work on "obit" material on Nixon'.

Another example of such stockpiling occurred when an interview with the former French Prime Minister, M. Couve de Murville, was conducted by the Paris correspondent on 11 July 1973 in anticipation of a French nuclear test on Bastille Day, 14 July:

> This, with a piece to camera, is intended to be used as part of a film package incorporating French defence ministry footage of the nuclear force.

In the event, the explosion occurred on 21 July, a week later than expected. The interview was used in the evening news bulletin on BBC-1, and, the following day, at greater length, the 'voices' were used by the radio current affairs programme *The World this Weekend*.

Deployment of correspondents is also a matter of considerable discussion at these meetings. The ramifications of the April 1974 *coup d'état* in Portugal for its African colonies were seen as newsworthy; the Radio News futures notes read:

> Mozambique is emerging as the most interesting story area. [Our Southern Africa Correspondent] is remaining there for the time being and will be making a trip to Beira where there was White v. Black rioting at the weekend. He may then go on to Tanzania where an important Frelimo gathering is thought to be about to take place.

This story provoked a good deal of discussion. Some thought the correspondent should not go to Tanzania because he might not then manage to return to Mozambique where the situation was unstable, and anyway, asked the Foreign News Editor, 'Would they let him into Dar?' He went on to inform the meeting of the purpose of the Frelimo gathering: a decision to move out of guerrilla warfare and to enter the political arena was likely. The Editor wanted to know how long the meeting would go on because they would still have to cover the Mozambique situation. It was decided that the Frelimo meeting should be 'covered by a stringer' (non-staff reporter) and that the newsroom would write the necessary copy to be 'voiced by the FDE' (foreign duty editor). A correspondent just returned from Rhodesia was then asked to fill in on the reactions to the Portuguese *coup* there. After citing his contacts, and their reliability, he summed up by saying that there was 'increasing concern though it's still a minority of Whites who're anxious'.

Foreign futures meetings combine, then, logistical and evaluative concerns. Much of the comment centres on the performance of given men in the field, and such reports as they are likely to be filing. The meeting, like the others discussed in this chapter, acts as a forum for pooling intelligence. It provides a basis on which to plan coverage for the coming fortnight.

NEWS-GATHERING

News-gatherers consist of, on the one hand, specialist correspondents and, on the other, of general news reporters. There are two distinct teams in the News Division, one of which serves the Television News Department and the other the Radio News Department. This division of labour is of only very recent origin, and marks a definite stage in the development of the BBC's domestic news services.

Until the beginning of the 1970s, a pool of general news reporters rotated between Broadcasting House and Television Centre. By 1972, however, they had been divided into two separate groups each of which worked primarily for either radio or television. In the same year the specialist correspondents began to be split between the two services. At first they rotated from one to the other, but after about a year were finally formed into two separate teams.

Many newsmen saw these changes as the outcome of a power-struggle in which Television News finally asserted its rightful place and shook off the 'dead hand' of Broadcasting House. There is some truth in this, as in the view that a major cause lay in the empire-building of the then Editor, Television News.

It was Radio which had to give ground. Without doubt, part of the reason for change lay in the expansion of radio news and current affairs outputs after 1970. The proliferation of outlets on Radio 4 turned reporters and correspondents into what several called 'circuit-fodder'. In addition, the main BBC-1 television news bulletin's time-slot expanded in 1972. The reporting staff were severely pressured, and the Editor, Television News, successfully argued that he needed more manpower for 'his' bulletins alone.

The competing demands led to the present rationalization of staffing. Until 1972, specialists were still controlled by Broadcasting House, through a special Department of Home and Foreign Correspondents, which serviced both the Television and Radio News Departments, and arranged overseas postings. This Department no longer exists. Now home specialists are under the direct control of the Departmental Editors of Radio and Television News. Foreign correspondents are linked to each Department through the foreign news editors, who generally supervise deployment. All correspondents work primarily for the News Division. although in radio they contribute extensively to current affairs programmes.

Political reporting is one key area which remains common to both services. This important exception to the rule is a considered matter of policy and was explained by one senior news executive as following the BBC's traditional line of speaking with 'one voice' on politics on both radio and television. The political staff are organized under the political editor, who is an important figure in the BBC since he acts as a gatherer of political intelligence, especially concerning politicians' views on broadcasting.

Home specialist correspondents cover defined areas of news interest. These are listed in Figure 3.5. There are eight specialists in television and nine in radio. In addition, there is the political staff of eight. The specialisms embody defined areas of news interest, and are expected routinely to generate stories. They all focus on major institutional spheres of British life, notably those of government and industry. One has simply to list the main areas to see what a staple diet they provide: Parliament and the major political parties; industry (the CBI and TUC), finance (the Stock Exchange and banks) and consumer affairs; Whitehall departments for education, labour, science and technology, home affairs, health, agriculture and fishing and local government; the Churches; the Monarchy. All are the stuff of the daily cycle of news.

News-gathering in this defined set of spheres contrasts with the generalist approach expected of reporters. There is a pool of twenty general reporters in Radio News, of whom half are at any time seconded to the current affairs programmes. A separate team of sixteen general reporters works for Television News alone. Both of these groups of reporters are centrally assigned by the intake desks. The London-based reporting staff are supplemented by regional

Figure 3.4   BBC FOREIGN CORRESPONDENTS, 1976

Area	Country & City	Number	BBC Service		
			External	Radio	TV
Europe	USSR; Moscow	1		1	
	France; Paris	1		1	
	Belgium; Brussels	1		1	
	Irish Republic; Dublin	1		1	
	W. Germany; Bonn; Wiesbaden	2		1	1
	Spain; Madrid	1		1	
	Austria; Vienna	1	1		
North America	USA; New York; Washington	4	1	2	1
South America	Argentina; Buenos Aires	1	1		
Middle East	Lebanon; Beirut	2		1	1
	Egypt; Cairo	1	1		
	Turkey; Ankara	1	1		
Far East	Hong Kong	1			1
	Singapore	1	1		
	Japan; Tokyo	1		1	
	India; Delhi	1		1	
Africa	Kenya; Nairobi	2		1	1
	South Africa; Johannesburg	1		1	
Australasia	Australia; Sydney	1		1	
	Total	25	6	14	5

radio and television reporters and the reporters of local radio stations.

Figure 3.5 BBC HOME CORRESPONDENTS, 1976

News Specialism	No.	Shared by both services	Television only	Radio only
Politics and Parliament	8	Political Editor, Political Corr., Scottish Political Corr., and 5 others		
Economics	1			Economics Corr.
Business Affairs	2		Business Affairs Corr.	Business Affairs and Labour Relations Corr.
Industry	2		Industrial Corr.	Industrial Corr.
Energy	1		Energy Corr.	
Science	2		Science Corr.	Science Corr.
Defence	1		Defence Corr.	
Diplomatic and Court	2		Diplomatic Corr.	Diplomatic and Court Corr.
Education	1			Education Corr.
Home Affairs	2		Home Affairs Corr.	Home Affairs Corr.
Religious Affairs	1			Religious Affairs Corr.
Agriculture and Fisheries	1			Agricultural Corr.
Sport	1		Sports Corr.	
Total	23	8	8	9

The BBC's domestic news services have 25 staff foreign correspondents posted abroad in various locations. These are listed in Figure 3.4. In addition, there are six foreign correspondents working for the External Services who also provide despatches for domestic use. There are also contractual arrangements with other correspondents who 'string' for the BBC. Foreign correspondents are generally posted in news capitals. Such locations, notably in the United States and Western Europe, provide staple news of, for example, the

American Presidency and the EEC. Together with news from conflict-ridden trouble-spots such as the Middle East and Southern Africa, routine foreign news gathering in the BBC, as in other media organizations, is set up in a way which is geographically limited. Although it should be noted that for a broadcasting organization it disposes of an exceptionally large number of foreign correspondents. Its main competitor, ITN, relies heavily on the practice of sending out 'firemen', and has one staff man in the USA and one in Europe.[10]

Like specialists in other news organizations, BBC correspondents have the status of an 'expert': they are internal pundits to be consulted by all non-specialists. The importance of this role is stressed in the BBC's *News Guide*, a codification of desired news practice:

> Any major story in an area covered by a specialist correspondent, e.g. education, should always be referred to that correspondent.[11]

The home correspondents are available for consultation in the London newsrooms. The foreign correspondents have routine discussions with London to assess longer-term trends and particular stories. Those stationed in Europe have a regular weekly 'hook-up' (irrespective of other contacts during the week) with the foreign news editors. There is also a daily exchange over a sound circuit with the BBC bureau in the USA at 2.30 p.m.

CONCLUSION

The production of broadcast news takes place in the context of a daily time-cycle. From the picture drawn in this chapter it is clear that there is a heavy reliance on a planning structure which creates a routine agenda of predictable stories which provide the backbone of each day's production requirement. There is nothing exceptional about the BBC's news operation in this respect. From such fragmentary indications as are available concerning its chief competitor in Britain, ITN, similar conclusions may be drawn.[12] Firm evidence is available about television news production practice in US networks in Epstein's account, and similarly detailed material on the major broadcast news operations of Ireland, Nigeria and Sweden is to be found in Golding and Elliott's work.[13] The analysis of routine practices given in these works shows the striking similarity of structure in different broadcast news organizations.

Most 'news' is constructed within a framework of firm expectations which are used to guide the deployment of available resources. For television in particular such planning is particularly important as there are technical requirements – such as having light to shoot film by, needing to wait for film to be processed – which make the time-factor particularly pressing. One might recall here Epstein's finding that despite the fact that news is defined by US television journalists in terms of immediacy, a high proportion of it is prepared in advance.[14] Most news is really 'olds', in the sense that it is largely predictable, but a powerful occupational mythology plays this fact down, as we shall see in the next chapter.

A noteworthy feature of the planning structure outlined here is that it is not one which easily lends itself to what journalists call 'digging' or 'investigation'. Diaries are assembled from sources available to all the media in Britain. Given similar news judgements about the same stories there is a tendency to homogeneity. Rarely does broadcast news present stories which are the product of investigation. It is not 'set up' for the task. To do this one would need to set aside resources – reporters, film crews, production teams. Again, this is not a point to be made about British practice alone. Epstein notes how US television correspondents do little in the way of originating stories, and how the bulk of coverage is reactive, being based on agency and newspaper stories.[15] Golding and Elliott suggest that 'being a monopoly, broadcast journalism is less concerned with the "scoop", the triumphant capture of an exclusive story ahead of rivals'.[16] To talk of monopoly, or, in Britain, duopoly, forces us to focus on broadcasting's relationship to the state, and its inbuilt tendency to caution. There is an ideology at work here about what broadcast news ought – and ought not – to do as well as a production structure stressing routine and predictability, which is pre-eminently oriented to meeting that day's deadlines.

There is little in the belief that news production is chaotic. Certainly, to the complete outsider it might look so. And to the complete insider it might feel so. But neither of these positions takes us anywhere. Bulletin production itself works within a structure of expectations outlined each day at the morning meeting, which is subsequently embodied in the various planning documents, and which will, if 'spot news' comes along, be disturbed. The tendency of this system is to produce an orderly picture of events, which, being 'news', are often themselves disorderly.

APPENDIX: THE BBC'S GENERAL NEWS SERVICE

The BBC works under competitive, or at least, duopolistic market conditions, in which a major criterion of efficiency in news-gathering is that of speed. One advantage of having a unified corporate structure lies in the possibility of operating a central clearing-house for news. BBC News is served in this way by what is described as 'our own internal news agency', the General News Service (GNS), which is based in the radio newsroom and operates on principles similar to those of other news agencies. There are two-way telex links between Broadcasting House in London and all of the GNS 'customers' – the various news and current affairs units in both the radio and television services.

Input and output

From the point of view of this chapter the GNS is most significant as a part of the *Intake function*, although it also sends information out. As a part of News Intake it falls under the responsibility of the Radio News Intake Editor.

Clearing information

The GNS team is headed by a senior duty editor who is responsible for its routine output, and also for ensuring that any special requests made by one or other BBC 'customer' are dealt with. In this way, news items of various kinds are directed through the desk according to the presumed interests of the audiences in question: these might be international, national, regional or local. The GNS has available to it all the agency- and BBC-originated news coming in to the output desks. The telex network is centrally co-ordinated by a computer and the sub-editors working on the desk code their copy so that it is automatically selected to meet both specific requests and general needs. If, for example, there is a House of Commons debate on steel, then the story will be cleared for all the steel-producing areas. If local 'personalities' from the regions or localities served by BBC stations are in London, then information and sometimes interviews are channelled to the interested 'customers'.

Desk organization

As the desk is concerned with transmitting 'relevant' news for internal BBC consumption a selection process necessarily has to take place; the chief sub acts as the copy taster as well as sending out material himself. There are two subs, one of whom has responsibility for local radio and the other for regional radio and TV. The copy which is transmitted over the wires is generally news agency material (particularly Press Association) which is re-written 'in radio style'. This sort of wired copy is known as a 'Rip 'n' Read' as it is intended to be taken directly off the teleprinter at the destination newsroom and read over the air. The copy has to meet the deadlines of news production in the local and regional stations.

'Beating the competition'

The relationship between London and the other newsrooms is a reciprocal one: the benefits of speed and accuracy are intended to work both ways. While the BBC relies on a diversity of sources for its news coverage its greatest preference is for its own. In coverage of Britain, until the GNS network was established there was a heavy reliance on the Press Association's copy which, being wired to every major news organization in the country, afforded the BBC no competitive advantage in 'tip-offs'. Now, according to the Deputy Editor, Radio News:

> We take a hell of a lot from local radio stations: it's really transformed our home news-gathering set-up. Previously we had to rely exclusively on PA other than staff reporters and special correspondents. Outside the main cities, London and the South-East, local radio has taken over as our main supplier.

From the standpoint of *national* BBC radio and TV news it is important to have the edge over ITN and the London commercial radio stations, which, it is claimed, is provided by the GNS network.

The earlier news of a story breaks the easier it is to accommodate it in the scheduled bulletin, and to 'fix it' logistically. For example, it was once pointed out with a great deal of pride, that a story about the death of a miner, who had been knocked down by a lorry while picketing, had been sent in by Radio Leeds and beat PA by ten minutes. Newsmen cite this sort of occurrence to vindicate the professionalism of their news-gathering system. The editor of the day is as a matter of course alerted to any such newsbreaks.

The GNS is on a loudspeaker hook-up to all radio and TV news and current affairs programmes and executives in Broadcasting House, Television Centre and Bush House. Whenever a news item seems to be of sufficient importance to warrant a place, the duty editor makes a brief newsflash – like announcement over the tannoy system – 'PA tell us that three miners were killed going down a shaft' – and then arranges for further details to be sent out over the teleprinters.

4

A stop-watch culture

Time is the substance of which I am made. Time is a river which
sweeps me along, but I am the river; it is a tiger which mangles me,
but I am the tiger; it is a fire which consumes me, but I am the fire...

(Jorge Luis Borges)

In the occupational mythology of the newsman time looms large
among the wicked beasts to be defeated daily in the battle of production. This chapter considers the nature and consequences of the
broadcasting newsman's obsession with duration and sequence. As a
feature of journalistic work it cannot be ignored, and not only
because journalists themselves assert its importance.[1] Rather, it is
because much of our sense of what is relevant, and therefore our
awareness of the passage of time, is structured by mass media
production cycles.

While the structuring role of the time-factor in production cycles
is almost invariably mentioned by sociologists who have studied
journalists at work, this theme is rarely singled out for separate
analytical treatment.[2] So far I have discussed how the routine
predictability of much news follows directly from the organization
of production. What is mainly considered here is the way in which
newsmen's production concepts are shaped by the constraints of
time, and the implications of this for the form and content of news.
In considering this feature of newsmen's occupational ideology we
are in the domain of the sociology of knowledge. For, as Gurvitch
has pointed out, 'the question of the ways to grasp intuitively,
perceive, symbolize and know time in ... different frameworks' is a
'central problem' of this field.[3]

THE TIME FACTOR IN CONTEXT

There are two contexts which must be outlined in order to understand the particular production system examined in this book.

The more immediate context is the occupational culture of the
broadcasting journalist engaged in daily production – one which

lays a particular emphasis on the stop-watch and the deadline as crucial features of work. In general, journalists are among those occupational groups in industrialized societies for whom precision in timing, and consequently an exacting time-consciousness, is necessary. Railwaymen are another.[4] Such an obsession with the passage of time is notable among those operating communication and transportation systems, which are dominated by a need for the exact co-ordination and synchronization of activities.[5]

To say that such groups are obsessed by time is but to point to exemplary cases of what is held to be a widely diffused fixation in Western cultures with the passage of the finer gradations of clock-time.[6] It is easy for us to understand such fixations as we are members of a society whose activities, notably work, are generally closely regulated by the clock. If it is true that 'the clock is surely the crucial machine of an industrial civilization'[7] then our looking at newsmen is simply a case of us the clock-conscious, watching the most clock-conscious. Our common denominator is an all too great familiarity with abstract time-reckoning which it is too easy to overlook, since it is taken for granted.

For cultures and societies which are not regulated by clock-time, the concepts and actions of newsmen must appear curious and alien, and probably quite pathological.

An apt instance came from one assistant editor in Television News who had spent a year teaching news production techniques in Libya on secondment from the BBC. The news was supposed to be trans-mitted at 9.00 p.m. each night, at the insistence of the Minister of Information. On one occasion, the programme before the news overran, so the news was forced to go on the air at 9.10 p.m. In keeping with the Minister of Information's instruction it officially went out at 9 p.m. This feat was achieved by the simple act of turning back the studio clock. The assistant editor had found it very hard to 'get them to take fast news seriously. They don't care about time there.'

Stories such as this underline the relative singularity of the value placed on time in developed Western societies[8] which, it is argued, has derived in part from the time-discipline progressively exerted upon the labour force with the growing dominance of industrial capitalism.[9] As Weber observed, time became just another commodity traded on the market-place, a further extension of ration-ality.[10]

This, then, is one possible framework for situating journalistic work: that of an occupation dominated by rationalized time-keeping within a society similarly so dominated. Within this context, newsmen travel along an astonishingly fast 'time track'.[11] This follows a regular cycle each day, the pace of which is governed by a series of deadlines.

A second, related context is that of the market for news in a capitalist society. As Raymond Williams has pointed out:

> The newspaper was the creation of the commercial middle class, mainly in the nineteenth century. It served this class with news relevant to the conduct of business, and as such established itself as a financially independent institution.[12]

These commercial market origins still inform the production routines of the press, and by extension, broadcasting. The production system described above, which is organized on the principle of delivering outputs at set times during the newsday, should be seen in relation to its market. Formally, at least, BBC News operates in a duopolistic market, in which competition is provided by the commercial radio and television stations of the Independent Broadcasting Authority.

Competition in production proceeds through each daily cycle. For the BBC's News Division, success in 'breaking' a story quickly or exclusively is principally assessed in relation to the outputs of the commercial network's national news produced by ITN. Newspapers are more of a source than a competitor.

NEWSMEN: VICTIMS OR CONTROLLERS?

> Both my organism and my society impose upon me, and upon my inner time, certain sequences of events that involve waiting. . . .
>
> (Berger and Luckmann)[13]

> There are long periods of doing fuck all, and then all hell breaks loose.
>
> (Television Newsman)

In an illuminating article, Lyman and Scott contrast two basic attitudes towards time. They write, on the one hand, of 'humanistic time tracks' where individuals feel they have mastery or control of their activities. By way of contrast, they point to 'fatalistic time tracks' where the feeling is rather one of compulsion and obligation.

Both these attitudes are exhibited by newsmen in their working lives. The reason for this lies in the peculiar situational constraints posed by producing news. News, despite much coverage that is pre-planned, is nonetheless felt by the newsman to be full of capriciousness. By definition, the unforeseen lies just around the corner. Newsmen are apt, therefore, to describe themselves and their work fatalistically. They see themselves as victims attendant upon events, and tell this kind of story:

The newsroom is quiet, activity controlled and routine. Then, 'the shit starts to hit the fan': a big story has broken; resources have to be mobilized and plans abandoned.

The tale is told in a way which reflects the way in which the operation is felt to move into top gear, suddenly, electrifyingly. The pace of work becomes frenetic, all-absorbing in its demands. Reporters find they must suddenly leave on an assignment – to report a bank robbery, an aircrash, to conduct an interview. Editors find they must make rapid selections. 'Everything is happening' in an episode of quick-fire activity. Utterances are clipped, sometimes rude; movements deft; the atmosphere tense; the noise level rises steadily. Sub-editors rush between newsroom and cutting-room, snatch a few words with the editor of the day and dictate their copy to typists. The TV news rehearsal takes place at a breathtaking pace. For reporters there is a great qualitative contrast between preparation ('fixing' interviews and 'doorstepping' sources), which involves waiting and holding back, and the act of reporting or interviewing, which is seen as the really authentic part of the job.

Newsmen oscillate, then, from victim to controller. From the valued, authentic aspects of news production – notably the hour before bulletin transmission – comes an idealized image of work as all-consuming action. From the direct experience of the structure of work at a given point in the production cycle the *entire* operation comes to be characterized as a feverish drama.

Such emphasis on action is an important feature of media professionalism. It is professional to be in control of the action rather than to be victimized by the pace at which it must, sometimes, be carried out. But oddly enough, being victimized is also something to be welcomed, as it is seen as what true newsmen feel in coping with an erratic force.

To be professional in this way is not simply to fulfil certain shared criteria of competence. It is as much a question of feeling certain things, of 'having the old adrenalin run'. Newsmen have, therefore, a specific cultural interpretation of the real meaning of their work, basic to it being the excitement and danger which arise from meeting tight deadlines. To become a controller, thereby transcending the victim-creating capriciousness of the news, is what makes newsmen's work so exciting.

The rhetoric employed by newsmen in describing their activities diverges, however, from the observed reality. In general, production is far from chaotic at anything other than a superficial level. Its rationale is to aim at control and prediction, while those who work the system celebrate its relatively rare contingencies. Indeed, there is a strange irony in the last-minute rush to fill the slot. Mostly, the intake of news items occurs during the last hour by design, as the later they arrive the more immediate they are. This means that anxious newsmen are working a system which can only exacerbate their anxieties. The contingencies are in fact created by the newsday cycle itself, and those values which stress immediacy.

IMMEDIACY AND COMPETITION

We become most clearly aware of the emphatic bias towards rapid turnover in broadcast new production when considering the key concept of 'immediacy'.

This is a temporal concept which refers to the time which has elapsed between the occurrence of an event and its reporting as a news story. Logistically, it relates to the speed with which coverage can be mounted. The pure type of immediacy, therefore, is 'live' broadcasting. In such cases, a TV camera or radio car is at the scene of the event as it happens, and the event is transmitted immediately to the viewer or listener. An added implication is the notion that the audience for news, can, via the technical means of communication, be present at the event. This idea is obviously fostered by contemporary broadcasting technology and the possibility of providing up-to-date actuality.

The very fact of having the technology can produce a spurious immediacy which is by now a familiar cliché. The rain-soaked industrial or political correspondent stands outside TUC Headquarters or No. 10 Downing Street and assures us that negotiations are going on at that moment. At this point, when X tells us that he is at a particular spot, and if he has a television OB unit, actually shows that he is there, we enter the realms of the absurd. But it is an absurdity which is broadcasting's own. Newspapers, by comparison, cannot be 'immediate' in this sense. They can, however, try to approach the ideal of rapid turn-over by rapidly updating stories in successive editions.

Immediacy acts as a yardstick for perishability. News is 'hot' when it is most immediate. It is 'cold', and old, when it can no longer be used during the newsday in question. Today's occurrences, those of this morning, afternoon, night, now, are what the broadcasting newsman wants to know about. Yesterday's story, in his view, belongs to the dustbin of history: the news archive. This value has been succinctly stated by Robin Day:

> More and more events are being transmitted instantaneously, direct and 'live'. This is the ultimate in news coverage, the real thing, seeing it happen as it happens.[14]

Similar observations, expressing the same sentiment, were to be found in profusion in the newsrooms:

> There's the feeling that if it's just happened it might be important.
> (Sub-editor, Television News)

> It's not really a news programme unless you have things bang up to date.   (Sub-editor, Television News)

> It's part of the professional side – you have to build up to a certain excitement for the deadlines without getting too edgy.
> (Foreign duty editor, Television News)

As immediacy is so central to news production as presently conceived it provides newsmen with a standard of logistical success. An apt instance occurred during fieldwork in 1972. There had been a dramatic aircrash in the London area. BBC Television News received an early tip-off about this occurrence and managed to send a film crew to the scene of the tragedy straight away. The main competitor, ITN, did not arrive so quickly, and the BBC team therefore scooped the story. The following assessment by the News Editor is immensely revealing of the dominant attitude towards the time-factor in news production (and also of news values):

> Professionally speaking, we were pleased that we were on the scene ahead of ITN, and got the film when the plane was starting to catch fire. . . . *When you've got news you should give it at its earliest.* You can't know all the contingencies.

This view was endorsed at the highest level in TV News. The Editor sent a congratulatory memorandum to the newsroom, commending the film crew in question 'for our extremely successful effort to get the Trident crash story to the screen. We gave a fuller and speedier news service than any other.'[15] From a professional viewpoint, this success in coverage was assessed as evidence of competitive competence based on speedy reactions:

ITN had no early coverage at all.

(Foreign duty editor, Television News)

We *had* to pull out the stops to beat ITN.

(Duty editor, Television News)

A similar example from 'the other side' is to be found in Tracey's study of political television. During the February 1974 General Election, the ATV newsroom in Birmingham, which was providing a results service for ITN in London, was briefed to get hold of the results first if possible: 'Constantly the need for speed was mentioned, and success over the BBC mentioned in seconds.'[16]

It is important not to underestimate the value for newsmen of having a yardstick such as immediacy for evaluating their performance. For, as will be seen in the next chapter, there is little meaningful interaction with the audience. Competence therefore becomes a professional matter – and what could be more simple and easily ascertainable than being able to measure it in minutes and seconds?

A slightly bizarre feature of competition is its occurrence within the BBC itself between the News Division and Current Affairs programmes. Thus, a radio Current Affairs producer told of programmes which would try to keep sources from the News so that they could interview them exclusively – credit going to those who put the voice on the air first. Programmes not only fight the News for this privilege but also one another. A similar tale from television quarters concerned the now-defunct programme *24 Hours* and the way it had spirited away a source intended for the News.

Immediacy, however, is in potential conflict with the value of accuracy. In the corporately cautious news judgement of the BBC, haste leading to mistakes, and thence to a loss of public esteem, ought to be avoided. This caution is given something of a public service gloss, as, for example, in the words of Donald Edwards, a former Editor, News and Current Affairs:

Sometimes we get hold of a piece of news which we know would interest the audience, but we are not absolutely certain of its accuracy. We have to hold it while we check. It is agony to a newsman to miss a bulletin, *but reliability and accuracy are more important than speed.* . . . It is not enough to interest the public. You have to be trusted.[17]

The tension is a basic one, giving us an insight into the way in which journalistic values (competition, speed) may conflict with a paramount organizational value (accuracy). In a context where the pace of output is rigidly governed by a certain number of time-slots, holding back a story until confirmation comes through means that the competition may well beat you to the draw.

The above quotation from Donald Edwards is echoed by the BBC's *News Guide* which lays down 'one-hundred-per-cent accuracy at all times' as the corporate ideal, notes that this 'must remain forever beyond our grasp' due to the 'fallibility' of people and therefore advises that 'If after checking as far as you can, you still have doubts about something, then leave it out.' This kind of policy is a practical counter-measure to what, to judge from the language cited above, is almost a state of original sin: the innate tendency to get the facts wrong. 'Accuracy' has characterized the BBC from its earliest days.[18] Being accurate, and therefore reliable, should be seen in the general context of the caution which characterizes the approach of broadcast news, not just in Britain, but elsewhere.[19] Such caution is manifest in the taking up of stories which have already entered the public domain via the press, or by steering away from some stories altogether.

Before considering some specific examples, it is pertinent to note how the need to make decisions under constant time-pressure brings about an evolution of rules of thumb concerning sources and their reliability. Until relatively recently, BBC newsrooms operated what was known as 'the two-agency rule'. This rule firmly prescribed that no report should be treated as adequately confirmed if it had not appeared independently on the tape of two news agencies. This rule gradually disappeared during the 1970s, and where doubt exists reports are transmitted using well-tried formulae such as 'Unconfirmed reports say that . . .'

Other current rules of thumb relate to news agencies, newspapers, newsfilm agencies, the Eurovision network, and the BBC's own internal sources. There is no attempt to suggest here that there is a set of uniform evaluations, but there are widely shared preferences and newsroom editors expect editorial staff to develop their 'instincts'. One editor of the day put it this way: 'The good sub develops antennae. He can spot it when things are wrong. It's important to know your agencies.'

Of the news agencies Reuter is uniformly spoken of as the 'quality' foreign news source, as unsensational and accurate, and it is therefore preferred to UPI and AP. Its staff are spoken of as 'men you can trust'. Probably one factor which reinforces these views is the BBC's special relationship with the agency: it has a liaison officer in the Reuter offices who relays special requests for 'follow-ups' of stories.

Of the two American agencies, AP seems to be the slightly more favoured by newsroom wisdom. With its rival UPI it is usually spoken of as 'good on America' or 'good for colour'. Both AP and UPI are thought of as 'slick' and 'sensational' which in BBC newsroom parlance is not a term of approbation. One newsroom editor described AP as a 'yellow press' agency, and another said its usual style was 'reds rape town'. Of the American agencies one editor said: 'You could use them as an "unconfirmed report", but not as an actual fact.'

The other international agency received in the newsrooms is AFP. The newsmen were suspicious of the link between this agency and the French government. It was accepted as 'good on France' but otherwise unreliable. The newsmen made a specific point of saying it was under government control, thereby revealing one criterion of what constitutes 'reliability'.

On the domestic side PA is the dominant British agency. It is the staple source of copy for the newsroom scriptwriters, and of tip-off and diary material for intake and reporting staff. It was described as 'reliable', if slightly 'slow'. As a matter of policy its Northern Ireland reports are never used on their own, but always have to be checked out with BBC-men on the spot – a point of some importance, as will be seen in Chapter 8.

Television has a consuming need for pictures. But not all the filming required by TV news can be done by its own crews. This is particularly true of foreign newsfilm where the cost of sending crews abroad is prohibitive unless the story is judged particularly newsworthy. Visnews is the principal agency for foreign news film. The BBC, together with Reuter's, is the main owner of Visnews. An arrangement which places it in a more favourable standing than 'stringer' or free-lance work. Regularity of association, as in the case of Reuter, is important in establishing trust. One member of BBC-TV's foreign news staff put the BBC's relationship to Visnews like this: 'They ring us to ask what are our priorities. They send a list, and it's decided what to ask for. We're almost cousins, and they're partly financed by us.'

Additionally, there are many sources of international newsfilm 'offers'. Among the range of foreign news organizations, the US network CBS is most frequently mentioned as a source, 'but it is not', as one newsman put it, 'quite as close as Visnews'. The third US network ABC is also occasionally used, but it was said that normally NBC and CBS materials suffice. Spain and Portugal were singled out as untrustworthy contributors to the Eurovision link, who would be unwilling to send film of civil disturbances or anything detrimental to the state. There was little respect for the news offers of Eastern

European countries, whose newsfilm is available via Eurovision's link with Intervision, its Eastern European equivalent. These were described as 'all fraternal solidarity meetings' and 'definitely no riots or good crashes'. Eastern European news services are anyway suspect *a priori*.

When newspapers are considered, a marked preference is to be found for the quality press. The news editor of Television News said 'We'd be doing a good job if the leads of *The Times, The Telegraph* and *The Guardian* got into the bulletin.' This view expresses a sense of the BBC's place in the media culture, and the kind of news values it admires. It goes further, however, to give indications of images of the 'reliability' of newspapers as sources of news in general.

The Times was widely described as 'authoritative' and 'reliable'. It could be described as one of the key yardsticks of excellence in BBC News. Indeed, this viewpoint has most recently been expressed in a document entitled *The Task of Broadcasting News*, which made much of the consistent similarity between the lead stories of *The Times* and radio and television news bulletins.[20] *The Financial Times* was generally respected, but not widely read by other than the economic and industrial staff. *The Daily Telegraph* while often referred to as 'biased' was praised for its extensive 'news service'. *The Guardian* seemed to occupy an odd place:. while evidently preferred reading around the newsrooms as a 'good writer's paper' with style, it was also labelled as having 'strong political attitudes', and therefore to be treated with circumspection.

Of the popular press, *The Sun* (apart from its compelling attractions on page three), *The Daily Mail*, and *The Daily Express* tended to be dismissed out of hand, and in an unflattering way. *The Daily Mirror* was thought by some to possess particular insight into the Labour Party, and to be a journalistically interesting paper.

The Morning Star was the only newspaper explicitly identified as ideologically motivated, though others might be described as 'biased'. The *Star* seemed uniformly to be seen as propagandist and therefore suspect. It was, however, thought to be helpful on labour matters by one of the industrial correspondents. The official BBC view of the newspaper is perhaps best crystallized by citing a memorandum from the Deputy Editor, Radio News, concerning the morning news feature 'Review of Today's Papers'. In this he wrote: '*The Morning Star* should find its proper place, but in view of its very small circulation should not find more than that.'[21] This message can be decoded as a warning to newsmen not to take too much note of the ideologically suspect; 'small circulation' should be read as a left-wing extremism which has little place in the consensual world of reasonableness and compromise which is deemed to characterize the views expressed in the British press.

Newspapers and news agencies are essential routine sources of news relevance. The newspapers are today's key to 'what everyone is thinking' in Britain, as well as 'what's happening'. The news agencies also provide an indispensable map of things worth knowing about. To have stylized judgements of the value of such sources, which in general prove 'right' is of considerable importance in a news organization, where time is always at a premium.

One strategy for making sure that reports fit the corporate criteria of accuracy and reliability is to expand the internal news network. The BBC has done precisely this in the case of its home coverage, by setting up the General News Service (GNS) which acts as a clearing house between the London newsrooms and regional and local stations. As a matter of policy the BBC has developed its local and regional newsrooms as extensions of its metropolitan news-gathering branch.

News received via the GNS thus affords two advantages: it has the standing of *reliable testimony*, pre-tested by BBC staff, and it is also fast, being unmediated by any outside agency. The tension between speed and accuracy is therefore resolved in this way. These points apply equally to the use of BBC staff reporters and correspondents. Having your 'own man' on the story is to use a self-authenticating source.

The BBC's monitoring of international broadcasts is another important source. It is used as early 'tip-off' material where important developments abroad seem to be foreshadowed or actually occur. Whatever is filtered through the BBC monitoring station is 'taken on trust' in the newsrooms. Examples of early tip-offs given by one copy taster were the announcements of Beria's death over Moscow Radio and that of President Nasser's death over Cairo Radio. The latter was received at 7.22 p.m. one evening and went out as the 'lead' story in the 7.30 p.m. TV bulletin.

One example of cautious news judgement occurred during field-work at Television News in 1976. A London correspondent of the American trade paper, *Aviation Week*, rang the intake desk with a tip-off. He was known as a good source on the basis of previous dealings with the Air and Defence Correspondent. He said that a Ugandan Boeing airliner had landed at Stansted Airport – at a time when Britain had just broken off diplomatic relations with Uganda. According to his sources it was carrying equipment damaged in the Israeli commando raid at Entebbe, and there were also rumours that the coffin of the missing hijack hostage Mrs Bloch was on board. The news desk was interested: the editors of the day said they would want to talk to the crew and film the plane on the tarmac being guarded by police. The flight was apparently a regular cargo trip between Stansted and Uganda. However, the story was classified as a possible 'good mystery' if the speculation was right. It was decided to send a crew to film the plane, and a reporter was asked to make some enquiries. Later that afternoon more details came from the airport source who said the aeroplane was alleged to contain President Amin's presidential suite and various trappings that flew with him, which had been sent to Britain for repair. The news organizer said that the story would be: 'Tonight police are guarding a plane from Uganda which contains some of President Amin's presidential suite.' It was not accorded much importance. However an awareness of Amin's previous attacks on BBC coverage was reflected in what the news organizer said to the tip-off man: 'It's the kind of story we don't want to get wrong. Amin'll use it against us. We can't take any risks.' The news organizer decided to check out the story with Stansted customs. The official source he spoke to said the story was based on rumour, since there was no possibility of knowing what was in the crates until documentation about their contents became available. The news organizer said: 'We can't broadcast speculation.'

The story was not run on television that night. It had not appeared on any news agency tape, nor did it in any other news organization's output.

The following day, the story was run by the *Daily Mirror* as a front-page splash with the headline: 'Idi's radar is here for repair: AMIN's load of cheek.' The news organizer told me that the *Daily Mail* had been offered it as an exclusive but had turned it down, and that if 'even they aren't running it it can't be much good'. According to the *Mirror*, Amin had sent 'a cargo of radar for repair'. The story was picked up by BBC Radio News that morning: it was mentioned in the 'morning papers' slot, and also briefly run as 'speculation continues' in the morning bulletins. At the morning editorial meeting at Television Centre the story was seen as very dubious. The news organizer said: 'The amazing Uganda aircraft. We're not sure about the crates. There are three – unmanifested. We couldn't stand up the story yesterday. We've got pics of it sitting on the tarmac.' The story was run later that day. Its form was, as on radio, a 'continuing speculation' story, in which there was a brief clip of film with a voice over.

The caution shown on this occasion was shared by the rest of the media, with the exception of the *Mirror*. What the example shows is that although Television News had the opportunity of breaking a story first, it chose not to. The basis of the caution lay in the failure

to 'stand up' the story adequately. A routine way of trying to
is by going to an official spokesman – on this occasion a
official. However, in anticipation of running the story, 'actuality
was acquired: namely, film of the aircraft on the tarmac. The story
was not the result of a BBC investigation – rather it was 'reactive'
in the sense that the tip-off came from an outside source. In the
event, it was run only after it had entered the public domain via a
newspaper, and then its speculative aspects were stressed by both
Radio News and Television News.

The judgement also showed a sense of the BBC's special place
among the media and an awareness that it should not leave itself
open to criticism. It also, incidently, showed a reluctance to create
any diplomatic embarrassment for the British government.

Some quite different points can be made about the handling of the
publication of a report of a public enquiry. The enquiry, by Robin
Auld, QC, concerned the conduct of teaching at the William Tyndale
School in Islington, London. This story should be seen in the general
context of the considerable mass media attention which was currently
being lavished on the theme of 'progressive education' and 'whither
the schools?'. The story was seen as a *national* one in terms of the
interest it aroused, although it was situated in London. The case had
been much-publicized, and so when a copy of the report became
available on a Friday morning, it was clearly going to be covered.
However, the publication was to be 'embargoed' (that is, deferred)
until the following Monday, by request of the Inner London Education Authority (ILEA) who were publishing it. At the morning
meeting it was suggested that the intake desk keep in touch with the
main protagonists in case 'we have to break the embargo quickly'.
Over the sound link, Radio News said 'It won't hold until Monday'.
It was expected the embargo would be broken, but at the BBC-2
desk which I was observing no action was taken in preparation for
this.

At 3.25 p.m. the desk was informed by PA that the embargo had
been broken by the *Evening Standard*, which had printed a full
account of the ILEA report. The sub chosen to handle the story went
to talk to his opposite number on the BBC-1 desk who had done some
preparatory background work. They discussed the story, the BBC-1
sub saying: 'There's a lack of ILEA policy on schools. The report's
three phone directories thick. There're no inspector's recommendations.' Their first action was to view archive film of the educational
dispute: there was an 'establishing' shot of the school's exterior;
pictures of striking teachers picketing the school; parents of children
affected being interviewed; pictures of the teachers going to County
Hall for hearings (which was seen as inadequate for identifying key

individuals). During the viewing, the BBC-2 sub was given all his briefing on 'background' by the BBC-1 sub; namely, that there had been a clash over the introduction of new teaching methods, two of the characters being Messrs Haddow and Ellis who had introduced the new methods. All the information came from press cuttings. During the strike of the 'new methods' teachers, teaching had been continued by supply staff, said the BBC-1 sub. By 4.30 p.m. the viewing was complete, and the two subs had worked out a chronological order: shots of the school; the strike; the County Hall hearing. The initial orientation to the story line was worked out in the first ten minutes, and the subs agreed to use a common version of the library film for both channels.

Back in the newsroom, the editor of the day came over to the BBC-2 sub with the *Evening Standard*, which led with the William Tyndale story. 'I've marked up a few things,' he said. In fact the *Standard*'s line was followed in putting the story together; and a similar line was to be found in a number of dailies the next day: 'Criticism all round for Tyndale School affair – THE HEAD WHO LOST CONTROL' ran the headline.

The marked passages were meant to guide the sub in writing his script. One ran: the head 'lacked the judgement, strength of character and ability to organize, required in the running of an already struggling school'. In later discussions with the Home Affairs correspondent who was giving a studio spot on the story, the editor of the day was disappointed to discover that these phrases, referring to Mr Ellis, the head, were not in the report itself but rather the *Standard* reporter's gloss on its findings. They nevertheless found their way into the script, word for word. A second passage focused on the 'doctrinaire and aggressive' attitude of Mr Haddow, Mr Ellis's colleague. A teacher who had complained about the use of progressive methods, Mrs Walker, was also mentioned in the *Standard* as being criticized for 'improper conduct'.

Concerning the visual realization of the story, the editor of the day gave instructions for there not to be 'too much library film'. The main focus was to be the report – *today*'s news. The angle was 'What's going to happen now: repercussions'. It was given an overall slot of three minutes, just over one-fifth of the time for the 5.45 bulletin. The visual components consisted of library film and stills, together with a report from the correspondent, since it was impossible to obtain and process interviews in the remaining time. The logistical factor thus affected the content. By 4.18 p.m. the 'blame all around' angle was being followed, reproducing the news line of the *Standard*. The editor of the day outlined the story structure to be followed: 'We'll start with a little headline: it hits everybody, particularly the head, Mr Ellis. Still of Auld QC, and general lack of judgement quote. Haddow – quote *Standard*. The woman who complained is also being criticized – improper conduct. We'll have a split screen with supers. Right. We've put the knife into three, there's also the ILEA – this back in vision. We'll have Tindall (the Correspondent) over the library film and PA background. An intro of half a minute with library film of the teachers going to the enquiry. Back to Tindall in vision, a sentence on teaching standards and then What Now?'

The Home Affairs correspondent said to me that he was worried about the possibility of distortion when 'it goes out so fast'. They had hoped to have the weekend to package the story, but 'We can't do anything with the story after today, since it won't stand up in news terms'. He divided his labour with the sub; he was to 'give what happened'. Again, the editor of the day was involved in drawing the main outlines: 'Teachers went on strike, forty seconds history, some quoting the report, ILEA meets next Wednesday pay-off.'

While the scripts were being written, the BBC-1 editor came over to chat with the BBC-2 editor, and said he wanted 'Ellis and the woman for interviews'. The BBC-2 editor said: 'We haven't got them in our hot sticky hands yet.' He was annoyed, saying he should have foreseen the fact the *Standard* would break the story on a Friday night, as they did not print at weekends. The BBC-2 editor looked over the sub's script asking him to emphasize certain points – 'It's a North London school; introduction of new methods, taking children away' – which found their way, subsequently, into the introduction. The BBC-1 editor said that he wanted a 'magic quote' in the *Nine O'Clock News* which summed it all up: from a mother who complained to an interviewer that her child could play chess, but he couldn't read or write. This came from the library film and it got in. In the later bulletins the story 'firmed up' with reactions from the NUT, and ILEA and the Education Minister, and interviews.

The story was broadcast along the lines indicated here. ITN had no report in their early evening bulletin, much to everyone's satisfaction. What occurred in a period of some two-and-a-half hours was the reduction of a report 280,000 words long into a three-minute story. Standard production techniques were thrown into relief: the focus on personalities who could be represented visually by stills; the use of ready-to-hand resources and ideas, namely, library film and press cuttings. Television News went for the story once the embargo had been broken by a newspaper. This was in line with what was described to me as a general reluctance to break embargoes first. Shortage of time inhibited any measured consideration of the story, which was seen as necessarily dead 'in news terms' after that evening. Thus the natural tendency was simply to take the reporting

D

of the story as it appeared in Press Association copy and in an evening newspaper. A good deal of satisfaction, however, was afforded by having beaten 'the competition'.

TIME SLOTS AND NEWS VALUES

Each newsday consists of a number of time-slots, each of which is clearly demarcated. The existence of news slots is public knowledge (available from newspapers, *The Radio Times, The TV Times*). For the news producers the existence of such slots poses a problem: they have to be 'filled' with news. A slot presents newsmen with a *goal*. On the other hand, on days when a lot is happening (in news terms), they might find that they have too much news on hand. The slot is also, therefore, a *constraint*.[22] Thus, time-slots carve up the day, presenting a set of formal targets for the production team. To cope with time-slots newsmen have first to meet their deadlines.

News stories are ranked according to estimates of their news value. This is at the same time a process of according a story a time-value. Time-values take two forms: they slot a story into a sequence, and fix a particular duration. Such time-valuing goes on throughout the production process.

A story's duration in a news bulletin therefore indicates its news-worthiness. As slots cannot generally be exceeded, the editor of the day is forced to express his news judgement through rather rigid *temporal* directives to sub-editors and reporters. Thus, he might ask for 'a one-minute piece on the industrial situation', or for 'Twenty seconds on the Queen'. The limit posed by the slot is thus always vividly present.

Editorial instructions to sub-editors and reporters set a time-framework for the newsman. Each individual contribution to a bulletin emerges from the experience of working within a temporal constraint, for every newsman knows that his 'piece' is part of the available total time-slot, and that to exceed it, or to fall below it, would prejudice the overall balance of the bulletin. In practice, not all stories remain statically within their initial duration: as a story grows in importance its time-value increases, and it will decrease if the story is deemed less newsworthy. The BBC's *News Guide*, a codification of desired news practice, ordains: 'Each sentence, each word, must be made to count, We learn to handle words as if they were gold. . . .'[23] A news bulletin takes a serial form, in which each sequence of words to be spoken by the newsreader and reporters has to be precisely timed. It is a standard assumption in the BBC news-rooms that the newsreader's pace of delivery will be at a regular three words-per-second. This might seem a ridiculously crude way of pacing such a technically sophisticated production as a television news bulletin, but it does in fact lie at the basis of the broadcasts we see and hear. Again, the time-slot operates in an intimate and personal way to control individual output in the direction of economy and precision. The practical importance of this rule was observed when one television newsreader was vociferously criticized as being 'hard to write for': his offence lay in a tendency to alter his pace of delivery, which 'threw out' the timing of the entire bulletin, and made a nervous wreck of the studio director. The incident illustrated the collective nature of production, and the reliance placed on accurate timing if it is to run smoothly.

There is a link between the story allocated to a newsman and his estimation of his own status. The stories which lead the bulletin or are given the longest duration, go to the most senior sub-editors, and reportorial pickings to the specialist correspondents. Prestige is conditioned by two factors: duration and placement in the 'running order'. The longer the story time, the greater the possibility for the newsman to exercise his skills in combining words, graphics, sounds, photographs, film. Given that news is seen as inherently unstable, with one established story being often superseded by a more immediate later one, there is an element of fragility about the status structure on any given day. The time-value of a story has important consequences for the satisfaction experienced by individual newsmen.

Concerning time-value, one senior news executive observed: 'What we leave out is what in our judgement doesn't rank as news in the context of limited time and space.' This remark is revealing, for it shows how scarcity of time may work as a defence: newsmen claim their own prerogative to decide what stories are worth. This tactic was used, on one occasion, by a reporter negotiating the relationship between his source and the Television News Department. His interviewee, the Minister of Transport, complained that a previous interview had not been used. The reporter replied that he was not in ultimate editorial control, and that anyway there could never be any guarantees as time was always short. Moreover, the Minister was told that as it was Sunday (with a short main news bulletin) the interview would have to be kept inside one minute. Again, the time-consciousness of the newsman can be seen to have a striking effect on his basic practices.

As has so far been indicated, there is a constant problem of controlling the work processes to meet output times, and of keeping within the slot. There is a detectable element of goal-displacement at times, when slot-filling becomes an end in itself. This was given archetypal voice by one editor of the day who said to his team: 'I'm in the shit length-wise. What've you got?' At such moments newsmen are trying hard to be controllers rather than victims. Although being a victim is quite enjoyable since it makes life authentically tense.

The two senior newsroom editors are supposed to have an overview of the entire programme. As bulletin time approaches, what tends to happen – notably in television where the programmes are longer and their constituents more complex and numerous – is a shifting of the editor's focus from the content of the programme to its sequence and duration. One senior duty editor noted in an amused way that the timing dominated his thoughts in those last minutes: 'The question you're asking yourself is "What can I drop?" ' He also drew attention to the adding and subtracting of minutes and seconds both before and during the transmission, which he felt was 'primitive', when he was trying to convey complex information. By the time production is at an advanced stage, newsmen no longer 'see' or 'hear' the programme due to their involvement in getting it on the air. As one editor of the day put it: 'You come out (of the studio) and ask "How was it?" You've an idea how you'd *like* it to be, but you don't know what's happening while you're coping with the problems arising.'

TIME AND NEWSMEN'S LANGUAGE

Newsmen make fine conceptual distinctions concerning time. This is only to be expected as the temporal dimension of their occupational culture is highly elaborated. A brief account of some of their most important working ideas follows.

The immediacy cluster

There is a cluster of notions derived from, and related to, 'immediacy', which suggest upheaval, suddenness, unpredictability. Whenever new information on a story comes into the newsroom it is up-dated. New facts and interpretations have to be integrated into the story, if it is to be used, prior to transmission. Such revision is a continual process, and contributes to the feeling that news is naturally without a resting place. Hence, news stories are talked of as 'breaking'. Ideally, they should break well before the deadline to be covered.

It is highly important to newsmen that stories have this apparent capacity to rupture the skein of existing expectations. And they have ways of signalling this to the news audience. Some stories, in their view, just cannot wait until the next scheduled bulletin. For these the 'newsflash' is used: the news item is given separate treatment in its own time, which confers an aura of urgency and importance on it. For example, when it first became clear that James Callaghan was elected Leader of the Labour Party (and thus Prime Minister) in succession to Harold Wilson, this event was thought important enough to merit its own little slot before the next scheduled radio news bulletin.

In general, though, the tendency towards immediacy is contained within regular time-slots. However, since a 'late' story is always prone to appear, there is an ever-present danger of disturbance. While this could unbalance the existing bulletin, immediacy is so valued as authentic, that the upset, stress, excitement, and drama created by the arrival of 'late' news is not only desired, but also regarded as ideal. It is possible to accommodate an unexpected story by leaving the sequence intact and by prefacing it with 'We've just heard that . . .' This formula stresses the immediacy of the new story. A further way of handling this type of occurrence is for the newsreader to say 'And now some late news . . .' just before the close of bulletin. Honour is saved: the story may be simply a few brute facts served without dressing, but the temporal imperative has been obeyed.

A further, quite distinct, way of coping with stories which are both immediate and 'big' is for the editor of the day to request an extension of the time-slot. Thus, for example, when the Watergate Affair first broke in Britain, ITN's *News At Ten* added a third quarter of an hour to accommodate reports from Washington as well as the rest of the news, the newscaster making it clear why the slot has been extended. A similar extension took place on the *Nine O'Clock News* when the BBC obtained an exclusive interview with President Idi Amin of Uganda following the raid on Entebbe airport by Israeli commandos.

Given the expectation that there might always be a new lead story heading down the wires, we find that the immediate story is treated almost reverentially, being full of potential, at least in principle.

Outside immediacy

Stories which are unexpected and unplanned for are called 'spot news', and concern events which are of their nature unforeseeable: aircrashes, collisions at sea, rail disasters, fires, assassinations, political coups, earthquakes, deaths. These are distinguished from 'diary' stories which might be known of months in advance: news conferences, space shots, state occasions and visits, elections, budgets. All of these are predictable 'future events' for which early arrangements can be made. Spot news, by contrast, involves 'instant' editorial decisions. It is very important to be sure that the means exist to cover such stories, to know that, for example, reporters and film crews are available who have not been committed to other stories.

Rapid decision-making and the atmosphere of upheaval which both derive from responding to the spot news story contribute to the general evaluation of this kind of story as nearest the bone of true news activity. Diary stories are often denigrated as 'set piece', or as simply routine with no element of surprise.

The running story

Another relevant category reflecting working patterns is the 'running story'. This category embraces all stories which transcend a given newsday cycle, and are pursued on subsequent ones. Examples are: The Watergate Affair, The Cod War, The (Lambton) Call Girl Affair, The Lebanese Civil War. A running story is one which is expected to be covered for a number of days at least. It appears for a sequence of days on the News Departments' planning documents. The best example of how a particular category is embedded in day-to-day planning is the 'Ulster Crisis'. During fieldwork this was a permanent category in the planning documents, indicating that the newsmen had become sensitized to both Northern Ireland and Eire as news-source areas. It was firmly expected that things would happen there in the future because of regular incidents (bombings, assassinations, demonstrations, etc.) in the past. This example provides a limiting case. One cynical old hand observed: 'It's been a crisis for so long you can't call it a crisis any more.' The concept of the running story reflects a tendency in production for some newsworthy items, on some occasions, for periods ranging from days to months, or even years, to become institutionalized. But, as with other stories, what one is likely to find on any given day of the running story are the most immediate 'facts' about it.

TIME, AND NEWS AS CULTURAL FORM

Broadcast news has a specific cultural form.[24] Time concepts can play a role in structuring the presentation and style of news bulletins.

A key idea is that of 'pace'. As broadcasters are in a capitalist market situation, where success is, in the last resort, determined by the size of audience they can attract, they feel themselves impelled to try and 'hook' the audience's attention. Bulletins, they argue, have to be so constructed as to achieve this goal. Orchestrating an interesting sequence of news items becomes, therefore, a dominant aim in production.

Each news bulletin is structured according to a concept of the right pace. Thus, for example, one editor of the day said that he approached the problem of constructing his programme by thinking in terms of a 'dramatic concept', according to which there would be 'peaks and troughs' during the course of the broadcast. He observed: 'You have to keep the interest moving: it's no good doing a flat 2-D newspaper. You have to give presentation some thought.' The kind of style adopted is thus justified by an appeal to the presumed psychology of the audience.

This style is closely linked to the concept of news as today's happenings. The idea of 'moving it along' has a temporal basis: dramatic items are placed in a sequence according to *when* it is thought the audience's interest is likely to flag. This view, it should be noted, expresses an ideal as, given the stress on immediacy, it is always possible the most balanced presentation will be upset by later developments. It is clear, though, that the rhythm of presentation is seen as needing judicious control.

Newsmen's approach to pace is based on this broadcaster's axiom: 'the audience can't go back over what it's just seen or heard'. Frequent contrasts are drawn with print journalism: the newspaper reader may re-read a paragraph or sentence if it is not at first understood, but the broadcast word perishes on the instant. Because news bulletins have a serial form, it is felt that their content has to be grasped at the moment of transmission. Newsmen are therefore aware of the broadcast media themselves as creating inherent difficulties.

Problems of pace are more acute in television news production than in radio. This stems directly from the time-slots available to each of the two media. The longest BBC radio bulletin lasts for fifteen minutes (on Radio 4); the longest television bulletin (on BBC-1) has a 25-minute slot, and, as TV newsmen never tire of saying, is seen as well as heard, and thus, they argue, needs to possess a sustained visual interest.

Changes of pace are provided in various ways. One relatively simple means of changing the focus of the audience's attention is to use two newsreaders as joint presenters. ITN's *News at Ten*, following American network news style, has used this technique since 1967.

BBC's *Nine O'Clock News* introduced a slightly different version in November 1972, dropping it in March 1976.

Pace is also varied by the placement of stories. Thus, in television news, film stories will be spaced out during the sequence so that they do not 'bunch': they might alternate with the 'talking head' studio-based reports of correspondents. In radio, variability is provided by the interspersing of the newsreader's monologue with the voices of reporters and interviewees, and also 'natural sound'.

There are, in addition, more formal ways of structuring the bulletin. One convention is the 'headline' through which newsmen extract the main story angle, and present it in very brief compass. For example:

Mr David Steel says that the Liberals must decide on the leadership issue in weeks and not in months.

The headline is a dramatic presentational device. It varies the pace at both the beginning and end of the bulletin, and also rules it off from other programmes.

Another device is the 'catchline' which serves to break up the flow of the bulletin. Thus: 'Industrial News', 'The Commons', 'The Watergate Affair' are all phrases intended to swiftly cue in the audience to the content of the next story, while making the assumption that people are sufficiently familiar with its past developments to comprehend present ones. Catchlines contribute to a news style which both looks and sounds economical. It is easy to see, in view of the foregoing, why newsmen should take it for granted that 'A combination of simplicity, clarity, and urgency is the only possible style'.[25]

These ideas define and limit both the form and the content of news. The basic cultural form is framed by the conventions current in the existing occupational ideology. News is seen as distinct from 'current affairs' and from 'documentary', where immediacy is not such an overweening criterion.[26] News is virtually all foreground with very little background.

CONCLUSION

This chapter illustrates an important aspect of newsmen's occupational ideology. The emphasis on speed in bulletin production is quite clearly derived from the overall constraint of producing news for a market based on the concept of the newsday. There are therefore systematic links between the newsman's time-perspective and the demands created by the organization of work. The newsman's emphatic bias towards immediacy, though, is more than just a response to market conditions. It is a form of fetishism in which to be obsessional about time is to be professional in a way which newsmen have made peculiarly their own. To make this point clearly is important for any sociology of the journalist's occupational knowledge.

Production is so organized that its basic dynamic emphasizes the perishability of stories. Where a story carries over from one day to the next, it is assumed that the audience will, after one day's exposure, be adequately familiar with the subject-matter to permit the 'background' to be largely taken for granted. It is always *today's* developments which occupy the foreground.

The corollary of this point is that there is an inherent tendency for the news to be framed in a discontinuous and ahistorical way, and this implies a truncation of 'context', and therefore a reduction of meaningfulness. Where an 'historical' element is purposely introduced – as for example in the William Tyndale report discussed above – this largely means the utilization of materials which are ready to hand, and which accord only a sketchy chronology to the story. It is hardly to be argued that this kind of practice constitutes an adequate attempt at explanation. But then 'news' as it is currently conceived is not intended to be primarily explanatory.

Such strictures may be thought to be excessive. For news is, after all, not history. It is, if anything, history's antithesis. It is only by such observations about the nature of its form, however, that we grasp its inherent limitations.

5

The missing link:
'professionalism' and the audience

Well, let's face it – you've got to put a map up every time. Most people just don't know where Beirut is.

You're dead right. They probably think it's a vegetable.

(from a conversation overheard in the television newsroom)

In this chapter, I have, alas, nothing to say about the transition from ape to man. The 'missing link' refers to a structural lacuna between the producers and consumers of news. In fact, the title to this chapter holds the key to its argument: that broadcast news is the outcome of standardized production routines; that these routines work themselves out within an organizational structure which has no adequate point of contact with the audience for broadcast news; and that there is, therefore, no sense in which one can talk of a communication taking place which is truly alive to the needs of the news audience.

We have already seen the way in which news production is highly routinized in relation to a series of overwhelmingly important deadlines. We have also seen that newsmen in common with other media personnel inhabit what Burns has aptly termed a 'private world'.[1] It is the nature of this world which is explored more closely here, by focusing specifically on a key relationship – that between the BBC newsman and his audience.

In media sociology the communicator–audience relationship has received considerable attention. Its interest lies in the definition of *mass* communication in terms of the structural separation of, and consequent social distance between, the communicator and those ostensibly communicated with.[2] One line of questioning which has been pursued is: 'How can mass communicators take account of their relatively unknown audiences' needs, tastes and desires?'

Sociologists have often worked with the assumption that there is a 'problem' in cultural production for the mass media. McQuail, for instance, has posited a 'need' for the mass communicator to establish a relationship with his audience. He suggests that this is requited by various types of 'organizational adjustment' which he labels paternalism, specialization, professionalization and ritualism.[3] While his notion of the mass communicator's needing a relationship with his audience is decidedly dubious, McQuail's focus on the internal elaboration of production routines under the umbrella notion of 'professional' competence, is surely right. Certainly the evidence of Elliott's study of documentary production and Tracey's of political television fully support that view, as does what I present below.[4] Furthermore, the evidence of those studies, like this one, shows quite decisively that the 'problem' of the audience is not an urgent one for the communicator. You do not find people wandering around in a state of existential *angst* wondering whether they are 'communicating' or not. You do, on the other hand, find an intense obsession with the packaging of the broadcast, and comparative evaluation of others' goods.

The focus in media sociology has been on the organizational and occupational milieux as points of reference for producers. The evidence, so far as news is concerned, is that these are of overwhelming importance, while the mass audience is not. To over-simplify a little, the argument is that journalists write for other journalists, their bosses, their sources, or highly interested audiences.[5] The 'total' audience, however, remains an abstraction, made real on occasion by letters or telephone calls, encounters of a random kind in public places, or perhaps more structured ones such as conversations with liftmen, barmen and taxi-drivers.

There is some recognition of this relationship to the audience in the BBC's *News Guide*, where pious hopes are expressed that the public service traditions will not be erred from:

> We must beware of becoming slaves of arbitrary changes in fashion, or of becoming a cosy group, so engrossed with our own technique that we forget to ask ourselves: what do our listeners think? We must never reduce our contributions to broadcasting to the level of journalists talking to and for other journalists.[6]

One newsman, commenting on this chapter, and agreeing with its argument, observed that the above passage was 'the Bible of hypocrisy. The only thing you think about is what other journalists are going to think about it. And anyway, you write stories for the Editor, not the audience.'

The evidence shows that mass communicators' reliance upon their milieu as sources of meaning and orientation brings with it a concomitant distancing from, and even a devaluation of, the views held by members of the mass audience. Members of the audience who contact the communicator about his performance are viewed as 'cranks' or as idiosyncratic[7] in line with the apparently general conviction that 'the bulk of audience reaction is from cranks, the unstable, the hysterical and sick'.[8]

The broad picture available from production studies is one in which the mass communicator enjoys little 'feedback' from his audience, a feature of the work-situation which necessarily creates a heavy reliance on occupational knowledge and the cognitive support of the organization.

'PROFESSIONALISM' AND THE WORLD OUTSIDE

One way of understanding how newsmen pursue their work, given the absence of immediate interaction with their audience, comes from examining the role of 'professionalism', and the way it is used in asserting autonomy. A striking feature of this professionalism is in an immersion in what Philip Elliott has called the 'media culture'. Newsmen have to 'keep up with what's going on', and that means watching television, listening to the radio and reading newspapers. On one level this becomes a formal part of newsmen's 'search procedures',[9] as exemplified in my account of the Intake and Planning structures. On another level, there is a definite normative component: the committed newsman will monitor news as it is defined by other organizations, and so 'the man for the job' is one whose general knowledge

> needs to be a good deal wider than that of the majority of listeners. The good sub-editor keeps himself abreast of what is happening: he is able to relate to its background any story he may be given to handle. *He listens to news bulletins and current affairs programmes on his off-duty as well as his duty days and he reads newspapers and magazines.*[10]

This normative ideal does not, of course, apply solely to sub-editors, but embraces all staff. A Television News reporter, when asked 'What does being a general reporter mean?' replied,

> That you can do anything. Your standard of general knowledge is very high. You're expected to know the state of play in any country. I read all the newspapers and have really good general knowledge.

The committed, dutiful newsman has no 'days off'. This is an important part of the newsroom ethic – and there were numerous examples of such commitment. A duty editor in Radio News complained that when abroad on holiday he found the BBC's World Service broadcasts failed to give him adequate information to keep up with the nuances of events in Britain. An editor of the day noted,

> You spend an awful lot of time being saturated in the news. Even my six-year-old child talks news. People come to dinner and ask things. You have to read constantly – that's the only way you can make snap judgements.

He also observed that even on holiday you had to keep up with 'developments' in stories, and this was achieved by reading papers on the beach or listening to the radio. On one occasion he had been away when Lord Snowdon was ennobled; when back in the newsroom he had asked 'Who's Lord Snowdon?' everyone had stared. This example illuminates the close relationship between being 'professional' and an immersion in newsworthy facts.

When newsmen work their shifts they tend to view them as enclosed slabs of time during which stories have to be exhaustively discussed. While reporters and correspondents tend to follow through a given story each newsday, and to be immersed in the detail, the newsroom chat is broader, and encompasses the range of significant stories of the day. Part of the work ethic is to eat and drink news: in the BBC Club news angles are sometimes examined over a pint; and when newsmen find the pressure great they tend to spend their lunch hours or supper-times at the desk with both their sandwiches and their copy in front of them.

It is not surprising, given this kind of milieu, that newsmen need to be warned against becoming a 'cosy group'. The structure of work, which is organized around a series of deadlines, imposes strictures which make the satisfaction of the Corporation's demands pre-eminent.

It is also not surprising, given this kind of work situation, implicated as it is in the wider 'media culture', that the newsman should see the fact that he has 'kept up with the news' as legitimizing his exercise of power in deciding what has 'news value', a concept which is 'of key importance . . . as the basis of such occupational autonomy as journalists enjoy. . . .'[11]

Audiences

The newsman's sense of independence is tempered by an awareness of the outside world, of 'what the audience thinks'. At least the newsman believes that he knows what the public desires and thinks. An important source for such beliefs is provided by a monitoring of the media culture which newsmen also use as a plank in their argument from 'professionalism'. As one editor put it:

> The interesting thing is that pragmatically there's never any doubt: we'll all (all media) go for the same thing. We keep a careful check on what we lead and on what ITN leads.

There is a general awareness of the competitive structure within which broadcast news has to be produced. Successful competition is measured by the resourcefulness shown by the newsman's peers in other organizations, and by the extent to which the mass audience can be 'hooked'.

Audiences for broadcast news in Britain must choose what they want to see and hear from among products offered by the two broadcasting authorities. While the BBC's original inspiration lay in public service, since the passage of the first Television Act in 1954, it has had to face competition from commercial television. And in 1973 the first legally-sanctioned commercial radio stations went on the air. The creation of the present duopoly changed the rules of the game and Britain's competitive broadcasting system has a 'unitary character' in which the 'differences are less significant than the common basic assumptions on which both systems are grounded'.[12] Competitive assumptions are built into the everyday practices of the BBC, as a consequence of the fundamental economic logic of contemporary broadcasting.

A keen awareness of this state of affairs is present in the News Departments as elsewhere in the BBC. It could hardly be otherwise given the number of frank public utterances on this subject; Huw Wheldon, former Managing Director of BBC-TV, summed up the position before the BBC took the tyranny of the ratings seriously:

> In a word, seriously diminishing audiences put the very financial foundation of the BBC at risk.

Elaborating on a major strand in broadcasting history since the breaking of the monopoly, he went on to say:

> What the BBC then had to do during the Fifties and Sixties was to get back from the frightening and slippery slope of a 70/30 ratio in Commercial's favour, and achieve a position of at least rough parity. The central competitive instrument was the way in which programmes were scheduled.[13]

It is axiomatic, then, that this 'rough parity' must be maintained in order to avoid problems with politicians and the public over whether the Corporation's revenue from the sale of the broadcast receiving licence is adequately justified.

Audience research

Routine research

Certain kinds of information are routinely provided for the News Departments by the BBC's Audience Research Department, a unit servicing the entire Corporation. Audience Research in the BBC pre-dates the competitive era, and it has been rightly pointed out that the existence of such research is 'bound to inject an element of ambiguity into the determination of programme content.'[14] In the terms outlined at the beginning of this chapter, a tension is set up between the professionalism of the communicator with its implied autonomy, and the meeting of apparent audience demands and desires, with their implications for limiting autonomy.

The Editors of the News Departments are sent statistics on daily audience size and composition as part of a general service to all programmes known as the *Daily Audience Barometer*, described as the 'BBC's equivalent of the box office'. There is keen interest, even an obsession with this kind of figure throughout broadcasting.[15] News is in one respect exempt from great upswings and downswings: its very regularity has given it an established place lacked by more occasional outputs. But this does not mean that there is any the less of an obsession about how 'the competition' is doing. In the assistant editors' room at Television Centre a large wallchart traces the relative fortunes of BBC's *Nine O'Clock News* and ITN's *News at Ten*. ITN's outputs are closely monitored, and each day a list is drawn up comparing the two organizations' running orders. A senior editor in Television News, asked if the pressure of ITN's competition was felt, replied:

> The *spur* of competition rather. We ask 'why' and 'how' about their output. We are very conscious of what they produce. Not in a ratings sense simply – though we don't ignore these – but rather the comparative coverage of particular stories. There is also the question of priority – who gets on the air first.

Thus, apart from assessing the opposition's news judgement, there is also a qualitative appraisal. The Deputy Editor, Television News, was expressing a common view when he observed 'ITN's very

prestigious and very good'. At Broadcasting House, too, the Radio
News Department primarily sees ITN as the competition, even though
the advent of commercial radio has brought a more direct opponent.
A memorandum from the Deputy Editor, Radio News to the newsroom staff indicates how this competitive consciousness relates to a
conception of professional conduct:

> No serious news organization can afford to ignore competitors.
> We *must* monitor *News at Ten*.[16]

Special surveys
A further, irregular source of information for programme producers
is the special survey undertaken on request by the Audience Research Department. Three such major surveys have been made of the
audiences for both Radio and Television News (including ITN), and
one which deals with television news alone.[17]

Such surveys are very revealing documents, expressing clearly a
set of views about what the news organization ought to know about
its audience, in ways, as Richard Collins has put it, highlighting 'the
ideological frame of reference of the questioner'.[18]

A major theme dealt with in all the surveys is the 'standing of the
News services'. The differing results published in 1957, 1962, 1971
and 1973 provide interesting insights into the shifts in the public
image of BBC News in relation to ITN. All the reports show that the
News Departments are primarily assessed in relation to ITN – the
principal 'competitor–colleague',[19] and only to a lesser degree in
relation to the press. The relevant universe in which BBC News
evaluates itself is that of the media culture.

Taken as a whole, the surveys present an historical picture of the
decline of BBC News's dominance in the field of broadcasting, something already noted in Chapter 2.

> In 1957 BBC-Radio, and in 1962 BBC-TV, were by far the most
> frequently nominated as 'the main source of news'. In 1970 . . .
> BBC-TV no longer held the lead over ITN, radio, and the newspapers,
> in the numbers nominating it as their main source of news. Where-
> as in 1962, 38% said it was their main source as against 20% for
> ITN and 33% for the newspapers, in 1970 only 28% said so,
> similar numbers choosing ITN and the press. As in 1962, BBC *radio*
> proved to be the main source of news for only a minority (14%
> now, 17% then).[20]

According to the surveys there has also been a diminution in the
BBC's rating for presenting news interestingly:

Whereas in 1962 more than twice as many people chose BBC-TV as chose ITN (46% compared with 21%), in 1970 they were chosen by approximately equal numbers.[21]

In an area of 'standing' crucially important in the BBC, that of accuracy and trustworthiness, the 1970 survey found that BBC-TV still 'proved a clear leader'.[22] This affords some slight evidence for the belief, often encountered in the News Departments, that the BBC still somehow maintains a 'special relationship' with the British public. The Editor, Radio News, said, 'We're lucky. We still have the trust of a substantial part of the audience. Perhaps less than used to be the case, but people are more cynical these days.' Like a number of other newsmen he observed that at times of crisis or of great public concern, the BBC Radio News audience figures rose, as did those for Television News, and in the latter case more than those of ITN. No one ever produced evidence to support this claim.

In fact, to judge from the Audience Research Department's own findings the belief in the BBC's own faithful has little more than a limited foundation in actual audience behaviour; one survey identifies:

the hard core, 'blue chip' BBC viewers who are usually both older and higher in social class. They see the BBC as representing such virtues as solidity, sobriety and quality, and would turn automatically to it for the news, especially in time of stress or for information about events of gravity.[23]

However, there is some evidence that the belief that 'everyone turns to the BBC in a crisis' was well-founded *before* the rise of ITN. Crozier has noted that during the Suez crisis of 1956 'the BBC's fifteen daily bulletins (Home and Light Services and Television) had an audience of more than 50 per cent above normal; the 6 o'clock news heard by nearly 10 million; the 8 a.m. news by nearly 8 million.'[24]

The degree of obsessive concern with how news is rated may be gauged from a 1973 study, entitled *The Relative Standing of BBC News and ITN*, which entirely addressed itself to the 'reasons why (the) decline in the standing of the BBC's news services had occurred'. The report confirmed the BBC was no longer seen as *the* 'most accurate and trustworthy' news source, and that in the public's opinion it shares these qualities with ITN. Interestingly, it argued that the 'news is embedded in the totality of the channel; it does not stand out with any degree of isolation'.[25] Interviewees tended to work with overall images of the BBC and ITV within which the respective news services were located in a subsidiary way.

The findings of the special surveys are not generally disseminated in the News Departments. The reason for this given by the Editor, Radio News, was that they did not provide 'sufficiently clear conclusions to be of help'. A view echoed by the Editor, Television News, who thought they were 'not particularly useful', as they were 'not practical'. If they had been distributed it would have seemed that their contents were 'vitally important' and this would have been misleading. He had no worries about or objections to the distribution of the findings, he said.

Other sources of information

The News Departments have other non-routine indications of 'what the audience thinks'. The Deputy Editor, Radio News, said that in a standard week audience reaction yielded about 30 letters. The Editor, Television News, thought there might be some 20 per week which 'required answers'. There are also some half a dozen telephone calls made daily to the newsrooms. These reactions mostly fall into the category of 'complaints' which, said the Editor, Television News, was 'not a vastly useful response'. Asked what sort of audience research material is made regularly available the Deputy Editor, Radio News, confirmed that it was,

> Not much more than the figures. There's nothing in detail on listener reaction; audience research is too expensive.

Among the newsmen the awareness of audience *figures* was pre-eminent, and their size was taken as a criterion of importance; as an editor of the day in Radio News observed:

> All the audience peaks on Radio 4 are at news times. By any standards, news is the most important output, and it's not accorded recognition.

There is little awareness, however, of audience *reaction* in the newsrooms and among reporters, as letters go directly to the senior editors for handling. Synopses of their contents are only sporadically made available. The Editor, Radio News, said that this was done when listeners made 'valid points' which ought to be known about. For most newsmen, the 'objective' evidence for any beliefs they might hold about the audiences are the synopses of letters and telephone calls which go into the 'Newsroom Log' and these are seen as coming 'from a particular type of person, one who feels strongly, a small minority' as the Editor, Radio News, put it. Images of the audience are also built up from private interactions, and in the case of reporting staff through interaction with sources. There are newspaper criticisms of the news output, though because it is so routine (apart from occasional cosmetic changes), critics find other media outputs more worthwhile.[26] Letters to newspapers and the *Radio Times* also provide information about what some members of the audience think. This relative insulation from the world is widely acknowledged at the operational level in remarks such as these:

> There's no direct feedback; there're only letters and calls and these are usually cranky.

> All you're left with ultimately is a feel.

Some sociologists have perceived such a situation – one in which the mass communicator operates in conditions of uncertainty about his audience – as a 'problem'. Observation suggests otherwise. In the BBC's newsrooms as elsewhere, there are beliefs and routine strategies available for coping with the social distance between communicator and audience.

Routinizing production for an audience

Herbert Gans, reporting on a study of newsmen in the United States television news networks, emphasizes their ignorance of the audiences they are addressing:

> Television broadcasters know little about their audience. Although the networks which employ them conduct studies of the characteristics of the audience, its viewing patterns and program preferences, news broadcasters rarely see these, and have no desire to see them. They are presenting the news, not trying to satisfy an audience, and the less they know of the audience, the more attention they can pay to the news.[27]

Gans has pinpointed the professional attitude, and evidence from the BBC newsrooms suggests there is no reason to qualify his view. Most of the data collected on newsmen's conceptions of the audience had to be elicited in interviews or discussions. That it was not volunteered is highly significant. If the newsmen observed had been acutely and pressingly aware of their audiences as a 'problem', they presumably would have said so. In fact, production routines embody assumptions about audiences. There is not a problem in the way sociologists sometimes have presented it, rather *'the audience' is part of a routinized way of life.*

Reporters and newsreaders are sometimes buttonholed by members of the public who know their names or faces and tell them what they think about particular items. Newsreaders particularly, who in fact have no editorial role at all, complain of being saddled with responsibility for the entire output. But sometimes this kind of reaction from the public does not even yield specific criticisms about the bulletins, but merely confirms that someone, somewhere, is watching or listening:

> People that you know will come up to you and say, 'We heard you yesterday! Don't know what it was you were saying though. But we heard you.'
>
> (Reporter, Radio News)

When it comes to thinking about the kind of news most relevant to 'the audience' newsmen exercise their news judgement rather than going out and seeking specific information about the composition, wants or tastes of those with whom they are communicating. In this context making a news judgement *is* thinking about the audience because the presumption is that the professional's selections are those which meet the desires of those who are being addressed. This brings us to an important belief underlying the routines of selection.

'Audience interest'

Newsmen customarily reply to questions about news judgement by saying that they select either what is 'important' or 'interesting'. There are two different strands in the argument from professionalism here. To talk about the public's 'interest' is to say that news is selected in line with what is generally wanted. Newsmen do not doubt that they know what is wanted. And they explain their knowledge by invoking the related notions of professionalism, commitment, and experience. It is a circular argument: because of skills in discrimination deriving from his immersion in the world of news the newsman is best placed to discern what is interesting – an explanation which provides no independent criteria. It is in this context that we have to see the audience as issuing imperatives to the newsmen: as an explanation of selection it has rhetorical force rather than descriptive accuracy.

When newsmen explain particular choices by reference to audience 'interest' the logic is one of justification as well as of explanation. Rules of thumb define what is of interest, or what is not. In one particular case the notion of public 'interest' has been codified in a more or less firm 'rule' concerning disasters. 'McLurg's Law', named after a legendary woman duty editor, lays down scales of relative newsworthiness for disasters: if crashes occur far away, say in Asia, they are not as newsworthy as if they occur in Europe; and they achieve paramount value if they occur at home, preferably in the Greater London area. It is not only crashes, but also natural disasters of any conceivable kind which are subsumed under the 'law'. A subsidiary clause relates to skin colour and cultural proximity: the following death tolls, in two individual variants, are of roughly equal news value:

One thousand wogs, fifty frogs, one Briton.

One European is worth twenty-eight Chinese, or perhaps 2 Welsh miners worth one thousand Pakistanis.[28]

The 'law' is usually propounded in the context of a joking situation, but as one newsman remarked, 'It's a joke that's relevant. It's dictated by the facts.' An editor of the day gave a succinct explanation of the rationale behind McLurg's Law:

It's a question of the impact on people. A coach overturned in India the other day and sixty or seventy people were drowned, but I ignored it. An Indian airliner crash would rate it – it's more exciting.

In view of the fact that national news services are first and foremost concerned with items of domestic interest the existence of such a 'rule' is not surprising.

This particular example – 'foreign human interest' – splits beliefs about audience interest into two component parts, foreign stories and human interest stories. It is a general conviction in the News Departments that foreign news is hard to sell, that the British public has little interest in it:

The EEC's grinding on like the mills of God, and when I was in Vietnam a while ago I could never interest people. It was a quiet period – there were a thousand casualties a day. Nobody cared;

they'd heard it all before – you couldn't tell them anything new.
(Diplomatic Correspondent, Television News)

A TV reporter quoted 'the old news editor's maxim: one home story is worth five foreign'. In a similar vein a chief sub-editor in Radio News thought that the British public was not very internationally minded. They were bored with the Watergate Affair. That was why good dramatic home stories were needed.

The human interest story is something of a catch-all category, one component of which is the disaster story. Here again the notion of impact is invoked. When newsmen are asked why so many plane and train crashes make the bulletin, an answer frequently given is that it accords with the audience's desires:

It's not just a ghoulish streak; the general public do feel themselves involved. They can identify with these. The landslide in Hong Kong doesn't involve them so much. It's far away. The public see themselves in it – it's a talking point.
(Foreign Duty Editor, Television News)

To take another example, that of murders. On one occasion the editor of the day selected a story about two young girls being murdered; it was interesting to the public, he said, because it related to family life:

Two eleven year old girls – that's news; young girls alone are always getting murdered on the way home, or leaving home.

Another kind of story seen as linked to family interest is that of the baby snatch; a television reporter who had covered a celebrated case gave a detailed account of why the public was likely to be interested:

Every mother, or grandmother, would identify with that story. It's the sort of thing that happens. A mother gets taken short six weeks after being pregnant and has to go to the toilet. She knows she shouldn't leave the baby on its own, but she does, and then it's gone. It's a six week old baby – tiny, new. The fact she needed medicine added extra pathos.

Stories which involve British Royalty to some extent fall into this same category. When the Duke of Norfolk's retirement from the stewardship of the Jockey Club was announced, the television sub-editor writing about the story justified coverage by saying 'the story is of general interest; there's a nostalgic element'. On another occasion, at a futures meeting, it was decided to obtain pictures of the Queen at a Highland dance; newsworthy, as one newsman said, because 'they'll show what she's wearing; she'll twirl her knicks around decorously'.

Such ascriptions of 'interest' are premissed upon a model of the newsman-as-audience:

> I can only take what goes in my own home as an indicator of interest. There was a great thing about the Prices and Incomes Board folding up, but everyone was bored. But when there was an item about typhoid-carriers, we had a half-hour discussion. We're supposed to be an informative medium, but we've got to entertain the public. This is more obvious with the style of news now.
>
> (Sub-editor, Radio News)

Newsmen see themselves as in a position to take the role of the audience in respect of standards, taste and comprehension. As noted above the news judgement is merged in practice with the question 'What does the public want or expect to see or hear?' The news-producing milieu fosters the belief that newsmen are audience members, albeit of a specialized kind, because of the normative pressure to immerse themselves in media outputs. And, if the newsman is an audience member, then his family functions as the 'typical' audience group, and for some, this is an important source of response:

> I'm really writing for myself and the wife. Otherwise you'd think of that 18 million viewers [sic]. The wife's my hardest critic, by the way; always saying, 'Why did you do that?'
>
> (Chief sub-editor, Television News)

These observations crystallize an essential attribute of professionalism in the newsrooms. There is a certain need for strategies to cope with the ambiguity of affirming on the one hand that 'audience interest' is in the last resort the arbiter of what is included in the bulletins, and on the other that of maintaining an autonomous stance. It can be resolved this way:

> P.S.: Is the news geared to the audience?
>
> We prefer to use our own intelligence. The basis is 'What is going to appeal to the majority of people?' For example, chess has become news. We make adjustments according to the fluctuations of interest in a given story.
>
> (News Editor, Television News)

The newsmen remain the controllers, the definers of news value, although a statement such as this appears to make the audience all-powerful. Not all newsmen feel bound to advance such arguments in defence of their professionalism, and some occupy a frankly agnostic position arguing that pragmatically they seem to be producing the right sort of thing.

> You wouldn't want to know what the audience wants – it might tie your hands too much.
>
> (Editor of the day, Radio News)

The argument forwarded to support this position is couched in terms of the professionalism of the communicator: it is far better to know little, since untrammelled judgement may then be exercised on behalf of the public. Naturally, it is admitted that on occasion this judgement can be imperfect:

> In the end it's professional judgement and we're not always right.
>
> (News organizer, Television News)

> No matter what you do, you bore some of the people some of the time.
>
> (Foreign duty editor, Television News)

The latter variant shifts the onus on to the audience to some extent. In general, the appeal to professionalism asserts the newsman's autonomy and rightful control over the product, and the total audience does not enter as a significant consideration in other than exceptional situations – such as a dramatic fall in viewing or listening.

Should the 'problem of the audience' arise at all it is always in the very practical circumstances of coping with routines. For example, one problem which faces newsmen is that of knowing when a story is so widely diffused that it should no longer be included in the bulletins. It is necessary, therefore, to make assumptions about the audience's knowledge of a particular story. This problem arises particularly at Radio News where outputs are more frequent than in television. A duty editor at the Radio News summaries desk posed the issue this way:

> We ask 'when has everyone heard about it?' That's how we judge when a lead story is played out.

But this tells only what sort of judgement is exercised and not the basis on which it is made. Since on any given day editors cannot know what their audience know, the answer has to be derived from 'news nose' or 'professional' judgement. In this way *not* actually knowing what the audience knows presents no problems: it is resolved by making certain, possibly very plausible, assumptions about its state of knowledge. An editor of the day asked whether such assumptions were made replied:

> Yes. Take the example of the Irish shootings. When we talk about the burning of the British Embassy in Dublin we have to get in a reference to last Sunday's events ['Bloody Sunday']. We don't talk about it as though it didn't happen. We know the audience knows about it.

In newsman's terms, this is the problem of providing adequate 'background'. In current practice, because of the pressure of deadlines and the shortage of time available and, in addition to this, the concept of news-as-front-page, the routine practice is to keep such background to a minimum. There is also an impetus to ring the changes, one which derives from newsmen's values rather than any independently-informed appraisal of what the audience wants or needs: 'We're always looking for new stories, minute to minute.' Observation in the newsroom suggested that the impetus for change came partly from boredom with a given story after a long newsday: immersion in the detail seems to make editors convinced that the public is somehow equally familiar and equally bored.

An assistant editor in Television News, in self-critical vein, gave an example of how newsroom perceptions can become distorted by an obsession with immediacy. The dramatic raid by Israeli commandos on Entebbe airport in Uganda, to release hijack hostages being held by Palestinian guerillas, had dominated that day's news. The hijack story had led all of the bulletins until in the evening another story came through of nine people killed in a motorway crash. According to the editor, in the newsroom, where everyone was very familiar with the details of the raid, there was a feeling that they should lead the next bulletin with the motorway crash. This decision was severely criticized by his senior colleagues the following day; justly he thought. But, he argued, they had not been living with the one main story all day.

A chief sub-editor in Television News gave a clear description of how assumptions about audience knowledge become embodied in the production routines:

> You work on the assumption that the public *do* read newspapers, they *do* listen to the radio. You forget explanation. It becomes,

after a few days, 'The Container Dispute', 'Northern Ireland', 'The Common Market': [the issue] becomes a side heading, and then you go into the day's news. I don't know what people expect.

The channel for which news is produced provides one rather vague discriminant which is sometimes cited when talking about interested publics. Here is one way in which what Walter Lippmann so aptly called the 'phantom public' can be made more real. In Television News, the BBC-1 outputs are seen as the main news output as they attract the largest audiences. The BBC-1 team has therefore to produce 'the national news', on the broadest possible basis of appeal. This influences the selections: BBC-1 is seen as needing to give comprehensive coverage. By contrast, in the days of the late-night programme *News Extra* on BBC-2 (axed in September 1975) the production team took for granted an audience *au fait* with the news of the day which wanted more background:

> We expand the important story of the day with ramifications using experts with personal knowledge. We go for a totally different set of stories which are reduced on BBC-1, which are news in themselves, the vaguely scientific, social story which needs exposure and time. We pull together the strands on international stories, comparing them.
>
> (Editor of the day, BBC-2)

The BBC-2 programme concept was in part determined by the image of the audience as: 'more "intellectual", more informed, and prepared to sit through a half-hour news presentation!' (Foreign duty editor, Television News).

Similarly, for radio newsmen distinctions can be made in terms of the channels for which news is produced. Radio 4 is directed at the audience 'really interested' in news. The aim here is comprehensiveness, as on BBC-1. By contrast, the audience listening to Radios 1 and 2 are perceived, in the words of one duty editor, as composed of 'people listening to pop who don't want the finer details'. This view affects the approach to newswriting:

> Generally speaking, the story is kept short. It's literally the bare bones. We keep it fairly simple without patronizing, without going into the jargon used in the Parliamentary Report.

In its turn, the Radio 3 audience is seen as more interested in 'cultural stuff, artists and composers dying'.

These classifications are vague, telling very little about actual audience wants. But they are, and this is crucial, serviceable in the sense that they provide an orientation and presumptive touchstone with the world outside.

OBLIGATORY COVERAGE: NEWS AS A PUBLIC SERVICE

You've got a duty, if they're talking about something – you've got to supply them with information to let them talk sense.

(Senior sub-editor, Radio News)

It worries us quite a lot if there are a lot of complaints or attacks – and it's not just by isolated individuals. We take it seriously when there're a lot. We think about things; we're sensitive to criticism. You're bound to get certain complaints. For instance, I could've predicted that people'd say George Best is getting too much attention. We don't worry if it's an isolated nutty person, but we do if it's a steady flow.

(Deputy Editor, Radio News)

The last section has indicated how, despite their lack of an immediate and concrete relationship to the broadcasting audience, radio and television newsmen nevertheless find an adequate number of sources of orientation through beliefs and strategies deriving from the concept of 'audience interest'. There is a distinctive set of beliefs which, this time, derives from the BBC's Charter obligations to inform, educate and entertain the public which finances it. The duty to inform is invoked particularly in times of crisis. Recently Northern Ireland coverage has fallen into this category. The public service element in the notion of professionalism emerges clearly in this statement by the Deputy Editor, Radio News:

There's a fair number of letters which say: 'Stop telling us about Northern Ireland. The Irish are bloody foreigners, and nothing to do with us. Tell us more about home stuff.' Our reply is: *'Sorry, we don't like it either, but it's damned important, and we've got to tell people about it.'*

In this formulation the BBC professional is governed by an imperative of what it is proper for a concerned and responsible newsman to do. The imperative may not always be an agreeable one but it must be obeyed, even if the audience protests. Northern Ireland was frequently mentioned in this connexion:

Take Ulster: we've got a duty to do a daily round-up. Though there might be a small explosion – we mustn't be complacent and say 'There's another one', if it's something affecting us all.

(Reporter, Television News)

Other stories were also justified in terms of the duty to the audience:

We did a three-minute piece on the Bangladesh abortions. I thought that was an interesting story. *24 Hours* did a very similar piece to ours, but their audience is about two million. ITN didn't cover it. One consideration in covering it was that ours is a ten-million audience. Something of that importance deserves to be seen by more than two million.

(Editor of the day, Television News)

The size of the news audience is seen as conferring obligations, particularly when a monitoring of the media culture indicates an absence of competing coverage. An additional argument is that high costs of TV production ought not to be a deterrent from covering stories right up to the limits of the budget:

We can't think, for instance, that we won't go and cover something because we can't afford it. Take Watergate: that's our financial Golgotha. It's crucifying us in terms of back-up costs, satellites. We've practically taken over a local TV station in Washington who're doing little else but work for us. In budgetary terms we should have stopped coverage a fortnight ago. It's a major constitutional crisis in the United States. *We unequivocally have to cover it.*

(Deputy Editor, Television News)

Such 'mandatory' stories differ somewhat from the *News Guide*'s lists of categories of 'public service information' pure and simple, which are identified in terms of their 'immediate concern to sizeable sections of listeners': The Weather, The Financial Times Index, Cancelled Events, Special (official) Messages, SOS Messages, Thames Flood Warnings and Public Transport Alterations and Power Cuts. Taking the last example, during the electricity, gas and railway workers' strikes of 1972 and 1973, BBC bulletins contained detailed information of considerable interest to travellers and power users. A Radio News reporter covering the electricity workers' strike in 1972 observed:

The BBC is a public service as well as a news media. We would be leaving people to wonder if we don't say anything.

The public service argument, although distinctive, clearly has points of contact with assumptions about news interest amongst the audience. It is not always personally agreeable for newsmen to cover certain stories, but they perceive their duty to do so as originating from the audience's independent desires:

> I'm just arranging a one-minute wrap-up of the One Thousand Guineas. I'm not a betting man myself, but I know that a lot of people will be interested.
>
> (Home News Editor, Radio News)

> There are some things which I wouldn't want to put in. *I'm* not interested in football; it's a bloody obligation. But the public's interested so we should be carrying the bloody thing.
>
> (Editor of the day, Television News)

The picture is one of a caring communicator who has to cover a wide range of stories: from crises to football matches. It becomes a duty, using this argument, to present any, and all, the news, however unpalatable.

A MODEL FOR COMPREHENSIBILITY

Trainee journalists in BBC News were told by their chief instructor to bear in mind 'the Sheffield bus-driver's wife' as the kind of person who would have to understand whatever they produced. Such an image serves as a reminder, as an institutionalized caution to be lucid.[29] Once again the underlying notion of the newsman as representative recipient of messages comes into play:

> Our strength and weakness is that *we take it that if we can understand it, then so can the public*. At times we get carried away. We sometimes think that certain forms of words are understood when they are not, and it's just a sort of journalistic shorthand.
>
> (Chief sub-editor, Television News)

The 1971 Audience Research Department report, noting that 60 per cent of interviewees considered BBC-TV News was 'always clearly worded', pointed out, even if listeners do regard the bulletins as clearly worded, this constitutes no proof that they were, in fact, comprehensible. Research in this area, which has been widespread abroad, could usefully be undertaken in this country.

In broadcasting, which by definition reaches a global audience, the problem of comprehensibility is more acute than in the case of newspapers or magazines which have clear profiles of their readerships. As with other aspects of the selection process, the choice of vocabulary is routinized, and internal definitions of what constitutes clarity are available in the newsrooms. For example:

> We've found a way of simplifying the description of the trade gap which is reported as a matter of duty every month. 'The balance of payments': 'the difference between what we buy and sell abroad'.

> P.S.: How did this phrase come to be adopted?

> Someone thought of it, and we hear it and say, 'yes, that's good'. Then we have to use it again, and so we ask, 'what was that phrase that was used the other time?' and go and find it. The phrase perpetuates itself, it becomes shorthand. It's the nearest phrase to what we think people will understand. It's not quite right, but it passes for the best because it's *spoken*: you can't re-read the TV script to find out what it said until you understand it, as with a newspaper.

> (Chief sub-editor, Television News)

Such readily-accessible phrases obviously speed up the process of giving shape to the bulletin, and reflect the dominance of time-pressure in production.

Other clarity routines relate to the way in which news bulletins are 'sequenced' to make consumption easier. One technique relates to whether a story falls into the home or foreign category. It is common practice to have a 'foreign round-up' which ends with the newsreader saying 'And now, home again' after a series of stories which have the common (and usually sole) characteristic of being located outside the United Kingdom. Northern Ireland is another such category and stories from there are normally run in a sequence. The technique is used for a wide range of stories: 'industrials' which concern, for example, pay-claims or strikes in different industries may be handled this way. So might disasters: say, two air crashes in quite different places, and with different circumstances surrounding them. The effect of this sequencing is to package together the bulletin – which is a series of generally unrelated events – into a more meaningful combination.

Obscurities in reports and written stories are meant to be removed in the process of passing through the editorial system. Part of the newsreaders' role is to act as everyman by checking the scripts and seeing that he can understand everything; one radio newsreader described himself as:

> a middle man, not a specialist, a gatherer or writer. We have to protect the public from the specialists – it's good that we're not journalists. We have to understand the news straight away if it's been successfully compiled. I'm an intermediary between the listener and the producer.

Achieving clarity is a particularly intense obsession amongst broadcasters and is related to the specific problems of non-print media such as radio and television. Outsiders are told countless times that 'there's no going back' in broadcasting: the message has to be understood immediately or not at all. Frequent comparison is made with newspapers: there a reader can return to a point which has eluded him; in television and radio the impact has to be simultaneous with the audience's act of perception. The *News Guide* derives from this constraint the necessary style: 'there is no room in radio news for complexity, vagueness, ambiguity, obscurity. We must know what we want to say. *And we must say it with directness, simplicity and precision.*'[30]

A related assumption is that the audience's attention needs to be stimulated if it is to be held. This view emerges clearly from the following remark, made by an editor of the day in Television News:

> We do put some things in simply because they are pictures. If there was a three- or four-minute speech, you'd want a good picture story to revive flagging interest.

The concept of clarity is related to beliefs about which presentational forms are best suited to effective communication with the audience. These beliefs are somewhat ambivalent. On the one hand newsmen stress their autonomy, and the self-sufficiency of their milieu, yet on the other they are aware of a competitive reality in which the number of viewers or listeners attracted, or retained by broadcasts is the truly significant yardstick. This awareness finds expression in the routinization of production, rather than in an urgent preoccupation with form.

News is produced in presentational formats, or packages, which appear to satisfy the audience. Of necessity, there are direct links between programme concepts and practice, and assumptions made about the psychology of the audience. There is a desire to communicate in an optimal way. But the optimum is professionally defined by the producers.

In both News Departments, broadcasts are constructed in accordance with what, at any one time, amounts to a production formula: that is, a relatively set and stable way of selecting, ordering, treating and presenting news. A central concept is that of 'actuality': the notion that the TV camera or the microphone can act as vehicles which convey the reality of the event they are transmitting.[31]

Actuality

Moving pictures are for the TV newsman a form of actuality, a medium through which reality can be genuinely and authentically captured and presented. There is a conventional wisdom concerning the role and significance of pictures for television news programmes:

> Being TV, we want to put film to [the story] if possible.
> (News Editor, Television News)

> I suppose the main difference [between radio and TV] is that being a visual media we have to fit some sort of picture with what is going out, even if it's only a still, or a quarter screen overlay . . . If there are floods in the Sahara you have to show a picture.
> (Senior TV engineer, Television News)

> TV is pictures. It feeds on them. It must always have them. There can be silence on the screen: no words, no music, no sound effects: but there must be pictures. This is the first datum that all TV journalists have to come to terms with.[32]

Optimum television news coverage is defined in terms of obedience to a pictorial imperative. It is the moving pictures of events which are felt able to convey the truth in a way best suited to the medium. Filmed, videotaped or 'live' accounts are the optimal modes of presentation available to the TV journalist. The remarks cited above make this clear. A former Editor of ITN, Sir Geoffrey Cox, has spelled out with clarity the sort of production concept with which his news organization has worked, one which differs only in nuances from that encountered at the BBC; writing about picture value he has noted that:

The most obvious way in which TV is a strong news medium is its
ability to depict on the screen an event exactly as it happens, or as
it happened . . . Where natural sound of the event is available the
impact is even more effective.[33]

This expresses the basic belief that television is a medium which does
not interfere in what it transmits and that 'live' TV is the most pure-
from-the-source form. Despite telling criticisms this view is still
widely held, and has been expressed somewhat extravagantly by
Kenneth Adam, a former Director of Television, BBC:

The event without reconstruction, or editing, or interference –
this, putting sound with picture, is the unique quality of television
transmission; because it is the transmission of experience. News
is no longer what it has always been, something heard or seen or
reported upon after it has happened. News is not then, it is now.
After President Kennedy was killed, while millions watched, all
the old definitions went by the board. Truth is not only stranger
but stronger than fiction.[34]

The second best concept

If live dramatic television and the good film story represent television
at its best, anything which is not realized in those terms falls into
the category of second-best, or worse. Sir Geoffrey Cox, expressing
the ITN view, has said:

There is no doubt that in TV, as in the popular press, when you
have the pictures that tell the story you must give them the space
to do their job, even if the other news has to be boiled down to
headlines.[35]

On this view picture value should be used as a selection criterion for
deciding what counts as the news of the day. While this is clearly a
view also obtaining at the BBC, senior newsmen were careful to
stress the responsibility which governs selections.

The second-best presentational mode which receives most op-
probium is the 'talking head'. This is the dismissive phrase used in
the TV world to describe a person in vision (on the screen) who is, in
one way or another, speaking to camera. Thus, for example, newsreaders addressing the public are talking heads, as are people being
interviewed or giving speeches. Robin Day has described the

E

talking head as 'what TV professionals tend to regard as a second hand and a second class way of presenting issues'.[36] The idea, there-fore, of transmitting an entire news bulletin in such terms is seen as

a waste of opportunity. It is what Madison Avenue men call 'radio with a light to read by'. *The picture adds nothing*: indeed it may subtract, in the sense that it distracts. If the special talent of TV is to be exploited, the pictures and the words must reinforce each other. *The watcher must see what he is hearing about, and hear what he is seeing.*[37]

This kind of view contains an implicit theory of the informational success of a visual as opposed to a purely auditory medium. The disapproval of what is seen as a shoddy form of presentation is often expressed in terms of that pliable notion, professionalism. To commit the sin of 'thinking radio' is to have less than the requisite consideration necessary for the goal of maintaining audience interest. To bore is to run the risk of people switching off or even, far worse, switching channels. At yet another level it is not really a question of holding the audience, but rather one of respecting a value which in part defines the technically proficient programme. Sir Geoffrey Cox, while acknowledging that diagrams, stills, maps and other graphics are useful presentational aids significantly ranks them below moving pictures. He also notes the absence of optimal television when presenting a 'situationer', or scene-setting story, from locations such as conferences:

This is a story which the cameras cannot tell, and for which TV is *forced back on what is virtually a radio report with the reporter in vision.*

Such reports, he observes, have to be kept short and pointed to retain the viewers' attention.[38] The comparison with radio again is not fortuitous; it expresses definitively the view that TV has its own technical repertoire and that this *has* to be used. To judge by evidence from the special Audience Research reports commissioned by the News Departments, there is indeed a desire amongst the viewing public for film stories. However, the typical quotation which follows is hardly a basis for making assumptions about the general psychology of attention:

Adults were asked to say whether they would like film to be shown more or less often, presumably in place of stories read by the newsreader or spoken by special correspondent . . . a little

under a third were content with things as they are, but (predict-
ably) nearly all the rest (59%) would like film 'more often' or
'a lot more often'.[39]

The distinctiveness of the television concept of news is illuminated
by an example. In July 1973, one TV bulletin carried the story of a
father in an American town threatening to kill his child with a knife.
There were dramatic pictures of the police closing in and ultimately
rescuing the child, watched by crowds on the pavements. In terms
of strict news value a story of this category – American small-town
crime – is of minimal interest to journalists producing news for a
British public. This is clear from the following views expressed by a
copy taster in BBC Radio News:

> You discard most of the foreign immediately. About 15% of all
> copy is about minor incidents in the Middle East. Another 15%
> is from the States: *murders and things like that which are common-
> place.*

As the commonplace does not typically make news, clearly some
other criterion was at work: namely, picture value. Questioned
about this specific story, the Deputy Editor, TV News, agreed with
this assessment: 'It was bizarre, out of the ordinary. There was
danger.' However, like other newsmen in TV News, he was at pains to
stress an awareness of the 'dangers':

> We're always on our guard about running a story because there are
> good pictures. But it's wrong to think we choose things just because
> of this: for example, the other day we led with the Pound and the
> IMF . . . Again, in the case of the baby snatch we did that by
> interviews. I'm not denigrating wall-paper film since frequently it
> does convey the feel of the story; it heightens public awareness.
> Radio can't convey the feel of five hundred police tramping
> around Bristol. And it can't show the empty prams outside all the
> shops in Bristol. There's not one mother who leaves her child
> outside. On the other side there are strict picture stories: there's
> the 'end of the bulletin story'.

By this account, then, there is something of a tension between news
values proper and picture value. Whereas on the one hand news
judgement tells newsmen that a given story is important and deserves
prominence, on the other they recognize that the 'best' story from
the point of view of television as a medium might be a different one.
During fieldwork in Television News many of the newsmen referred

to the danger of giving too much play to the pictures and of forgetting
the real story which they are meant to illustrate. To quell any doubts
on my part, the News Editor noted, in much the same vein as the
Deputy Editor: 'We always go for the big story, *even if we haven't
got the pictures*'. This statement encapsulates the ambivalence.

However, awareness of the need for pictures did not prevent
some from recognizing that those self-same pictures frequently
failed to communicate effectively the true nature of the issue or
events in question. The issue mentioned most frequently was
Northern Ireland: 'Lots has been done on Northern Ireland, but the
impact hasn't come across.' (Senior duty editor, Television News)

Pursuing this theme, one television reporter said that he had been
subjected to culture shock on first arriving in Belfast, and that he
did not see how anyone who had not directly experienced the
situation could grasp it: 'The population over here [in Britain]
doesn't accept it as a real situation.' Television, despite the pictures,
had not, he thought, conveyed a comprehensible message.

Programme concepts

The study of organizational procedures has shown that the production process involves a progressive narrowing of options as stories
are fitted into slots.

The editor of the day, in his producer's role, is responsible for
building the programme, for realizing, so far as possible, the conception embodied in the final running order. The running order
contains what one newsman aptly called a 'hidden skeleton': it
imposes order on a selection of stories and prescribes how they
should be handled. The running order is subject to progressive
modification as the newsday continues. Editors stressed that the
order chosen for radio and TV bulletins did not follow a strict
ranking of importance in terms of straight news value:

I write stories, firstly in a rough notional order of importance, and
then I take each one and see where they hang together. You try
to draw a balance between the order of importance on the one
hand and coherence on the other. No bulletin could be based
entirely on the order of importance: it would be absurd. You
try to make it look like a designed programme rather than an
accident.

(Editor of the day, Television News)

There is an underlying aesthetic ideal of how the well-constructed programme looks or sounds. There are explicit links between the programme concept and the interest which has to be maintained in the audience, and this is in turn linked to the goal of maintaining audience size.

While the above quotation comes from a television newsman, the same basic notions apply to radio news. An editor of the day observed:

> You don't want the bulletin to be a succession of jumps. You don't want voice pieces all to come together. You put foreign stories together in a small group. But all these tidy arrangements can be destroyed at a moment's notice – that's part of the attraction of the job.

Programme concepts, therefore, incorporate assumptions about the presentational forms which will command the audience's attention, even, newsmen hope, where the stories are 'difficult' or 'boring'. Formats are deliberately varied through time to try to maximize audiences – a point dealt with in detail in Chapter 9.

In general, news programmes or bulletins are seen as needing an internal dynamic supplied by variety and drama. One senior duty editor in Television News summed up this entire perspective when he remarked 'keeping the audience interested is our *raison d'être*'. There are, however, as Elliott has pointed out, inherent dangers in clarity and presentational routines which tend to simplify media content in order to hold the audience's attention, for they produce a 'relationship between production and audience based on audience satisfaction rather than the communication of meaning'.[40]

CONCLUSION

The data presented in this chapter support the argument that there is a missing link between the producers and consumers of news. This raises doubts about whether we can talk about the process in question as one of 'communication'. The newsmen studied know little about their audience's levels of information and knowledge. There is no satisfactory method of feedback which enables them to become more aware. Audience research is sporadic and ambiguous, and where it is not simply concerned with the size of viewing or listening publics, or their class composition, it has tried to pinpoint why BBC News has been 'in decline', rather than how well people understand what it tells them about the world.

Other sources of information are rough and ready – telephone calls and letters, mainly – the unsystematic garnering of evidence produced by self-selected informants. There is also the rather diffuse attention which the BBC attracts because of its symbolic place in British culture, and this serves to make newsmen aware that the BBC is being watched, but tells them little about how well they are doing their job.

The evidence also tells us a good deal about the way in which the gap between producer and consumer does not pose severe problems because it is filled with the conventional wisdom of a professionalism which is largely self-sustaining. Johnson has noted the general structure of uncertainty prevailing in producer–consumer relationships which derives from the social distance between them. The indeterminacy of this relationship creates a potential for autonomy in which 'Power relationships will determine whether uncertainty is reduced at the expense of producer or consumer'.[41] The power here lies with the newsmen who assert their possession of the necessary knowledge for effective communication. When pressed, they produce vague ideas about their audiences, based on their view of the kinds of people who listen to or watch particular channels, or from interactions with neighbours or people on trains. Ultimately the newsman is his own audience. When he talks of his professionalism he is saying that he knows how to tell his story.

6

The mediation of control (1): the editorial system

A persistent focus in sociological studies of news organizations has been the modes of control applied to ensure that specific editorial policies are followed.[1] The existence of such policies implies that each news organization constructs news in identifiable ways, in terms not only of the selection of stories, but also their angling and mode of presentation. To put a construction on the news, impose a meaning on it, is inescapable, since the production process is one that at all stages involves the making of value-judgements.

In the BBC, 'policy' was not a term much used, being hard and definite. More appropriate, it was felt, was 'guidance', since the policy-making machinery is quite subtle and empirical. This preference is not accidental, being an indication of the BBC's style. The official position is that the BBC's news is a neutral, factual construct. Talk of policy tends to contradict this line, suggesting explicit value-judgements.

To talk of the existence of a policy-making machinery raises the question of ensuring that policy is adhered to. The degree of conformity in the News Departments was striking. In this chapter, and the next, an explanation for this is advanced. Here, it is argued that various features of the BBC's editorial system act routinely to ensure broad conformity with the desired approach to the news. The reviewing function of the formal bureaucratic hierarchy and relations of power and status in the newsroom are crucial here. In Chapter 7, controls embodied in the individual newsman's need to adhere to corporate ideology and to assume an appropriate professional identity are examined.

Many newsmen who read earlier drafts of this study expressed surprise at the pervasive nature of the control system depicted here. They did not, in general, consider themselves kept on a short leash, and were unconscious, most of the time, of the highly ramified nature of the editorial system, and its impact on their work. They espouse, as it were, the BBC's micro-myth of independence. This stresses the autonomy of the production staff, and delegation of responsibility downward from the Director-General. The macro-myth of the

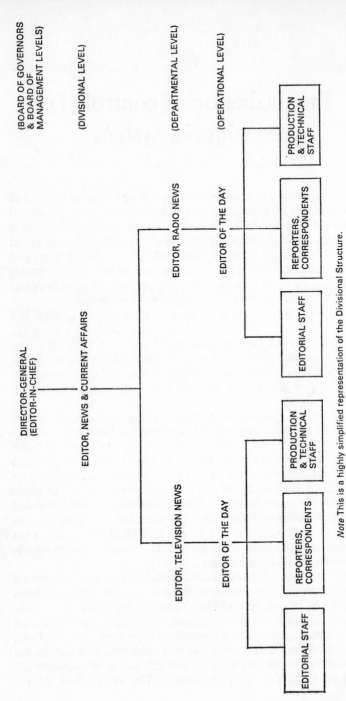

Note This is a highly simplified representation of the Divisional Structure.

Figure 6.1: Hierarchical organization of the BBC news division

BBC's independence, is, of course, the view that the BBC is largely socially unattached. Together, the two myths support a considerable sense of autonomy.

Just as the macro-myth is injected with reality by reference to the BBC's social responsibility in a democratic society, so is the micro-myth tempered by the notion of reference upwards as limiting the scope of every individual's action. As a senior editor in Television News described it:

> If you pick the right people you get broadly the right decisions. There are established areas where reference upwards is desirable and required. The onus is on the person to whom the responsibility is delegated. A failure to refer is a reflection on your judgement. People grow into the situation; they know when the moment comes to take a second opinion.

The concept of reference upwards points us towards the BBC's bureaucratic hierarchy, and an examination of how it mediates control. On examination, it becomes apparent that 'reference upwards' does not adequately describe the editorial process. More accurately, there is a continual process of reference downwards, of judgements and decisions, which goes largely unacknowledged. It is only the difficult marginal cases which are the actually visible occasions on which advice is sought. Otherwise, unacknowledged, the invisible framework of guidance is omnipresent. How does this come about? To answer this requires an examination of the BBC's command structure.

THE BBC'S COMMAND STRUCTURE

Board of Governors

According to the BBC's charter, the Board of Governors is the paramount authority in the Corporation. In fact the Governors *are* the BBC. Their role, and particularly that of their Chairman, has varied at different points in the organization's history. For a long time Reith's conception prevailed. For him, the Governors were public trustees, having *de jure* authority over the BBC's activities. The Director-General (DG), however, as the BBC's chief executive, and his managerial support staff, being the experts in broadcasting, would exercise *de facto* power. This view held sway until 1952, when the Reithian conception was revised by the Beveridge Committee on broadcasting, which redefined the role of the Governors as a more active interventionist one. This approach was endorsed by Lord Normanbrook, who as Chairman of the Governors from 1964–67 argued that they had an essentially ministerial character with an executive role to play.[2]

Wedell has suggested that the Reithian system of control (weak Chairman, strong DG) persisted until well into the 1960s. Something of a shift in the relationship between the DG (Board of Management) and Chairman (Board of Governors) occurred in 1967 with the appointment of Lord Hill as BBC Chairman. In a case study of the retirement of Sir Hugh Greene, the then DG, Tracey has suggested that the appointment should be seen as an attempt to push the BBC into a greater orthodoxy and into the 'middle ground' after a period of some quite unorthodox broadcasting. The Governors, being appointed by the government, are an important point of articulation between the state and broadcasting. Thus, Tracey argues, 'a re-definition of the overall purpose of the BBC was intended to flow from a marginal redistribution of power and control at the very highest levels of the Corporation.'[3] Lord Hill's appointment was Harold Wilson's intended instrument for 'taming' the BBC.

Certainly, to judge by Lord Hill's autobiographical account, he did quite expressly set out to challenge the power of the DG.[4] This active approach to the Chairmanship would appear to have been continued by Hill's successor, Sir Michael Swann.

But the Board of Governors, while formally supreme, is not the main instrument in the formation of BBC editorial policy. Very occasionally the Chairman may take an editorial decision. An example of this occurred in 1965, when Lord Normanbrook decided that Ian Smith, Prime Minister of Rhodesia, should not be inter-viewed by BBC television's *24 Hours*, as it might pose political problems.[5] But this decision was made in the DG's absence. The Board of Governors, moreover, meets fortnightly, and does not have as its sole and specific purpose the making of editorial decisions. An internal document makes it clear that the Chairman 'is continuously involved in discussion of matters *arising from editorial decisions*'.[6] Generally, in other words, the decisions have already been taken. Our key focus, therefore, is rather on the DG, and his chief editorial aide, the Editor, News and Current Affairs (ENCA).

Director-General and Editor, News and Current Affairs

The Director-General of the BBC is its Editor-in-Chief. Sir Hugh Greene was propounding the Reithian, strong DG thesis when he wrote;

no matter how responsible a Board may be and no matter how often they meet and how much interest they take, they cannot be responsible for the day to day running of an organization. They must have a chief executive, an editor; and that editor or chief executive is me.[7]

So far as the BBC's news staff is concerned that statement holds true today. Few in the newsrooms knew very much about the high politics of the BBC's boardrooms. The DG, however, was universally considered to be the BBC's Editor-in-Chief. The Board of Governors, as one newsman put it, was thought of as 'a distant mythical authority' and the names of most of its members were not common knowledge. Much of the DG's editorial power is delegated to a key figure in the BBC's news hierarchy, the Editor, News and Current Affairs. It is ENCA's level in the hierarchy which newsmen are most familiar with, as he acts as the general co-ordinator of news and current affairs activities for the radio and television services.

From the time that 'controversy' was first routinely found in the output, after 1928, a specialized bureaucracy has existed within the BBC to deal with problems of editorial control and policy.[8] Such institutionalized vigilance has persisted in various guises. The present 'controversy committee' is chaired by ENCA, as we shall see. But there have been changes in this area, which are worth noting.

During the Chairmanship of Lord Simon, in the late 1940s and early 1950s, editorial control of controversial matter was plainly thought worthy of special attention. Simon wrote:

Talks are held to be so important, so controversial and so dangerous if they go wrong, that a special Director is almost essential and certainly very desirable, to guide policy and to maintain top contacts within the government, the opposition, and many varied external interests. . . .[9]

This special role was then played by the Director of the Spoken Word (DSW) who had close links with the DG. Coatman gives an example from the late 1940s when the DSW monitored forthcoming programme content by asking producers to submit advanced information on talks.[10]

Since the early 1950s, with the 'news explosion' and the growth of television current affairs, the need for control has become even more imperative. It has also become more ramified. Harman Grisewood, who held the top post of DSW in the early 1950s until its abolition under the DG-ship of Sir Ian Jacob, has described the creation of the substitute co-ordinating role of Chief Assistant to the Director-General. The DG, he says,

> was to be especially watchful over the current affairs and news output in television; and from now on, I was as much interested in the domestic life of party politicians as in the well-being of the BBC. . . . Someone in the BBC has to know the political world from the inside and not only draft answers to the politicians' letters.[11]

In pursuit of the BBC's well-being, Grisewood established the practice of intimate discussion with politicians, and set up informal relations between the BBC and the party whips' offices, which have been maintained by his successors in the chief assistant's role.[12]

Later in the 1950s, another new role was created when Hugh Greene became the BBC's first Director of News and Current Affairs (DNCA). Grisewood complains that his post of Chief Assistant had not allowed him adequate power over the television producers. Greene's entry to the post of DNCA may be seen as the answer to Grisewood's wish for someone who was, in effect, 'Deputy Director-General' in matters editorial. Greene's brief was 'to weld together the news and current affairs elements in radio and television so that they could carry out their respective functions against a background of shared policy and journalistic assumptions'.[13] The BBC's answer to the problems of editorial control in the 1950s was, therefore, to maintain and develop Reith's centralism, in the spirit of 'One Corporation, One Voice'.

Recent attacks on news and current affairs programmes, most notably calls for a 'patriotic censorship' concerning Northern Ireland, caused further centralization in the late 1960s and early 1970s, and a strengthening of the role of the Editor, News and Current Affairs (successor to the DNCA).[14]* It is this structure which was operating during my fieldwork.

Editorial control in the highest reaches of the BBC is routine in character, and is based on two weekly editorial meetings, one chaired by ENCA, and a subsequent one, much more exclusive, chaired by the DG. Both of these take place on Friday mornings. I did not have access to these meetings, which are restricted to the most senior of the BBC news and current affairs editors, but they are not an entirely closed book, as there are minutes of their deliberations, which I was, on occasion, able to read – though unofficially.

---

* As this book goes to press (July 1977), the BBC has announced the re-creation of the post of DNCA; its incumbent will sit on the Board of Management. Evidently, the DG will in future be 'sharing' the function of Editor-in-chief.

In addition, half a dozen of the editors who attend the meetings spoke about them in general terms during interviews.

The first meeting is known as 'ENCA's meeting'. It brings together the most senior editors from the domestic radio and television services, and there is also a representative of the BBC's External Services. Among the thirty or so present are the Editors of Radio and Television News, the Heads of the Current Affairs groups in radio and television, the Political Editor, the Chief Assistant to the DG, the Head of Outside Broadcasts.

The meeting runs through the previous week's minutes, and the editors are then invited to make comments and to raise problems. One source described it as 'a forum in which colleagues are informed and reactions given to programmes'. The role of ENCA is that of giving 'overall guidance on content' as one editor put it. The Editor, News and Current affairs, said that his role was to respond to the existing output rather than to initiate new departures. He said he 'would draw attention to gaps, deficiencies, imbalances, unfairness'. The approach is that of retrospective review.

The subsequent meeting in the DG's office deals with more confidential matters, and is attended by the top half-dozen editors, and several members of the Board of Management. The DG is given a résumé of the earlier discussions and told the sense of the meeting. Where there are unresolved matters for his decision he decides on what is to be done. There are discussions about particular programmes, and as one editor described it 'DG says "Liked that", "Didn't like that"; "That was good; that was bad". The policy emerges from that in the form of very broad tramlines.' Like ENCA, the DG draws attention to areas of coverage which he thinks have been overlooked or overexposed, but, informants said, rarely lays down hard prescriptions.

The deliberations of these two highly select meetings are diffused throughout the news and current affairs production units by means of the News and Current Affairs Minutes. These minutes have a restricted circulation within the BBC, but the dissemination of much of their contents is ensured, because, as we shall see, the system is deliberately leaky. The importance of the minutes is spelled out in an internal document, *Principles and Practice in News and Current Affairs*:

One of the Director-General's main instruments of communication on matters of editorial policy is the minuted record of the News and Current Affairs meeting. These minutes are circulated to 150 addressees throughout the BBC. Nearly every person on the list has some degree of managerial or editorial responsibility for

News and Current Affairs programming. The minutes do not simply record decisions; they give full accounts of discussions of difficult editorial problems, so that those who read them may understand the factors which influenced the making of the decision in each case.[15]

The issues dealt with at the meetings and style of the minutes are best conveyed by citing a typical example. The minutes for 16 July 1976 were eleven pages long. They made constant reference to previous minutes. Thus, to interpret them fully would require the possession of an entire series of these guidelines. Below, I list the subjects dealt with on this occasion, quoting at length from those most comprehensible without further background. My own summaries of unquoted sections are in brackets. The main minute refers to discussions taking place at 'ENCA's meeting'. 'Later' refers to the more select discussion in the DG's room. The numbers are those of each separate minute.

611. Broadcasting from Parliament;
612. Broadcasts on Racial Matters;
613. Regional Television Fees;
614. Angola;
615. Report on Lonrho;
616. Liberal Party Leadership election;
617. Programmes about the House of Windsor: 'a member of the Royal Family had asked to see an interview with him before deciding whether to give permission for it to be broadcast'.
    [This practice was to be maintained].
'*Later*: DG said it must be remembered that the Royal Family was in no position to reply to mistaken information or opinion . . . it was essential to get matters right before transmission.'
618. India;
619. 'House' stories about the BBC [Mr Callaghan, the Prime Minister, had made a speech at the opening of the new Broadcasting House, Manchester. The issue raised in the minute was whether the BBC's news and current affairs teams should use such stories]. 'ENCA observed at present the tendency was to fall over backwards to include criticisms of the BBC but to be shy of favourable items.'
'*Later:* DG said that if a decision was taken to report hostile comment [about the BBC or any other organization] one must be sure to report the reply. [The minute went on to give advance warning that the DG and Chairman] would in the autumn be speaking publicly about the factors relating to an increase in the licence fee.'
620. Broadcast reference to persons who become targets of violence [There had been a request from the police not to use stills on screen of prison officers accused of assaulting IRA prisoners in the event of their being convicted at a current trial]. 'ENCA said it was best not to direct attention to those who became targets for violence. He acknowledged that in this case the names of the prison officers were already known, but the general public did not know what they looked like.'

621. The pharmaceutical industry;
622. Programme complaints commission;
623. Mr Erik Rydbeck – News letters from South Africa: '[his] views [on racial matters] were completely one-sided and should be ignored'.
624. BBC accreditation in East Germany;
625. Alleged instances of BBC overstaffing [This was an exceptionally long minute. It referred to an article in *The Guardian* which alleged that the BBC had fifty-nine staff covering the Democratic Convention in New York]. 'ENCA said the number was "not far wrong". . . . ENCA repeated his insistence that departments should cut down their staffs by themselves.'
     '*Later* [The Television Service was going to give details of staffing in New York to the Home Office – the Ministry responsible for broadcasting. There was to be a 'central point' for departments to apply to.] DG urged that all the BBC staff concerned should keep a check on their tongues for their own sakes. . . .'
626. Prison Officers [had been referred to as 'warders' on the *Today* programme: they considered this derogatory];
627. 'DG asked why Jimmy Carter's acceptance speech had been described as a "good" one, without any attribution for that adjective in the R4 9.00 a.m. news bulletin that morning. Editor, Radio News said he would look into it.'
628. Mrs Sally Oppenheim, MP [was pressuring for more broadcasting facilities];
629. Mrs Thatcher [was reluctant to broadcast until a General Election was imminent];
     '*Later:* [DG said] The BBC could not withhold invitations to Mr Callaghan because of Mrs Thatcher's reluctance to appear. DG agreed with ENCA that, despite that reluctance, Mrs Thatcher should continue to be invited to broadcast in the usual way.'
630. Information about Central and Southern America.
     At the 'later meeting in DG's office' two matters were considered:
631. The UDA in Glasgow [the DG asked whether there were any programmes in progress on this; there were not];
632. Hospital cockroaches [there had been protests about an item on *Nationwide* from hospital circles].

The picture emerging from a consideration of these items is primarily one of pressures feeding in to the top of the BBC's hierarchy. These come from politicians and from various organized lobbies. The BBC's own corporate image is of obvious importance to its controllers, as may be seen from the immense concern shown about *The Guardian* report; it is also apparent from the discussion of House stories, where it is clearly implied that reports of speeches concerning the licence fee should find their way into the output. There are also various instances of 'problem' coverage; obviously Mrs Thatcher had to be seen to receive invitations, otherwise there would be accusations of BBC bias against the Conservatives; the decision concerning prison officers took the line that they ought to be protected from the IRA; and coverage of the UDA in Glasgow was evidently of special interest, presumably reflecting fears encountered in the BBC that it might be 'the next Belfast'.

It was illuminating to compare reactions in the newsroom with policy decisions at the ENCA/DG level. For example, the minute concerning the prison officers was put into effect during my field-work in Television News. At a morning meeting the Editor said they would not be showing stills of the prison officers in question. He made the point explicitly that this was in response to a police request, expressing concern that the men, or their families, would be open to retaliation. One warder was interviewed – after permission had been sought from the Editor, Television News – on the late-night news bulletin, but apparently at his own request, and not at the BBC's initiative. I was also able to observe the reaction to *The Guardian* report on the shop floor. It was hardly treated with the high seriousness of the minutes. Most newsmen were well aware that there would be a fuss when they first saw the report. But it was essentially seen as a joke, and there was envious carping about those who were on the gravy train.

The diffusion of 'guidance'

The way in which the minutes' contents are diffused downwards through the organization illustrates the BBC's managerial style. The DG and ENCA are the legitimate sources of editorial control, and the authoritativeness of the minutes is recognized by every newsman. But not all are privy to the contents of the minutes – not officially, anyway. As a restricted document, they are not meant to go below the level of duty editor in the newsroom. But on the other hand, there is no formal bar on any staff newsman actually seeing them. This means that getting hold of them lies in the individual's initiative.

There is a considerable desire to control the way in which the minutes are seen outside the Corporation. One very senior news executive chafed at the idea that they were seen as 'ENCA's Orders of the Day'. In delivering an official reaction to the previous draft of this study he drew attention to a point I had made in a *footnote*, in which I said that a sub told me he was shown the minutes 'illicitly' by an assistant editor on the way home. This way of putting it was 'not quite right'. It would be wrong to say that people looking at the minutes were penalized for doing so. But there was a preference for them to be passed on informally.

Two reasons were advanced for this preference. First, it was said that people at a lower level tended to take the points too literally, and they could become hamstrung, obsessed by detail. This was counter-productive as you wanted 'maximum autonomy flowing downwards'. Secondly, the minutes tended to be rather condensed, the details of the discussion were not there in every case, and 'you need to know how to read them'. It was stressed that they were not 'some kind of secret directive' as 150 people were entitled to read them.

That the minutes do involve skilled interpretation may be illustrated by this instance. One editor of the day showed me the minutes for 20 August 1975. There was a reference there to the then Prime Minister, Harold Wilson's Ministerial Broadcast of the week under review. The Head of Current Affairs Group (Television) pointed out that Wilson had stayed for a little while to chat after the broadcast. Expounding, the editor said: 'It's interesting that that has to be mentioned. Most people would do that as a matter of course. Yet in the case of the BBC that merits comment.' This observation was placed in the context of tense relations between Wilson and the Labour Party, and the BBC. This example shows, incidentally, how taking the political temperature is a routine part of the Corporation's intelligence.

Some further points were made about the diffusion of the minutes. One assistant editor saw his role as follows: 'We have to pass on the thinking. We discuss it with the boys in the [BBC] Club, and everything.' He believed the minutes ought to be restricted and mediated by senior staff, as they often contained criticisms of senior producers and their programmes; to let these loose would undermine respect for the line of command. Another assistant editor took a different line. He thought that all news staff ought to have access to them, but they 'oughtn't to float around the newsroom as there's a security problem.' There was at one time 'a strong *Private Eye* interest in the minutes'.

The minutes possess an ambivalent status therefore. Their contents are important for everyone to know, but their official diffusion is restricted. Word of mouth plays an important role in conveying guidance. This leads to what one newsman described as 'a curious choreography of manners'. A television newsman said that he, and everyone else, knew that a copy of the minutes was kept in the Home News Editor's drawer. In an account supported by others he said:

> You can turn up in the newsroom and say 'Well, what do you know! So-and-so's got a bollocking in the minutes.' Everyone *knows* you've sneaked them from the Home News Editor's drawer – but you'd never say so. You'll sneak them back there, and you'll never say you got them from there. And you'll never out and out ask the editor of the day what was in the minutes.

A plausible interpretation of all this is that the content of the 'ENCA meetings' is a useful kind of open secret. This 'secret' is open enough to defeat the conspiracy theorists both inside and outside the Corporation. Yet it is closed enough to permit a good deal of policy to be worked out at an implicit level. One would have to know a good deal more than finally goes into the minutes to realize their full significance – indeed one senior editor said that as their distribution had widened they had become more emasculated. Nonetheless, there are enough skilled and licensed interpreters around, in the know, to make sense of them, and informally to mediate guidance through the formal structure of the editorial system, to which we now turn.

EDITORIAL RESPONSIBILITY

Looked at in the round, the BBC's editorial system is articulated in two distinct ways. At the newsroom production level described in Chapter 3 there is a complex working out of editorial control between several craft groups. This will be returned to shortly. Distinct from this, but locking into it, particularly through the key role of the editor of the day, is the bureaucratic editorial hierarchy which has so far been the subject of this chapter. Its Reithian style of construction, that of the 'logical pyramid' of formal responsibility,[16] puts one in mind of Max Weber's discussion of bureaucracy. Weber could have been describing the BBC's system of 'reference upwards' when he wrote that the

> principles of office hierarchy and of levels of graded authority mean a firmly ordered system of super- and subordination in which there is a supervision of the lower offices by the higher ones.[17]

Supervision and subordination tend to be played down, however, in the orthodox account of editorial practice. The editor of the day is, according to this, as newsmen sometimes say 'God for the day'. His godliness is limited, however, by the fact that the newsroom's performance is under continual scrutiny by those of an even more elevated status. The style of intervention may in general be unobtrusive but it undoubtedly acts to check editorial autonomy, as pointed out by the Deputy Editor, Radio News:

> You leave people basically to get on with the job, and don't do much more than to slip in when there are complications. You occasionally interfere to the point of saying 'I wouldn't do that'. For example, on Monday at 6 o'clock there was a report about

Nigeria packed with clichés, rather gory blood and guts. The Editor went in and said 'I wouldn't run that again'. This ties up with responsibility. Some papers would happily run that. We don't want to thrust the blood and guts at them.

In this situation, the Editor was acting as the arbiter of good taste. The Editor, Radio News, said that he expected editors of the day to refer to him if they had any worries concerning the following areas: Ireland, which was 'difficult'; stories dealing with the BBC's politics; stories involving legal problems; stories about violence. Editors of the day are also expected to trim their sails when cost factors have to be considered, as a senior executive in Television News put it:

> All the major decisions, especially financial commitments, would be referred. For example, sending a reporter and crew to Karachi means the commitment of several thousand pounds. . . . Within the UK deployment is much more a day by day and hour by hour affair in the hands of the editor of the day.

These are, however, marginal cases, and actual interference is rare. The style of control is one which relies upon responsible editors, who have been so thoroughly socialized by long exposure to the *mores* of the Corporation that they will 'instinctively' make the right decisions. It is the effectiveness of this system which has led Wedell to talk of production in broadcasting as 'proceeding largely "on hunch" and by light of the institutional ethos of the organization'.[19]

Editors of the day, while apt to stress their independence of action, are also very aware of being entrusted to produce an output which is 'reliable', consistent through time, and indistinguishable from that of their fellows. To ensure this they too diffuse 'guidance'. An editor of the day in Radio News described the approach: it was not possible to supervise everything, but he would give 'overall policy guidance with tricky stories – the controversial ones – Northern Ireland, where carrying stories might result in crowds going out simply because they heard something on the BBC. If necessary you can refer it upwards. The Editor or the Deputy Editor will ring this morning or later in the day – just to keep themselves informed. We can ring them at any time – but it happens very rarely: we're usually in a better position to assess and take decisions.'

The same editor went on to describe the retrospective review function exercised by the Editor, Radio News, in terms reminiscent of those used about the DG and ENCA:

He doesn't interfere very much – he lets us get on with the job. He's fairly receptive; he usually notices the weak spots, and that gives us a different light on what we're doing – that you're pushing a story too hard, crowding out others.

The newsroom editors stress their autonomy by pointing out that they make the decisions, as the observer can see. They also emphasize their reluctance to refer upwards and seem to find it difficult to think of examples of when they have done so. However, one gave the following instance. During the 'Land Deals Affair', when various political and personal associates of Harold Wilson were accused of speculation, Wilson's political secretary, Marcia Williams (now Lady Falkender), had given an interview to the *Daily Mirror*. The editor of the day wondered whether to try and get a taped interview covering the same ground. But being aware of the sensitive relationship between Wilson and the BBC, he had phoned the Deputy Editor, Radio News, to ask for the go-ahead. He was given it, but Mrs Williams refused the interview, so in the end he had to quote the *Mirror* in the bulletin.

Affirming the orthodox account of autonomy, editors are eager to disparage any suggestions that internal pressures are applied:

Lots are convinced that the bosses say 'Do that', that the Chairman and the DG are looking over your shoulder. We make mistakes but we try and look at everything objectively. But the human element comes in.

Another editor stressed that the *operational* reality, as he experienced it, invalidated criticisms that a premeditated censorship existed. BBC News was not, as many people seemed to think, a 'high-powered committee sitting back and reviewing things', but rather 'a group of half-educated journalists' who did their work under pressure: 'You have to remember the conditions under which decisions are made'. While this last view is somewhat deviant in laying such stress on the fallibility of the news producers it nonetheless works defensively in stressing the pragmatic, and hence uninterfered in, side of the activity: 'It's a last-minute rush. There's no conspiracy.'

The stress on editorial responsibility promotes the general feeling in the newsroom that it is the editor of the day's programme which is being introduced. The framework of 'guidance' finds its way into the newsroom unobtrusively. Priorities and policy decisions worked out at the ENCA and DG meetings become taken up as their own by those making major decisions in the newsroom. The process was summed up by one senior duty editor:

The Editor says '*I* think we should cover . . .' The editor of the day says '*I* want us to cover . . .' Then the senior duty editor says to the subs '*We* want to cover, we're doing . . .'

The possessiveness of editors about their programmes is curious because they are not permitted much scope for individuality. Editorial soundness is identified by its consistency. For example, at one morning meeting, a part of the output was criticized for sounding too idiosyncratic. Later, an editor of the day explained: 'It mustn't be too obvious that someone else is doing it every shift.' But there is another aspect of editorial possessiveness which is in subtle contradiction to the pursuit of consistency. Many newsmen remarked that they could tell who was sitting in the editorial chair on any given shift. There were hints which could be picked up from the ordering of news items, occasionally from their selection, treatment or the language employed. Thus, within the context of the house style there are variations enough for editorial identities to be sniffed out by insiders. This quite minor point is revealing about the stamp and scope of editorial authority. The pursuit of consistency and safety does not entirely neutralize the individuality of editors of the day. But the hints are such that only insiders can pick them up. The fact they can do this, however, makes them feel even more that it is really the editor's programme.

Departmental Editors and editors of the day, therefore, give an orthodox account of editorial practice which stresses that editorial control actually plays itself out on the newsroom stage. Most newsmen would go along with this, and agree with the long-serving duty editor who said, 'Power is operational at the desk level – you can't get away from that.' In the sense that *virtually all* decisions concerning the handling of news stories are taken there, this view is perfectly correct. But in the sense that the value framework for the taking of those decisions has already largely been developed at higher levels of control, to which most newsmen have no access, the orthodox account misses an important point. It concentrates on reference upwards when the full picture requires us to acknowledge the greater importance of reference downwards.

OTHER FEATURES OF CONTROL

Apart from the diffusion of guidance, there are a number of factors which ensure the conformity of the news staff. First, it is important to realize that BBC News has a high standing in the Corporation. It is prestigious, commanding large resources, and ideologically central to the Corporation's 'mission'. Crucially, all its operatives are staff members of the BBC, with the exception of a very few free-lances.

Staff members are hard to dismiss, and all newsmen go through an extensive probationary period before they go on to the establishment. Each year an annual report is written on staff members which, if unsatisfactory, may result in the withholding of an increment. But this is rare, and such marginal financial sanctions are not particularly important. More significant is the attractiveness of a stable job in one of the bastions of the national culture. At a time of increasing casualization of labour in the media industries, with ever more production staff going over to short-term contracts, BBC News is often viewed as a career structure in its own right. For many deskmen, the ultimate goal is one of the coveted assistant editor posts, and for reporters a move into a specialism or foreign posting is often an attractive option, if it can be achieved.

The diffusion of guidance and the attraction of a well-remunerated job tend to ensure conformity in the newsrooms. An important additional mode of control built into the editorial system is the power of senior editors to assign news staff to stories.

Sub-editors have devolved control over discrete parts of the output, and the disposition of this control results from assignments made by the senior desk editors. As one put it: 'It's a complicated business taking into account preferences, ability, skills, knowledge, training.' By and large we can translate this into the crucial and opaque occupational criterion of 'experience'. The way assignments are given reflects the newsroom status structure: there is a pecking order for the allocation of stories. This order is based on an assessment by senior editors of a given newsman's reliability. As the Corporation is an exposed organization, some stories pose greater potential dangers of outside criticism than others. Of especial importance are those dealing with parliament/politics, industrial conflict, race, and Northern Ireland; also there are stories which need scrutiny in terms of the law of libel, contempt, and the possible infringement of official secrets.

Such stories are routinely placed in the hands of more senior (experienced) subs. Subs would not be assigned to them if they had shown themselves to be in some way incompetent. It is possible to acquire various labels and to damage career prospects by mishandling stories; this constitutes a strong pressure to conformity. One example given me in Television News concerned 'an Oxford chap who always tried to put down South Africa'. He was damned as unprofessional, and an egg-head to boot. A very experienced radio current affairs editor observed in another context that there were always ways of saying what one wanted in an acceptable (i.e.

inconspicuous) way. He gave the example of a newcomer who had wanted to say that 'Nkrumah is the uncrowned king of Ghana'. That could not be allowed. But he could quote others and thus not implicate the BBC. Yet another instance came from a television newsreader, a reporter of many years' standing himself, who told of a sub who had 'insisted on damning the American presence in Vietnam. It never got through. It's a bad thing to let your own feelings emerge, or take sides in either writing or presentation.' This touches on matters of professional identity dealt with in the next chapter. For present purposes, it is important to realize that assignment is based on reputation and that it operates as a mode of control.

In the allocation of work, the views of senior newsroom editors, especially editors of the day, are quite decisive. One sub told me how he had been labelled 'unpromotable' by one editor of the day because their news judgement constantly diverged. The editor of the day had said he could not feel confident that the sub would make the same decisions as he would in his place. The sub had set out to become more 'reliable', and had consequently been promoted. To be seen as reliable is a necessary not sufficient condition for advancement.

When a newsman's performance is felt to be inadequate he is put on a periodic report, with reviews of progress every three or six months. This means that his reporting superior (usually two grades higher) is required to keep an especially close eye on his work. Such sanctions are exceedingly rare, and only three came to my attention during fieldwork. One concerned a contravention of the staff regulations, the second unprofessional conduct, and the third inefficiency. (The first two will be dealt with in detail in the next chapter.) The more usual sanctions, apparently, are subtle ones. Thus some younger newsmen in Radio News whose ideas on news were too unorthodox were shown their superiors' displeasure. One sub was 'exiled to archives – rather like Siberia'. Another 'found I was doing the premium bonds and the cricket scores. That was a heavy hint.' Another ploy, apparently, is to give people no work at all, or to put them on stories which are never used.

Being assigned to a good story is one type of reward. Another is receiving some form of perk. Thus, for example, during the summer of 1976, Television News created a new team to work on the *Newsday* programme. This programme was to involve newsmen in producing in-depth stories with the possibility of a good deal of foreign filming. There was a clamorous scramble in the newsroom to be seconded to the programme, and the choice of team was clearly used as a way of 'bringing on' potential high-fliers Other such perks for newsroom staff are being assigned to make 'specials' or to cover party conferences. Reporters try for foreign postings. Systematic exclusion from such prestige projects, or from promotions, is a potent sanction.

Evaluation of the subs' performances is similarly matched by continuous assessment of the reporters. One can resolve this, rather roughly, into two major components. First, there are technical criticisms. In radio, for example, if the cue preceding the report overlaps with the report itself this is seen as poor workmanship. Some reporters are seen as having poor voices or boring ones, or unsatisfactory personas. Lateness in filing reports is particularly worthy of odium: here one can see a criterion emerging directly from the editorial need to control the pace of work. (As one news organizer put it, he could not abide cliffhangers.) The second set of estimations is what one might call journalistic. This has to do with not 'getting the weight of a story right'. One example given by several newsmen concerned reporting from Portugal during the upheavals following the overthrow of fascism there. One of the correspondents was criticized by more radical newsmen for 'being too close to the story' and letting his anti-left prejudice show. Of another, it was said by one of the foreign news staff: 'We won't be sending X again to Portugal. He had an unfortunate history of getting there before or after riots.' Another journalistic malpractice, according to a news organizer, is not keeping in touch with the desk: 'There's one rule: always keep in touch with the office; don't move until you get the word.'

From evaluations such as these a structure of reputations emerges, one which fluctuates with time. It is probably not true, as one television reporter said, that 'You're only as good as your last story'. But a number of serious errors in news judgement would indicate someone was slipping. And that would mean he was worthy (whether a sub or reporter) of consideration for 'a shunting spot'. It is clear that something of a minor star system does operate among reporters. Of one it was said he was totally reliable, he was 'not much of a human being – nothing matters to him except getting the news back': but this was what made him so good. A news organizer at Television Centre said there were some who would never be given a foreign assignment if possible, and others were only good for 'sticking their big feet into doorways'. Reputations are a matter of gossip, especially matters such as who will next 'make correspondent'.

At this juncture it is appropriate to point to the differences in the formal role attributes of reporters and correspondents. The central significance from the point of view of this chapter is the degree to which they differ in their *control* over work.

The reporter, like the sub, is a generalist: he sees himself as everyman who can be sent anywhere and be asked to report on anything. Reporters are centrally assigned by the newsdesk and come more closely under the instructions of the editor of the day. They are expected to report on the news stories listed in the daily diary and do not have the role of initiating stories for the bulletins. The resultant vagaries of deployment are one of the facts of journalistic life: 'The disadvantage is that there's a rota to fill: if anything happens you go. That's the way all newsrooms work.'

Reporters do have a sense of relative deprivation when they compare themselves with correspondents. The following remarks made by radio and TV reporters give the flavour of the distinctions involved:

> Reporters rarely scout out stories of their own. It's dealt with by the Intake desk – a very institutional operation.

> The editor of the day will tell you what to do even before you've thought about it.

> Correspondents are on a higher grade. They're paid to speculate in some sense, to interpret. He stands or falls by it: it's more risky, but he gets more authority with extra money.

This status difference is organizationally routinized in the different treatment accorded the two categories of reporting staff. A news organizer in radio said that 'You can be more dictatorial with reporters' but that with correspondents 'it's more a matter of negotiation, a bargain needs to be struck. You try to argue them into a position where they can't say no.' Correspondents, like the more tried and trusted senior subs, are better placed to take the pick of stories. Within the status structure of the News Departments, correspondents are identified as experts, and therefore exercise a greater degree of control over their work, operating at home in defined specialist fields, or as regional/national pundits abroad, with considerable freedom to originate stories. Non-specialist newsmen are advised to consult a correspondent whenever a story falls into a relevant province, and senior editors consult them at planning meetings.

The specialists are obviously aware of their standing. For example, one Home Affairs Correspondent observed that if he said 'something doesn't rate, it's old, I've done it before, these are largely accepted as reasons. They normally accept it if I say I've got something.' One of his sales pitches to the news desk went like this: 'Drunkenness figures're out today: cold percentages – nothing more. Tomorrow's much better. Battered wives report: men shoving pokers down their wives' throats.' Evidently, he was expressing something of a preference here.

Where correspondents have their defined fields, reporters operate in a pecking order structured by the mutually reinforcing criteria of age and experience. For example, a reluctant young radio reporter was assigned to work with the pop current affairs programme *Newsbeat*, one poorly thought of by newsmen. The older set of a half-dozen or so reporters had been exempted from consideration by the Editor.

However, correspondents are by no means immune from fluctuations in their reputations. The Economics Correspondent, who once served both media, was allegedly eased out of television appearances because of his 'on-screen personality'. Abrasive comments made about this indicate the atmosphere in which such assessments are built up. One duty editor said the correspondent made his wife laugh; she wanted to know where the strings were. On a quite separate occasion during gossip at the dinner-table, when the economics brief had already been taken over by a new Business Affairs Correspondent, it was conceded that the Economics Correspondent had improved: 'His head doesn't jerk around so much.' During the same conversation it was observed that a woman political correspondent had been officially banned from television because her presence was poor.

The political correspondents were generally thought of, both in Radio and Television News, as entirely separate from the News Division, and as rather pleasing themselves in what they did. The Political Staff, working largely from Westminster under the Political Editor, a respected figure himself, were widely resented, and described by one newsman as 'so sold on the Westminster set-up that they hardly ever produce anything critical'. Others said that there was an acknowledged tendency for Westminster staff 'to show too much enthusiasm for the Club', that they were 'insiders talking about insiders like insiders'.

A digression: women and the status system

The following observations are not central to a discussion of the news-room status system. Yet they do concern a distinctive and interesting feature of the way stories are allocated.

The starting-point is that there are very few women in the newsrooms. Or more accurately, there are few women who are not typists or secretaries. In Radio News in September 1975 there were six women subs; in Television News in July 1976 there were only three.

Most of the women interviewed felt that there was a special category of story reserved for them: the 'soft story'. Such stories were – and this list is a composite of items produced by a number of women interviewed – abortions, lost babies, the Royal Family, fashions, the Cruft's dog show.

The existence of a kind of female ghetto has to be explained in terms of the dominant attitudes towards women in the News Division. A P.E.P. report, published in 1971, a little while before this study began, found that in general women's career prospects in the BBC did not match those of men. News and current affairs were singled out as among the areas in which women had done poorly. The beliefs present then were consonant with those found in my own study, as I illustrate below. The report argued: 'Hard news gathering is considered to be a man's job – not only in radio and television, but also in newspapers.'[19] A senior official, according to newsroom folklore, made the same observation but slightly differently: 'A good reporter needs to have a pair of balls.'

As in other walks of life, and doubtless throughout British society, the newsrooms boast their own large quota of male chauvinist pigs. For example, one veteran senior duty editor said bluntly: 'It is a fact that the women just aren't as good as the men.' He did concede that one of his girl subs was 'pretty good', and observed there had been change of late (this was in 1975) for at one time 'it was impossible to be promoted if you were a woman'. This point about recent and rapid change will be taken up shortly. Another newsman, a correspondent, confessed an unrepentant *machismo*, which he affirmed (no doubt correctly) was widely shared in News. In his view, women just gave rise to 'tampax problems', and men were more uniformly reliable. 'A woman reporter has to be 25 per cent better than a man. She's only half a reporter – no use in Belfast where you have to lean against a bar with army officers and swill down pints. They just can't get the right sort of information.'

It is not especially surprising, in the face of such views, that women feel they have to prove themselves. Standard assumptions about women and their career potential underpin the dominant viewpoint: that they cannot really be committed as they will go away and have babies, and that they are frivolous. An interesting example of this latter view arose in relation to female dress. An opinion attributed to one Editor was 'X in hotpants is good for the newsroom's morale'. Such a view is double-edged. A quite different girl was not taken seriously on the ground that she wore 'provocative clothing'. In yet another case it was alleged that a particularly stunning sub had been in part taken on because of her 'decorativeness', although, as it transpired, she was very able. The following observations, made by women, can readily be understood in this context:

> The only woman who got on here looked like a man. There's a legendary story about her news sense; the Russians were exploding a bomb, and all she said was 'Where are the pictures?'

and

> I hope you won't think I'm stupid, but they're anti-female. If you look around you'll find all the women are typists: [on this shift] there's one woman sub and one woman film editor, and there's no chance of a woman making the editor's seat.

The first quotation contains a model of how the hard-nosed newsman approaches a story – no flap or emotion, let's get the facts – to which women have to conform, if they are to succeed. The second quote suggests the belief that career opportunities are not equally available to even the most committed virago. Certainly, such beliefs are not without foundation. A different informant told me that a middle-ranking editor had made a point of seeking her out and saying that if she were ever to run the desk he would absolutely refuse to work with her.

One rather hoary view often encountered in the newsrooms was that women made poor performers in hard news terms. This view was also noted quite independently by the P.E.P. report:

> It is argued by men, that 'the audience' would not like a woman newscaster or reporter on television, particularly for political or economic items, or for distressing items.[20]

Now, despite the fact that during the fieldwork period this piece of conventional wisdom was challenged – both in Radio News, which began to use female newsreaders, and in Television News which gave Angela Rippon a star billing on the *Nine O'Clock News* – it was clear that to many newsmen it was no less wise.

It was still held, after these changes, that when women broadcast there was a 'technical problem' with their voices. This meant that what they said, as one correspondent put it, 'doesn't sound quite so true, and since it's BBC News they have to sound authoritative'. Another correspondent agreed: 'Either they sound too upper class – like the head girl at Roedean – or they lack authority.'

One woman newsreader made it clear that she was aware of especially critical attention; if she were to make mistakes people would point to the fact that she was a woman. Essentially she was trying to be 'professional' and to gain acceptance as a good journalist, in which case her sex would be irrelevant.

Women as a group labour under a disadvantage. A woman reporter in Radio News was widely described as a disaster – and not just by men. However, it was felt that because of her poor *journalistic* performance, she had now made it harder for other *women* to become reporters in future. In similar vein, a female Parliamentary correspondent was also seen as a poor performer. Commenting on a report she had delivered, an editor of the day said that her voice was 'not authoritative enough for Parliament'. His chief sub agreed: 'She's OK for battered wives.' 'That's right – Women's Lib.'

As a concluding point, one might note that one NUJ father of chapel thought he discerned an overall improvement in women's career possibilities over the years under review here, although the ABS has argued that the position is still one in which only token successes have been won.[21]

Journalists and non-journalists

Collectively, the *journalists* of the News Division are the arbiters of the content of the news at production level, an organizational reality reflected in their relationships with the non-journalists who service the news operation. To draw an analogy with a quite different type of work: non-journalists relate to journalists in ways similar to the relationships between paramedical staff and physicians. The news judgement has primary status, just as 'the tasks performed by paramedical workers tend to assist rather than replace the focal tasks of diagnosis and treatment'.[22]

These relationships, while fundamentally the same in each of the media, do differ in specific organizational detail.

As production techniques in radio are far simpler than those of television, technical intermediaries intrude far less in the process of assembling bulletins for transmission. The editor of the day performs what in other outputs would be the role of producer: he decides not only upon editorial content but also upon style, format, and last-minute changes. The news bulletins are serviced by a pool of technical officers known as Production Operations Assistants (POA's). In theory, a rigid distinction is made between technique and content: technical officers play no role in determining the content of news broadcasts. In practice, the POA can sometimes play an advisory role: where there is no threat to the newsman's expertise, no 'news point' to be made, the technical officer can proffer advice about how the broadcast might be better realized. It is clear that at this point there is something of a clash of craft values. The technical and engineering branches of the BBC have traditionally been concerned with 'good broadcasting standards', whereas newsmen have typically been more interested in transmitting the news quickly.[23]

While the engineering and operations staff might well resent their position, they recognize the legitimacy of the newsmen's claim to determine content. And because of the special nature of the news – its need for immediacy – they accept that the standards of good broadcasting, which ideally require the best possible sound reproduction, must to some extent go by the board.

This is to put the position at its most negative: that some engineering and operations staff do not like working for the News Department because they feel they are selling out on their skills. There are those, however, who do accept the constraints more willingly. And these non-journalists internalize newsmen's values to the detriment of their own. Thus for example, one technical editor said: 'Time's the big factor. We're less fussy with news tapes because of the speed.' While the implication here is that less fussiness or mere adequacy falls far short of good broadcasting, this point is nevertheless made from within the *newsman's* perspective.

Some engineers rub shoulders with the newsmen for so long that they develop a considerable feel or news sense. One veteran sound engineer told how he had helped a new reporter to transmit a quick report from a radio car. Another example of the positive contribution engineers can make came from a reporter who observed that at set-piece news conferences or political speeches the engineer while making his recording 'has quite often learned to mark interesting passages'. Such examples diverge from the role conception of the engineer as a technical expert sensitive solely to gaps in continuity and fluctuation in sound levels.

The power relations of the editorial system are very clearly defined for newly-inducted members of the journalistic staff. During a production training session, one news trainee said she had been 'overruled by the POA'. The trainer pounced on this admission, and delivered a homily about how you could not tell the Editor that you had been overruled: if something went out over the air, you alone had to take responsibility.

By contrast with radio the mechanics of television production are very intrusive. While as in Radio News the editor of the day has a producer's role, he cannot simply walk into the studio and present the newsreader with his script. Transmissions require skilled direction. Bulletins are transmitted under the supervision of a studio director. The relationship between the editor of the day and the studio director was described by a senior news executive:

> The man who puts it on the air is in charge of transmission. He's working to plans/scripts provided by other people. He's operationally in control. The editor will make changes but will not issue commands other than through the studio director; *he executes his orders through the studio director.*

The studio director acts as an arm of the editor of the day: he orchestrates the transmission in line with the detailed production instructions embodied in the scripts. One studio director described his role in terms of the constraints posed by the power structure: 'The editor decides *what* he wants and the *order*; the director tries to make it work.'

The greatest scope for autonomous action comes when something goes wrong:

> In an emergency you must have knowledge of the importance of stories. If there's an early OB or a film break you have to make instantaneous decisions. It's based on editorial judgement; *the proviso is that you're pretty certain that this is what the editor would want.* In half the programmes you put out a mix that's not on the script. The editor lays down the guidelines: what *should* be – the rest is to try and make it happen, or the next best thing.

This account recognizes the legitimacy of the editors and in parallel with that given in Radio News, the primacy of news judgement rather than of optimal televisual values. As bulletins are rehearsed, and the studio director is responsible for the operational readiness of the entire range of sources (OB units, videotape machines, telecine machines, cameras, sound tapes, and so forth), his hopes of a smooth production lie in making as few alterations as possible to the script. However, in news production upsets to the running order are normal and expected; one studio director noted: 'The worst time is when there's a pre-set programme, and a major story breaks ten minutes before. The thing collapses and you don't have time.'

This production perspective was endorsed by a news transmissions assistant, who is responsible for timing the individual items and keeping the studio director informed of any dangers to the sequence:

There's not much sympathy between production and editorial staff: they don't know what it is to bring a script three seconds before you're going out.

A further perspective needs to be taken account of in discussing editorial legitimacy. The news studio is manned by engineering and operations staff (cameramen, sound men, vision mixers, engineers) who work under the studio director. A view of the power structure commonly accepted among the technical staff was stated by one senior television engineer: 'The editors say *what* goes in; the directors say *how* it should be done; we actually *do* the thing – that's us.'

So, while editorial control of content is recognized, from the studio perspective, the director is the most significant source of commands:

We're responsible for technical matters, not content. The director will try to warn us if anything is going wrong. We will try and set up alternatives if the link fails – then we have the alternative means of communication.

From the editorial point of view this complex interlocking of roles and competences is seen as a technical service designed to permit the transmission of bulletins. However, as in radio production, there is some scope for blurring the distinction between technique and content. For instance, the studio director may contribute to the selection of visuals, though in a rather marginal way. As one duty editor put it: 'The contribution made by the studio director depends on him. It depends whether he wants to be just a machine putting out film.' Similarly, film editors cut film to editorial instructions from journalists. Yet like the veteran sound engineers in radio, many have an interest in news which complements their purely filmic skill. For example, when on one occasion the editor of the day was viewing incoming agency film with the chief film editor (who recommended a particular story) he said half-jokingly, 'If a splendid chap like you says it's a good story, I'll take it.'

The Editor, Radio News, formerly a television journalist, stressed that comments by technical staff were always worthy of note: 'They were another listener or viewer.' He had found that technicians' reactions to a programme in the TV gallery gave important indications: 'If they went quiet you'd done well, whereas if they kept talking a lot you knew you'd made a cock-up.'

Similarly for reporters out on the road, as one of them put it 'a friendly association with the cameraman is a *sine qua non*'. While the presence on screen of the television reporter gives the story journalistic credibility in the traditional sense, it is heavily reliant on the news judgement of the cameraman. A cameraman's journalistic ability is critical and determines preferences for specific working partners.

> Some crews instinctively cotton on. The chemistry's right. With others it's a drudge. The best *camera* teams are the best to work with: *they have good news sense in terms of pictures.* X . . . Y . . . knows a great deal about Northern Ireland. He reads around a lot. He likes to know about the country he's going to.

And, 'The best cameraman will switch on before you've started.' The importance of creating effective crews was underlined by a film operations organizer, a former cameraman himself:

> Some you get on with; some not. There's a little friction, sometimes disagreements over seeing the story in a different light. Say an articulated lorry has crashed: the cameraman thinks – first thing, get the film. The reporter's first thought may be to talk to the driver. A big part of my job is putting people together who'll harmonize.

In the event of disagreements, however, the legitimate journalistic power of *directing* the camera is in the hands of the reporter, who is responsible for the newsfilm sent in, just as *editorial* power is exercised in the cutting rooms.

The overall picture, therefore, is one in which there is some scope for non-journalists to contribute to shaping the content over and beyond the simple execution of technical commands. But (with the exception of cameramen) this is a somewhat marginal contribution. We can see, therefore, how the system of devolving editorial power, but retaining it in the hands of the 'responsible' element of the News Division reproduces throughout the craft structure of BBC News one basic approach toward the control of content.

CONCLUSION

Dissidence and non-conformity are not the accepted style in 'hard news' production. While newsmen in other areas of broadcast journalism – notably some current affairs teams – may be permitted a more maverick approach, 'the news', with its flagship function, is the home of the conformist.

BBC newsmen, while often noting the journalistic orthodoxy of

F

their departments, nonetheless see themselves as working in a system which offers them a high measure of autonomy. They often deplore the omnipresence of the editor of the day as inhibiting their initiative, but accept the legitimacy of his interventions because it is 'his' programme which they are producing. The above account has shown the way in which the allocation of stories within the status structure of the newsroom, and editors' assessments of journalistic expertise and reliability, function as modes of control. The journalists collectively act as controllers over the technical and production staff. In this way editorial control is articulated throughout the production system.

The role performed by the editor of the day is not generally analysed in the newsroom as one linked into the chain of editorial command running all the way up to the Director-General. In this regard its broad organizational significance is missed: namely, that it is the point of articulation between the immediate context of production and the editorial hierarchy.

The command structure does not usually perform its work of editorial control through obvious routine intervention at the production level. Rather, in general, it works according to a system of retrospective review, as a result of which guidance is referred downwards and becomes part of the taken for granted assumptions of those working in the newsrooms. The general unobtrusiveness of this system, through which orientations first defined at the top of the hierarchy become quite unquestioningly adopted by those at the bottom, permits an orthodox ideology of editorial control to flourish.

But the editorial ideology stresses autonomy in a way which does less than full justice to the substantive controls which actually constrain production. It has been argued here that the focus in the official ideology on devolution and reference upward underplays the actual impact of reference downwards in the formation of approaches to the news reflecting corporate policy.

While this chapter has focused largely on the workings of the BBC's system of imperative control – one which is ultimately coercive and reliant on negative sanctions – it is not this dimension which necessarily weighs most heavily in ensuring conformity. As we shall see in the next chapter, a commitment to the BBC's *Weltanschauung* is central to the mediation of control. But such commitment must be considered against the background of the formal system sketched out here.

7

The mediation of control (2): corporate ideology

The BBC thinks of balance and impartiality mainly in terms of political parties. Perhaps that is because political parties have stop-watches at the ready, in the hands of officials who are ready to cry 'bias' whenever they can see a party advantage in doing so. But the virtue of impartiality should be exercised between other opposites and shades of opinion.

(*Ariel*, The BBC Staff Magazine)[1]

In ten years here I've never had an explicit conversation with any of my colleagues on politics or religion. There's a feeling that you might limit your scope for action if you declare yourself.

(Television Newsman)

This chapter examines the central tenet of the ideology of the BBC's News Division – namely, 'impartiality'. This requires us to consider a highly ramified and well-articulated *Weltanschauung*. Like any other ideology, the one espoused in the BBC provides a cognitive orientation to the world, which, while it contains lacunae and contradictions, does, nonetheless provide solutions to most practical problems encountered.[2]

Impartiality is, of course, but one of the values characteristically invoked in liberal-democratic characterizations of the supposedly 'socially responsible' press of capitalist societies. This news media ideology contains a repertoire of terms – objectivity, balance, responsibility, fairness, freedom from bias[3] which may be thought of as a family. While, as linguistic philosophers will tell us, each of these concepts has a distinctive range of meanings, what is of sociological interest is their *total* justificatory role when invoked in the ordinary discourse of newsmen. For the most part, they are interchangeable, and arise in similar contexts.

Impartiality is the linchpin of the BBC's ideology: it is a notion saturated with political and philosophical implications. What the BBC claims, when it says it is 'impartial', is that it has achieved institutional detachment from the conflicts of British society, and that the Corporation is independent of all interests. The news is therefore held to represent all interests and points of view without an evaluative commitment to *any*. Such a position implies that the production process is simply a set of technical routines which enables the producers to secure an undistorted picture of reality.[4] Furthermore, the credibility of this position is predicated on the assumption that the news staff constitute a collective of 'neutral', non-partisan operatives, whose adherence to a particular model of professionalism in turn ensures that fact and value are held rigidly apart. Overall, therefore, the BBC's news is legitimated was the product of a community of disinterested and honest empiricists.

Such a position bears considerable similarity to the more simplistic versions of value-free sociology which have recently been the object of critical attack. Gouldner, for one, has pointed out that a misleading image of the technical specialist emerges from the espousal of such a value-free stance. The claim to be detached, however, is in fact premised on an uncritical and generally unarticulated commitment to the established order.[5] Value-freedom, on this analysis, is part of the professional ideology of some sociologists. In just the same way, it is central to the legitimation of much journalism in capitalist societies. A contrasting image to that of detachment which is often drawn, both in sociology and in journalism, is that of commitment. This approach denies the existence of a social space in which the intellectuals, or for that matter, cultural bureaucracies such as the BBC, can float freely.[6] As Charles Taylor has pointed out, the concept of neutrality 'to be meaningfully employed requires a background of value commitment; and this background while defining and enjoining neutrality in some contexts, forbids it in others, i.e. those where the background values are themselves attacked'.[7] And so it is with the cognate concept of 'impartiality'. It can only have a meaning in the context of an existing set of values, and in the case of the BBC the relevant complex of values is that of the 'consensus'.

Criticism of impartiality, and the related value of objectivity has focused not only on the theoretical shortcomings of the value-free approach, but also on its practical limits. Kurt and Gladys Lang, at the outset of the television age, showed very convincingly that television presents 'a refracted image of the events it reports'. In arguing this case they were taking issue with the journalistic view view that the technology of broadcasting is 'an ally in the quest for actuality'.[8] Subsequent research which has addressed the question of whether news is a 'mirror of reality', as it is often claimed to be, has emphatically endorsed the Langs' finding that it is not.[9]

News does not select itself, but is rather the product of judgements concerning the social relevance of given events and situations based on assumptions concerning their interest and importance. The 'reality' it portrays is always in at least one sense fundamentally biased, simply in virtue of the inescapable decision to designate an issue or event newsworthy, and then to construct an account of it in a specific framework of interpretation. News must be assessed as a cultural product which embodies journalistic, social, and political values. It cannot be, and certainly is not, a neutral, impartial, or totally objective perception of the real world. In the specific case of the BBC, the social cartography which the news may offer is structurally limited by the organization's place in Britain's social order. Ralph Miliband has summed up the scope and limits of impartiality as mainly operating 'in regard to political formations which while divided on many issues are nevertheless part of a basic underlying consensus. . . . Impartiality and objectivity in this sense, stop at the point where political consensus itself ends. . . .'[10]

To say that the BBC occupies a place in the consensus is to proclaim no great sociological discovery. It is a fact which has been recognized and, moreover, endorsed by the Corporation's own accredited theorists. The interesting issue is not *whether* it is so, but rather what its main *consequence* is: namely, that the outputs of broadcasting are, in general, supportive of the existing social order.

A classic statement to this effect came from Sir Hugh Greene when he was still the BBC's DG in the mid-1960s. He pointed out at that time that there were limits to the BBC's neutrality concerning basic moral values, and also said that it could not put democracy at risk by being 'impartial about certain things like racialism or extreme forms of political belief'.[11] This position has subsequently been reiterated in full in the BBC's internal briefing document *Principles and Practice in News and Current Affairs*, which stresses the Corporation's commitment to the established and legitimate institutions:

> there are some respects in which the BBC is not neutral, unbiased or impartial. The BBC cannot be neutral in the struggle between truth and untruth, justice and injustice, freedom and slavery, compassion and cruelty, tolerance and intolerance. *It is not only within the Constitution: it is within the consensus about basic moral values.*[12]

This consensual stance has a more explicit moral and political content in the following statement by Norman Swallow, a veteran BBC producer:

> A foreign visitor to Britain or the USA, who for a few months regularly watched television's coverage of public affairs, might justifiably conclude that their combined television organizations shared a common and positive viewpoint on many of the major

issues of the day. They are apparently anti-Fascist, anti-Communist, opposed to racial intolerance and violent crime, highly critical of the governments of the USSR, Communist China, Cuba, Spain, Portugal, South Africa, and Eastern Europe, Christian (especially in Britain) but tolerant of agnostics, friendly towards surviving monarchies, hostile to most social and political cranks, suspicious of professional politicians (but nevertheless enticing them into their studios as often as possible), and supporters of 'the wind of change' so long as it never reaches gale force.[13]

This was written in the mid-1960s. But it is quite possible to find up-dated versions of such working assumptions among newsmen who are aware and self-critical. Thus one young radio reporter said:

The Corporation's view is middle-class liberalism. Strikes, Communists, Black Power, Fascists are all bad. Social Democrats and Tories are good. But on the whole you discuss whether a story has been done well or badly in the context of the system. You rarely discuss whether the organization is good or bad, or what its global view is.

It is noteworthy perhaps that the last two quotations, which contain exceedingly explicit social and political positions, are not typical of the way in which the BBC defines its place in British society. Normally, this takes a more abstract form. As Kumar has pointed out 'Current BBC metaphors show a dramatic shift from those involving notions of leading and directing, to those involving far more neutral concepts: essentially the BBC is seen as the "register" of the many different "voices" in society, as the "great stage" on which all actors, great and small, parade and say their piece.'[14]

Such a vision of the BBC's place in British society presupposes a theory of the nature of that society: namely democratic pluralism. This is premised on the view that there are no predominant groups or interests in society, but rather that 'there are only competing blocs of interests, whose competition, which is sanctioned and guaranteed by the state itself, ensures that power *is* diffused and balanced, and that no particular interest is able to weigh too heavily upon the state'.[15] In this view, the state itself is above politics, and attempts to balance and accommodate all views and pressures, and to secure a just outcome. Just as the state is supposed to act to promote some hypothetical 'national interest' in balancing demands, so is the BBC supposed to be in itself a market-place for ideas and competing viewpoints, endorsing none, admitting all, a national institution above the fray.

But this form of legitimation becomes implausible, and poses problems for broadcasting at a time when the consensus is becoming increasingly strained. Indeed the very viability of the stance *presupposes* a consensus. As Hall has argued, polarization in politics, industrial conflict, the crisis in Northern Ireland have pushed broadcasting into an increasingly exposed position.[16] There is sharp competition over definitions of social reality, and over the general direction to be followed by British society, and hence it is increasingly difficult to sell the idea that there is some Olympian vantage-point from which the arguments below may be surveyed.

It is not without significance, therefore, that key figures in the world of broadcasting have more and more reiterated the view that the role of their media is to buttress the established order. Hence, Sir Charles Curran, the BBC's Director-General, has cited an utterance by one of his senior editors which he 'treasures': 'Yes we are biased – biased in favour of parliamentary democracy.'[17] And Sir Geoffrey Cox, former Editor of ITN, has expressed very clearly the grounds for this commitment. He has argued that in the social crisis of the 1970s that 'impartiality is not enough'. Rather, the 'primary duty' of the broadcaster is to sustain the democratic system and the rule of law, and he ought, moreover 'to probe the *bona fides* of those who criticize our present democracy, not to make it better but to supplant it'.[18]

The parliamentary model plays a special role in the BBC's thinking: indeed, it is central to the social philosophy informing the news operation, as is clear from this statement:

The basic principle of BBC News is that a mature democracy is an informed (not guided) democracy. The BBC takes it for granted that the parliamentary democracy evolved in this country is a work of national genius to be upheld and preserved. The BBC's primary constitutional role is that of a supplier of new and true information as defined above. It shares the role with a free press, but with one important difference, in that a newspaper has a point of view and a place of its own in the political spectrum. The BBC has none.[19]

What is extraordinary about this quotation is not just its inaccurate and sentimentalized view of British history. It is also the view that the BBC can at one and the same time be an organization within the constitution and yet credibly claim to have no place in the political spectrum. In the simplistic sense that it cannot readily be accorded a party political label, this of course is true. But to talk so clearly about a constitutional role is to set the Corporation among the established institutions of the state. If that is not a political place, then what is? Another point to be noted is the slavishly uncritical manner in which parliament is written of here. The obvious inference is that politics outside parliament are to be treated with a good deal of suspicion. Nigel Harris has given a most succinct account of the consequences of this stance:

> The complete identification of 'democracy' with, say, the British House of Commons at any given moment of time robs the language of effective criteria with which to judge that institution. The real is redefined to become the ideal. Opposition, logically must therefore always be 'antidemocratic', even if it seeks a greater popular participation in the House of Commons.[20]

Naturally, such a consensualist stance on politics (one taken by the BBC and other mainstream media) carries implications for the characterization of extra-parliamentary politics. As various sociologists have pointed out, the 'new politics' of the 1960s and after – student protests, demonstrations, urban rioting, urban guerilla warfare, squatting, rent strikes, ethnic protests, unofficial strikes, factory occupations – have become labelled as forms of political deviance. The celebration of consensus brings with it a depreciation of radical forms of action, their characterization as violent and irrational, and, moreover, obscures any understanding of why these should occur.[21]

There are several further points to be made. To venerate parliament as the central institution of the state is at the same time to posit a theory of where the efficient machinery of decision-making and power actually is. Does focusing on the formal gymnastics of parliamentarians really get to grips with the political process and where power lies? Some might argue that political control within liberal-democratic states is vested increasingly in certain sectors of the civil service.[22] Others, that a full understanding of politics and power needs to be rooted in an analysis of the class structure of contemporary capitalism, and the role which is played by ownership of the means of production.[23] This latter view in particular presents a fundamental challenge to the premises which underpin the BBC's legitimation.

In general, to pose such theoretical alternatives throws into relief the specificity of the BBC's commitment to a definite model of social and political reality. And no such view of society, nor the language for expressing that view, can be innocent or neutral. It carries its own evaluative baggage with it, and necessarily excludes alternative views.

On the one hand, therefore, the BBC's account of itself proclaims an ideology of detachment – corporate independence, and consequently, true impartiality – yet, on the other hand, the ideological commitment of broadcasting is clearly to the present social order, as it is *represented* by parliamentary democracy.

Such an overall position, one of general detachment within definite limits, is reminiscent of an extremely powerful (if implausible) sociological theory of the role of the intellectual in society. The BBC's self-image as that body which 'holds the ring in matters of controversy' is set into sharp relief by the social conflict taking place in contemporary Britain. To be *above* all conflict, to represent all relevant views, and to produce a journalism which will, in the long-term, 'heal' (as the BBC's Editor, News and Current Affairs, has put it[24]) is a theory of the BBC's social role closely akin to Karl Mannheim's thesis about the role of the intellectuals, first propounded some fifty years ago in *Ideology and Utopia*. It may be thought a little far-fetched to bracket the BBC's newsmen together with Mannheim's intellectuals. Certainly, purists such as Lewis Coser would argue that those working in the mass culture industries have little in common with 'intellectuals' properly understood.[25] However, media professionals are equally in the business of cultural transmission, and Philip Elliott's observation that they may therefore be considered as 'new-style intellectuals' is perfectly cogent.[26] Granted this is so, I would argue that the BBC's doctrine of impartiality/independence is nothing if not a latter-day Mannheimianism – a response to social cleavage which attempts to gain some measure of epistemological privilege for those who survey and report on it.

While Mannheim's theory of the 'socially unattached intelligentsia' has frequently been assailed, it nonetheless remains a most attractive doctrine for those who believe that there is some 'neutral' vantage-point from which to evaluate social change and the social order. A brief résumé of its main elements is sufficient to indicate its resemblance to contemporary thinking inside the BBC. Indeed, its relevance and appeal go well beyond the scope of broadcasting; it is also a characteristic argument of those who would assert that what is needed is more expert technocratic management 'on behalf of society' since political ideology is bankrupt.

Mannheim's theory was produced in the context of Weimar Germany, just prior to Hitler's accession to state power, a time when ideological warfare was rife.[27] He sought a position from which all competing ideologies could be impartially judged, and their truthful features extracted and utilized in an all-inclusive world view, a new synthesis or consensus, embodying a balance between tradition and change. Mannheim began with the premises of the classical Marxist analysis by arguing that ideologies were produced by social classes (capitalists and proletarians) which occupied antagonistic locations in the process of material production, and therefore pursued opposed interests. Such different social positions gave rise to mutually exclusive versions of reality, or ideologies. Mannheim tried to overcome the relativistic implications of this stance by seeking salvation in what he saw as a 'relatively classless stratum which is not too firmly situated in the social order'. The intellectuals, *déclassés*, and in virtue of their education exposed to the 'influence of opposing tendencies in social reality', would, Mannheim believed, be able to stand above the constricted horizons available to members of social classes.

According to this view, the intellectuals are held to be uniquely privileged, and able to produce, in principle, an authentic all-embracing form of knowledge. Thus, Mannheim created an 'independent', 'detached', 'neutral' social space for a particular grouping in society. The whole point of the exercise was to improve social integration: the intellectuals by their 'dynamic mediation' of competing ideologies were to pursue the social good by producing a new consensus. Real social conflicts were therefore to be resolved on the level of ideas by an impartial appraisal.

It is the claimed *detachment* from any particular view of society, therefore, which is the linchpin of the comparison between the Mannheimian intellectual and the BBC's official corporate role in British society. In keeping with this, the BBC says that it reports only 'unadorned fact' and 'untainted information'. This flow of 'pure fact' to the public, allegedly unhampered by the intervention of values is officially linked to the BBC's social purpose, that of informing 'a mature democracy'.[28]

At this point, detachment gives way to a commitment which is founded upon an overarching social value which necessarily limits the BBC's impartiality: namely, its obligation to support the established order. In fact, the ostensibly socially unattached BBC-man does have a political commitment: impartiality is itself predicated on the existence of the present British political system and its underlying social and economic order, and the BBC is required to sustain it. In this sense, impartiality and the domain assumptions it contains are closely akin to the supposed neutrality of the civil service – and this comparison, as will be seen, is by no means fortuitous.

TWO APPLICATIONS OF THE DOCTRINE

The concept of impartiality finds practical expression in a balancing of competing definitions of problems, the interviewing of opposing spokesmen, the presentation of differing claims about the truth. Newsmen feel reassured about their impartiality when they receive 'equal' pressures and complaints from right and left ('both sides') of the political spectrum. This empirical 'proof' of impartiality is as old as broadcasting itself.[29] From sociological studies of news organizations, it is particularly clear that an awareness of the political audience and its power to affect the future of the organization is institutionalized in production routines.[30] The achievement of impartial, or objective, coverage is asserted when certain formulae are adhered to or rituals performed which embody the organization's response to the exterior structures of political power.[31]

In the BBC, impartiality is supposed to characterize all news coverage, though in Britain today coverage of some aspects of Irish affairs are explicitly excepted from this constraint. The primary, or paradigmatic meaning of impartiality emerges when we consider the institutional forces of British political life. On the whole, being impartial in the specific sense required does not present a problem inside the News Departments, because the routines are so well-established, and the underlying principle so well-legitimized. The main characteristics of political impartiality have been outlined by Tracey in his study of ATV's handling of the February 1974 General Election. There he noted that the determination of the issues covered lay in the hands of the three main British parties rather than the television organization and that 'strenuous efforts were made to finely balance the three main parties – whether that was in terms of film reports, the audience in the studio or the panelists – a political symmetry had to be maintained and be seen to be maintained'.[32] The balancing act forces a form on political coverage, and also dictates its content. A result of this is that certain fringe parties, in Tracey's study the Communist Party and the National Front, are seen as unrepresentative of the mainstream of politics and to be treated with circumspection.

The Thurrock By-election

An illustration may be drawn from the fieldwork showing the same process at work. At the Television News morning meeting of Friday 16 July 1976, there was a discussion about how to cover the Thurrock by-election results. These had come in overnight – the Labour Party had retained a traditionally safe seat, but with a diminished majority – and the story had been covered by the morning press and the radio news. At the morning meeting the news organizer noted that 500 feet of film had been shot and that there were four lost deposits; interviews had been conducted with the Labour and Conservative candidates.

While coverage of the story took on the characteristic balanced form, it was not entirely without complications. These concerned the racialist party, the National Front, which was the subject of some discussion. The BBC-2 sub working on the story asked the Political Editor, who happened to be present in the newsroom, 'How are we to describe the NF? As extreme right-wing?' The Political Editor replied: 'Anti-Jewish, anti-black, racialist, all true. We don't label them at the moment.' In his last remark he was evidently reflecting the fact that no firm decision had been taken at the ENCA meetings concerning this group's characterization. A form of words agreed upon at this stage was 'the right-wing National Front which campaigned on a racialist platform'. The senior duty editor asked, 'Are we allowed to interview the NF?' The editor of the day replied: 'Oh yes. I suppose 3,000 was quite a lot of votes.' In fact the Front were not interviewed. The exchange illustrates, however, the way in which this group was regarded in the last resort as just another electoral party, a somewhat questionable perspective.

The by-election story was not dealt with on the BBC-2 desk until the early afternoon. The sub handling it listed the various standard techniques to be employed in actualizing the story: 'vision (the newsreader), a chart of the by-election results, still of Margaret Thatcher, someone from the Labour front bench to give the other point of view, film of the declaration of the result with the Tory and Labour candidates interviewed with supers giving their names'. This list was simply reeled off. For background the sub read the available PA tape which noted the swing to the Tories and a fall in the absolute vote. The story line was 'Labour squeezes home in Thurrock'. The Labour Party quotation to balance that from Mrs Thatcher was to come from Reg Underhill, its Acting General-Secretary, and was straight from the PA copy: 'This is another sad story of complacency in a safe seat.' The sub thought the Liberals' effort had been worthy but there was not space to give them a quote. The chart of the election results used for the 1.45 p.m. bulletin on BBC-1 was to be used again.

Next the sub viewed film shot after the declaration of the result. This showed the Labour candidate making a speech and the Tory candidate making a speech, and ran to one minute ten seconds in length. As the story was regarded as too old to lead the early evening bulletin, the film was trimmed down to thirty-four seconds, giving fourteen seconds to each major party candidate (Tory and Labour), and a few seconds for some scene-setting remarks in 'voice-over'.

The way the story was handled for the 5.45 bulletin shows clearly the established routines of 'impartial and balanced' news production. First, the story itself, concerning Westminster politics, was a mandatory one, covered since it reflected on the government's support in parliament and the country. The government's majority was raised from one to two. This was a *hard* event with a clear-cut structure. The focus was on the performance of the two main British parties, and 'balance' achieved by running film clips of exactly equal lengths. Established visual techniques were quite routinely deployed.

However, the coverage, though predictable in both form and content, was not entirely unproblematic. The National Front's platform was described in the script as an 'outspoken anti-immigrant campaign' which 'brought them six and a half per cent of the poll'. In a post-mortem the editor of the day noted his dislike for 'outspoken'. He thought this a very subjective term. The sub defended its use, saying that it had been endorsed by the Political Editor, who indeed used it in a studio spot later that evening in the *Nine O'Clock News*. Various joke permutations were suggested at the post-mortem such as 'pro-British' and 'fascist'. The label finally decided on was 'anti-immigrant'. However, this itself is hardly objective, since it is not only immigrants who are the objects of the Front's propaganda but minority ethnic groups, primarily black, whose members are resident British citizens. The label chosen reflected a common prejudice: namely, that all immigrants are black and that all blacks are immigrants, if not actually, then in the sense that they are necessarily apart from the mainstream of British life.

IMPORTANT

The Mozambique Massacre story, 10 July 1973

Coverage of British politics follows the model of balancing competing claims and ideological utterances. This model is not restricted to that particular context, however, but transposed to others where its use is more questionable. Balanced coverage – the practical expression of impartiality – was exemplified, as were some criteria newsmen use for establishing accuracy, in the following instance. On 10 July 1973, *The Times* (a newspaper thought reliable in BBC News) broke what briefly came to be a celebrated story, although since then it has been almost entirely forgotten. On the newspaper's front page was an account by a Roman Catholic priest, Father Adrian Hastings, based on information from local priests, which alleged that Portuguese troops on a counter-insurgency drive had massacred innocent villagers at a place called Wiriyamu in Tete Province, Mozambique. The scepticism which met the story on that day in Television News illustrated the way in which newsmen evaluate stories, and 'balance' competing claims to produce an 'impartial' story.

A collective attitude was first taken by senior editors of TV News at the morning meeting. The Deputy Editor who was in the chair set the tone when he observed that the story was 'too well orches-trated'. This was so, he felt, because Father Hastings's article had appeared in the week prior to a long-arranged visit to Britain by Dr Marcello Caetano, then Portuguese Prime Minister. The *timing* of the article therefore rendered it suspect: it could hardly be co-incidental, which implied a deliberate bid for publicity to discredit the visit (Criterion 1).

All the senior editors attending this meeting displayed a similar degree of scepticism. The deputy news editor thought that 'the left wing were waiting for this'. (Criterion 2). This criterion identified the story as a 'campaign to embarrass the government'. Another participant observed it was 'facile'. The most consistent theme in discussion was the story's timing: it was doubted because it had broken a week before Caetano's visit.

The Deputy Editor said 'someone must know' the truth of the matter; but until that information became available they were to be cautious. 'It's all too pat.' Criterion 2 was applied again when one of the editors of the day asked 'This priest: what's his background?' The deputy news editor was concerned that he might be a 'left-wing militant, or possibly a militant over Catholic rights'. These were obviously attempts to dig out the ideological motivations for the priest's story and place him into some recognizable slot.

The next step was to consider what sources were available. The Portuguese Socialist leader, Dr Soares, was giving a news con-ference in London that day in French. The news editor observed, 'there's no way of checking' as the alleged massacre had taken place in a village which was not on the map. Another criterion (3) emerged: to authenticate claims, a spatial location was needed. Because at that stage the newsmen did not know where the village was, the site of the incident lacked 'visibility' and threw the priest's account into further doubt. Over the sound link Radio News informed the meeting that an additional source was available. The Director of Information of the Portuguese government was due to arrive in

London. The Deputy Editor observed: 'That'll redress the balance a bit. We're trying the Lisbon end.' (Criterion 4.) After just a few minutes, therefore, the story's treatment had been sketched out in the conventional manner: if in doubt, give a balanced account. There was now an opposing viewpoint, and a reporter was to be sent to Lisbon to find out the official view there. Quite spontaneously, the chairman of the Radio News morning meeting observed 'The timing's a bit odd.' He went on to say that Radio News were 'trading on the possibility of an Opposition censure motion'. This remark implied that the incident was going to be controversial in terms of British domestic politics and would need careful handling. There was now a domestic angle as well as an international conflict of claims. Wariness of the complications of party politics was evident: 'Why is Father Hastings at this lunch at Transport House?' The Deputy Editor said in conclusion, 'Let's report it as it happens.' This apparently vacuous remark told the editors to be cautious in a specific sense: namely, to let the developments come in, and then report them.

In the newsroom, in the early morning lull, the 'Portuguese Massacre Story' as it was now known, was a topic of conversation. The editor of the day for BBC-1 wanted to know 'Does the place exist?' A reporter answered: 'There's only one way to find out – and that's to go there.' This indicates a further criterion (5) of assessment. An eye-witness account from a reliable source is taken to be a certain way of apprehending the truth. The editor of the day, briefing the chief sub-editor who was handling the story said: 'The BBC doesn't take a stand. At the moment we're between belief and disbelief.' He was being instructed to handle the story with caution, thereby putting into effect the policy decision taken at the morning meeting. The Deputy Editor and the news editor were present for some time in the newsroom. This was unusual as both are senior executives concerned with the managerial side rather than day-to-day operations. It was an indication of crisis. Even more unusual was the detailed discussion between the Deputy Editor and the editor of the day. They were both acutely aware that the story had domestic political ramifications.

By 10.55 a.m. the editor of the day was thinking in visual terms. More information had come into the newsroom over the agency tapes about the village where the massacre was alleged to have taken place. It now transpired that the village was called Williamo, not Wiriyamu, as villages in that region changed their names with the advent of a new headman. The editor of the day said to the chief sub-editor: 'We could probably get a map going. We can put the names of two places on the map – it's between them. Be careful who you quote: our man in Dar-es-Salaam has spoken to the FRELIMO commander.' In newsman's terms the story was 'hardening up' factually, being situated in space as well as time, and there were sources available to put both sides of the case.

The Deputy Editor was still in the newsroom. He observed: 'We don't believe it or disbelieve it. Father Hastings or the Portuguese.' The official attitude was defined as scepticism where balanced treatment had to be given to each side. The early criteria of evaluation were still being reiterated: the timing of the article was taken as central. The editor of the day said: 'The source isn't a left-wing trendy.' The news editor said to me: 'We're trying to get at something like the truth. We'll have an interview with the [Portuguese] Embassy about their version of what did or didn't happen. We'll go at it in a straightforward way.' The timing of the report was talked of as 'kindergarten primer stuff'. The Deputy Editor said to me: 'It might sound silly, but we've got a vested interest in the truth. We have to keep an open mind on it.'

Towards lunchtime both editors of the day (BBC-1 and 2) watched the ITN news programme *First Report* on which the Portuguese Ambassador to Britain was interviewed. Here was a further piece of testimony – namely, a denial of Father Hastings's story. One of them observed that although the timing was obviously set up this did not mean that the story was not true. By six o'clock, after two bulletins had been produced, he still felt that it was arguable both ways.

The basic guidelines for treatment had been set out early on, throwing into relief routine modes of appraisal. On the following day at a foreign news planning meeting, senior editors decided to apply for a visa for the Southern Africa correspondent. It was observed, 'The whole story smells.' In domestic news terms the story was about the elaborate precautions taken to protect Dr Caetano, and the political storm between opponents of his visit (notably the Labour Party) and the Conservative Government. At a home news planning meeting the same morning the Editor, Television News, laid down the angle to be followed: 'We'll look at the security story and keep an eye on the political side.'

One further incident, highly relevant in demonstrating the criteria of evidence employed by newsmen, was observed. Two days after the 'Massacre Story' first broke, the editor of the day for BBC-2 received an offer from Father Hastings of some film showing Portuguese troops burning down a village. It was previewed in a cutting room and was rejected as not having news value on the following grounds: (a) it was four years old, (b) similar film had been shown the previous day by the current affairs programme, *Midweek*, and the sequences available in this case were not of good technical quality, having been shot by an amateur; (c) there were no dead bodies. This last criterion meant that, in the editor's view, the film could have no direct bearing on the issue of whether a *massacre* had taken place (Criterion 6). The editor thought it common knowledge that villages were burned down in the Portuguese territories. Many journalists may have known this, but hardly the general public. The other two points had to do with the 'freshness' of the evidence: it was not adequately up-to-date, and had in any case been scooped the previous day.

By a curious irony, this editorial judgement became in itself a smallish news story. At 7.34 p.m. a PA 'snapfull' brought the news to the *News Extra* desk that the BBC had turned down Father Hastings's film. The Deputy Editor who was 'around' in the newsroom asked the editor of the day to telephone the Press Association and explain why the film had been rejected. By 7.40 p.m. an explanation had been set in motion specifying that the film had been rejected on grounds of news value. This was reported by some newspapers the following day. The editor of the day observed to me that 'it wasn't just corpses that were missing', but that the film had nothing to do with the massacre. Clearly he did not see it in terms of adding to *contextual knowledge* of conditions in Mozambique during Portuguese colonial rule, but saw it only in relation to the *immediate story* of the day. Had it been regarded as adding contextual knowledge it would have surely been more difficult to be impartial since it would have cast doubt on the Portuguese government's denial.

The use of evidence is particularly interesting. First, it is clear that the timing of this controversial story was important: the newsmen did not like to think they were being manipulated. Secondly, its source was important: if it could be pinned down as ideologically inspired this helped handle it. From the newsroom point of view it had party political implications, Labour versus Conservative, as well as raising a question of factual accuracy. Thirdly, the degree to which a definite observable location could be cited was an important factor in establishing the credibility of Father Hastings's story. It allowed an eye-witness (a reporter) subsequently to check the details. Fourthly, to satisfy the demands of balance, the newsmen felt impelled to find an alternative, in this case, opposing, viewpoint. Fifthly, reinforcing the need for eye-witness evidence, an important deficiency in Father Hastings's account was the fact it was based upon others' reports. Sixthly, the directness of the evidence was a crucial issue. Father Hastings's film was rejected because it was judged irrelevant to the specific claims which had been made.

The last point has illuminating implications. While the film provided hard evidence of military terrorism in Mozambique under colonial rule, oddly this was not seen as casting especial doubt on the Portuguese government's denials. A view of colonial oppression and its consequences simply did not figure as an interpretative possibility. Nor, therefore, was it seen as important to give the British public 'old' evidence to help it interpret the story. The facts were to speak for themselves in the clashing of opinion. The parliamentary model predominated. But this model could only limit understanding of why such a story should emerge at all, setting aside the matter of its truthfulness. Also limiting was the ahistorical tendency of going for immediate news value to the exclusion of relevant historical background.

THE BBC'S NEWS APPROACH

BBC News performs its permitted role like an actor in a morality play. For being impartial in terms broadly pre-defined by the state, it is rewarded with the gift of independence. This independence takes on a certain style, implies a particular posture. Of the two ideal typical images of journalistic activity in Western societies, the committed and the neutral, BBC News *must* choose the latter. The BBC, by its own official account, is corporately disengaged from that which it reports. But how is this ideology internally mediated within the News Department? Are there any who deviate from this basic commitment to neutrality, and if so what happens to them?

For the BBC to be politically uncommitted as a corporation in the narrow party political sense, but yet to be wedded to the prevailing order, clearly presents a model of individual professional conduct. This model is the one to be pursued within the Corporation by those working in its journalistic areas. Corporate disengagement entails personal disengagement on the part of the Corporation's staff when dealing with issues reported in the news. The argument runs thus: the news service has to satisfy the needs of the entire nation, and must therefore eschew taking sides in a conflict. Staff members must internalize this rule so that their beliefs do not affect their performances in organizationally unacceptable ways. This brings us to a discussion of a specific model of 'professionalism'.

The model in question is most explicitly embodied in a set of rules governing the political conduct of BBC staff, which in its conception is reminiscent of those presently prevailing in the British civil service. At the time of writing the relevant rules are those contained in Staff Instruction (S.I.) 206, which is dated 4 February 1963. A change in these rules has been sought since the early 1970s by the Association of Broadcasting Staff and the National Union of Journalists.

While S.I.206 dates from 1963, the basic stance taken in it was originally outlined in the 1930s and has survived revision in the early 1950s, and subsequently. For inspiration it draws on the myth of the civil servant as neutral executant of policies which are determined in the sphere of politics, and has, as such, a powerful rhetorical and legitimating role.

S.I.206 is a four-page memorandum from the Controller, Staff Administration, to all BBC staff, and its general concern is with 'Personal Activities'. Its rationale is explained in the following sentences:

> In particular, the Corporation must ensure that its reputation for impartiality and its standing as a public body are not prejudiced in any way by the outside activities of staff, and while the Corporation has no desire to censor the opinions of its staff, the public expression of political or other controversial views may obviously be open to objection. . . . In addition the Corporation does not consider that paid outside employment should be undertaken where the individual would have, in effect, two jobs or where the second interest would compete with his Corporation work.

The document goes on to make the point that 'in order to limit the occasion for which individual applications for permission must be made, staff are divided into two categories – Restricted and Unrestricted'. The category of particular interest here is that of 're-stricted' staff which includes those

> who because of their position in the Corporation must exercise special care with regard to political or controversial activities. This category includes all staff of Assistant Controller status and above, those carrying an important degree of responsibility for news and current affairs programmes and those who are well known as performers before the camera or microphone or whose prime responsibility is to represent the Corporation in its contact with the public.

The scope of the regulations is far-reaching. For example, S.I.206 stipulates that they 'apply to activities undertaken in the name of the individual, anonymously or under a pseudonym', and that where permission is sought for activities covered by the regulations this should be made in writing. Even 'unrestricted' staff, while being permitted to 'write books and occasional articles or give occasional lectures' have to obtain permission if they are making 'reference to the Corporation or broadcasting'. Restricted staff are specifically required to seek permission to publish subject matter which is 'political or in the realm of controversy', and for both categories of staff 'the Corporation may require to see the manuscript'. The same rule applies to letters and statements to the press.

There is certainly no encouragement for BBC staff to become politically involved. A restricted staff member seeking election is

> given up to six weeks' unpaid leave at the period of the election, and will be given a clear indication of whether or not he can expect to return to his former post should he not be elected, and, if not, an estimate of his chances of resettlement in some other suitable post so far as they can be foreseen. Should he be elected he will be required to resign. Should he not be elected, and should it not be possible for him to return to his former post, he will be given formal contractual notice when the election results are known.

Unrestricted staff, by contrast, may return to their former jobs. However, written permission from the BBC is required for either category of staff who wish to stand either for Parliament or in local government elections. Restricted staff are not even allowed to canvas or to take part in any 'minor political activity' without express permission.

The staff regulations provide BBC management with a set of restrictive rules which may be appealed to in disciplinary actions. As these rules have contractual force, they are, naturally, inhibiting, and their full acceptance is in reality a condition of continued employment by the BBC, and certainly essential for a successful career.

These propositions concerning 'neutral' professionalism may be made more concrete by considering a few cases of 'unprofessional' conduct. In BBC News proper, it was very difficult to find many tales of deviant behaviour, and similarly difficult to find many deviant believers. Naturally, there are those who think that prowling sociologists are up to no good, and that they might be management narks. But I do not think that in general I was victim to such paranoid labelling. Rather, I was faced with a mass of conformists. Their conformism lay not in personal style, dress or lack of sexual peccadilloes, but rather in their adoption of the model of corporate professionalism provided for them by the BBC by degrees varying from unreflecting acquiescence to the most full-blown commitment.

Being 'unprofessional': deviants

Three quotations from a long internal discussion of the presenter's role between the present Director-General and Senior News and Current Affairs Editors express some important principles:

(a) A good professional ought to be able to operate impeccably in areas about which he has strong personal views.

(b) When answering the question WHY, a Current Affairs man may start with a hypothesis but not with an evident commitment.

(c) Every time a man reveals a personal commitment he reduces his professional usefulness, until the moment arrives when he may be said to have used up all his credit-worthiness.[33]

Individual political commitments on the part of news staff are not in general talked about. Those who possess commitments know them to be damaging to career prospects. Thus, as one newsman put it: 'There's a feeling that it's *infra dig* to discuss politics. Personal views aren't aired.' The politics thus referred to are *not* the politics of the national scene, but rather what one believes in. And what one ultimately believes in becomes rather questionable. As a television newsman observed, and he had been in the BBC all his adult life, for some eighteen years now: 'You get so used to looking at both sides of the argument that in the end you don't know what you really believe.' I will return to this theme shortly, but in the meantime it is important to be clear that in the News Division the norm is, as an assistant editor in Television News put it: 'to be *above* politics in the party political sense. We're generally suspicious of commitment, of people with axes to grind. In this job you always assume people have axes to grind – you're sceptical about the interests which lie behind what they have to say.'

It is against this background that we have to evaluate known cases of deviance. One can put deviant activities, and the knowledge of these, into the context of a Durkheimian theory of normative regulation: the boundaries of the permissible are made clearer by the transgressions of the deviant. One well-known case concerns one of the BBC's Diplomatic Staff, who reported the Nigerian civil war. He showed, it is said, a clear bias in favour of Biafra, and was later dismissed, to become the author of best-selling thrillers. But this kind of deviance is exceptional. Newsmen rarely become explicit spokesmen for causes in their reporting.

The MacKenzie Case

A well-documented instance of deviance from the terms of reference set out by Staff Instruction 206 concerned a chief sub-editor in Radio News whose anti-Zionist and pro-Palestinian views on the Middle East conflict emerged in a satirical article he had written in a literary competition. The outcome of this incident was a severe reprimand and six months' demotion. As the case was something of a minor *cause célèbre*, albeit a brief one, in the quality press, and as it was often mentioned as a cautionary tale during fieldwork at Radio News, it is worth pursuing in some detail. It greatly illuminates the scope of the staff regulations, and the way in which the BBC's senior management would seem to have responded to quite extensive pressures from pro-Zionist groups.

The newsman in question, Mr Fergus MacKenzie,* had his prize-winning essay, entitled 'The Shortest Way with Trespassers' published in the *Spectator* of 17 July 1971. The essay took the form of an open letter to Mrs Golda Meir, then Israeli prime minister, from 'her esteemed servant Eli Krakwitz', and advocated numerous extreme solutions to Israel's 'Arab Problem'. In an interview, MacKenzie described his article as a 'satire intended for literary rather than political purposes'. He did, however, hold strong views on the Arab-Israeli conflict, and had developed the feeling during the Six Day War of 1967 that 'the Zionist case was the only one being reported here in Britain and in the West, and that the Palestinian case was going by default'. MacKenzie went on to say that the article was 'modelled on eighteenth-century broadsheets and written deliberately in an intemperate style'. MacKenzie vehemently denied that his writing was actuated by anti-semitism rather than by anti-Zionism. It is essential to distinguish these two positions if a dispassionate view of the issue is to be achieved.

On the day the article appeared, MacKenzie was called before the Editor, Radio News, Mr Peter Woon. He was reprimanded by Mr Woon on two counts, both of which made reference to the staff regulations: first, the article contained political matter and was not previously cleared with the BBC, and secondly, MacKenzie had identified himself as a BBC employee. He was warned against publishing any further 'controversial' material without the BBC's permission.

---

* I have departed from my normal practice of treating cases anonymously as Mr MacKenzie's received extensive publicity. He has left the BBC to work elsewhere, ans his leaving had nothing to do with the matter discussed here. Mr MacKenzie had had an opportunity to read and comment on these pages. I am grateful to him and to Mr Tim Fell of the NUJ for documentation and assistance.

On 5 August, while MacKenzie was away on holiday, a memorandum was sent to him by Mr Desmond Taylor, the Editor, News and Current Affairs. This reads as follows:

> My attention having been drawn (by the Chairman, Editor, Radio News, the Board of Deputies of British Jews, etc.) to your article in the *Spectator* of July 17th, I see that you promise that more articles are in the pipeline.
>
> This is to tell you that you must ensure that no further articles emerge from the pipeline contrary to the terms of your contract, before Editor, Radio News, has approved them. They must reach him before submission, and if he agrees to their publication, there must be no mention of your connection with the BBC, without permission.
>
> This is a formal instruction, a copy of which will go on your personal file. Could you please arrange to come and see me as soon as you return.

The reference to the intervention of the Chairman, then Lord Hill, and the Board of Deputies of British Jews is significant, and perhaps a little ill-advised given Mr Taylor's later observation that he was not responding to pressure. Of course, the dividing line between 'pressure' and having one's attention drawn to something is not a clear one.

MacKenzie's article had not gone unnoticed. It was criticized the week after it appeared by Dr S. Levenberg of the Board of Deputies as 'nasty, filthy, and bordering on anti-semitism'.[34] It sparked off an exceedingly acrimonious and extended correspondence in the *Spectator* during the remainder of July and the whole of August, in which supporters of, and detractors from, MacKenzie's views on the Palestine question argued their cases at length. MacKenzie had already been in bad odour with the Board of Deputies for having written an article in *The Listener* the previous year on 'the Zionist lobby' (as he put it in an interview), and this had also produced an extensive correspondence which continued for two months.[35] MacKenzie had not been identified as a member of news staff in this earlier article.

One member of the Board of Deputies, following its meeting on 18 July 1971, acted on his own behalf and complained to the BBC, as did Mr David Spector, Chairman of the Brighton Israel Friendship League. These complaints occurred before Mr Taylor sent his memo to MacKenzie. As MacKenzie was away on holiday at the time ENCA sent his note, he received it only after he had already despatched a letter to the *Spectator* defending his views and journalistic integrity. This was published on 14 August, and set out his political stance with considerable explicitness: 'Discrimination in an exclusivist society is unavoidable, and it is practised in the form of immigration laws, restrictions on residence and movement, in payment for labour, in education and in political participation.... I was lampooning the dual standard of morality of those who condemn these practices in Greece or Southern Africa but condone them in the Israeli occupied territory.' Certainly, it was far less common for such views to be expressed in 1971 than at the time of writing (1977).

This explicit rejoinder occasioned disciplinary proceedings as it was construed as a fresh breach of regulations. On 19 August MacKenzie was summoned by the Editor, News and Current Affairs, and demoted to senior sub-editor. From the BBC's point of view, apart from creating an embarrassment by engaging in public debate, MacKenzie's statement in the *Spectator* was unabashedly political. On 20 August, MacKenzie wrote a letter to ENCA in which he said that the decision to demote him 'raises issues not only of personal concern but of public interest'. A memo from ENCA on the same day took up the point about the public interest and rejoined:

> I must remind you, as I did recently in our interview of 19th August and in my note to you of 5th August, that you are not, under your contract, at liberty to submit for publication material of a controversial nature without my prior permission and authorization of the material in question.

Mr Taylor refused to budge on the disciplinary decision which had been taken to downgrade MacKenzie, but he noted the latter's right to appeal against it. MacKenzie's request for his demotion to be suspended until his appeal had been heard was denied.

MacKenzie's salary was immediately reduced and the newsroom duty rotas were changed so that MacKenzie became subordinate to the most junior senior sub-editor. The Radio News NUJ Chapel passed a resolution on 24 August which

> instructed their officers to seek the immediate reinstatement of Fergus MacKenzie as a Chief Sub Editor. They further deplored notification that his demotion is immediately effective despite his notice of appeal.

The chapel also noted its full support for MacKenzie, and it instructed its officers to seek a meeting with ENCA.

At a subsequent chapel meeting on 3 September, two resolutions were carried. One considered 'quite unacceptable the management attitude in demoting (an NUJ member) while an appeal against his demotion is pending' and it went on to urge 'the management to reconsider enforcing the demotion until the appeals procedure has been concluded'.

The second resolution criticized Mr Taylor for having written to Mr Spector of the Brighton Israel Friendship League as the letter 'formed the basis of a report in the *Jewish Chronicle*' and it noted that the NUJ had attempted to keep the MacKenzie affair confidential.

It is worth quoting Mr Taylor's letter to Mr Spector (or at least that part of it published in the *Jewish Chronicle*) because this establishes unambiguously the official grounds on which administrative action was taken: MacKenzie had broken staff regulations

in that he did not submit the article to his superiors and did not seek their permission to mention his connection with the Corporation. The permission would not have been granted and I need hardly say that he is now aware that he was wrong to do what he did.

Mr MacKenzie is not, as you described him, a Middle East reporter, but as stated in the *Spectator* a member of our news staff. He is not, however, in a position to influence news bulletins in any improper way and, indeed, we are satisfied that he never allowed his personal views to influence his news work.

It is indeed hard to see how such personal 'axe-grinding' would be possible given the BBC's editorial system. MacKenzie was clearly being disciplined for a technical offence – breaking the staff regulations – and not for the heinous unprofessional sin of producing 'biased content'.

The NUJ's protest against MacKenzie's demotion before his appeal was heard proved successful. The protest had been backed up by a threat to make the matter into an 'official dispute'.

MacKenzie's appeal was heard on 9 September by Mr Michael Kinchin-Smith, the BBC's Controller of Staff Administration. MacKenzie was accompanied by Mr Eric Blott, Deputy General Secretary of the NUJ, and Mr Tony Jay, his father of the chapel (FOC). At the hearing the union conceded MacKenzie's infringement of the staff regulations, but argued that the penalty was 'harsh, inappropriate and unprecedented'. It was agreed that the essay was quite obviously an eighteenth-century lampoon in style and not a straightforward political commentary; that the demotion would harm MacKenzie's career and that he would lose some £500 per annum in basic pay and overtime; that his professional competence was put in doubt; and that no similar demotion had ever occurred. Importantly, it was argued that the letter written by MacKenzie in his defence was not a separate offence, but directly connected with the article.

On the morning of the appeal a letter was received by Tony Jay, the Radio News FOC, from the Editor, News and Current Affairs. It read:

> You asked me to set down for you the reasons for Fergus Mac-Kenzie's demotion.
>
> He published, and allowed his connection with the BBC to be published, without permission. He was reprimanded by Editor, Radio News, and told not to do it again. Following this, a letter from him was published in the *Spectator* – again without reference to his editor.
>
> May I make it clear that I took my action, not because of any pressure from outside, but in defence of the BBC's own regulations and reputation.

These themes were to recur in the BBC's final judgement on the matter, embodied in a letter from Mr Kinchin-Smith to Mr Blott of the NUJ. This letter was dated 23 September. Following the appeal, it said, it had been decided to limit MacKenzie's demotion to a period of six months, during which he would have to give good service and give 'clear evidence that he had accepted, and would continue to accept, the BBC's regulations about outside writing'. The bulk of the letter is devoted to a ritual statement of the BBC's official philosophy, which might perhaps be explained as a pre-emptive strike against any leaking of its contents. It is worth quoting this as another definitive official statement of corporate ideology:

> As a public service the BBC must preserve complete impartiality in matters which are in the realm of public controversy. Unlike a newspaper, the BBC cannot have an Editorial opinion: its role is to be an impartial purveyor of news and information, so that the public may judge for themselves on the events of the day in the light of the best possible information available. Public confidence in this essential impartiality which the BBC has built up and preserved over the years can be prejudiced if senior staff in the News and Current Affairs field air their personal views on political or other controversial matters, and if in doing so their connection with the BBC is mentioned. This is the reason for the regulations on this matter.

This is an astonishing homily when one considers it was contained in a private letter and not one of the BBC's Lunchtime Lectures. Against this framework of assumptions MacKenzie's article, his publicly mentioned connection with the BBC, and his ensuing letter were all construed as serious breaches of the regulations.

The MacShane Case

Another instructive instance of deviance arose during my concluding fieldwork at Television News during July 1976. Even before it had occurred, I had been told about the man in question, who possessed a certain notoriety. In every sense of the phrase, this was a cautionary tale. The newsman in question was *not* with the News Division. This is in itself significant, because what occurred could not have happened in the closely controlled organizational context I have analysed. The newsman, Mr Denis MacShane,* was a member of the executive of the National Union of Journalists, and a known and outspoken left-wing labourite. He stood as Labour Party candidate for Solihull, Birmingham, in the October 1974 General Election. The BBC refused to allow MacShane to return to his job in Birmingham, and eventually, after an intervention by the General Secretary of the NUJ, he was given work at Radio London. He remained unemployed, but on the BBC payroll for some nine months before he secured the new job. This was contrasted with the different treatment accorded the Liberal and Conservative candidates in that election by a number of informants inside BBC News. It is also a point made by an associate of MacShane's, Tom Litterick, MP, in a brief document which criticizes the BBC's staff regulations for inhibiting open political commitment on the part of its employees.[36] In this document, Litterick points out that Alan Watson, the Liberal candidate, continued as a current affairs presenter and reporter after his electoral defeat. The Conservative candidate, Dick Tracey, however, did have problems which 'needed the intervention of William Whitelaw, Chairman of the Conservative Party, before he got a job again at the BBC and he lost money as a result. But he too made a come-back more easily than MacShane'.

MacShane was not simply a candidate for political office, but he also had the reputation for being a union militant, having been exceedingly active in organizing the NUJ's first-ever one-day strike in the BBC over unsocial hours, which took place in December 1975, and almost completely disrupted the news service. Most informants

---

* Here too I have departed from my normal practice of treating cases anonymously as Mr MacShane's was also quite extensively treated in the press. Mr MacShane himself has made no request for anonymity, and has had an opportunity to read and comment on these pages.

said that he had a lot going against him: a personal style which was far from bland, politics which were too outspoken and unorthodox, and a role as union activist which was profoundly irritating to management.

MacShane committed what was universally regarded as an act of unprofessional conduct, and he himself admitted it was such. At the request of a producer in Radio London, he rang a phone-in programme, *Platform*, which was dealing with the issue of electoral reform. He used an assumed name and spoke in a disguised voice, and held forth with some left-wing views. During the course of his remarks he made an unflattering remark (later held by the High Court to be libellous) about the former Conservative Minister, Mr Reginald Maudling. At this point he was cut off by the presenter.

The Radio London Station Manager, Mr Allen Holden, who was listening to the broadcast, recognized MacShane's voice, and rang in to demand an immediate explanation. A formal disciplinary interview followed which resulted in MacShane being given notice with three months' pay. The programme's producer was simply reprimanded.

The official NUJ account of the interview, based upon notes taken by two NUJ observers, gives considerable insight into the handling of the incident. This account was accepted as accurate by the General Manager, Local Radio, Mr Michael Barton. The NUJ document sets the scene by saying:

> A recorded interview between a BBC staff member and his Head of Department is an integral part of the BBC's disciplinary process. BBC employees are allowed to be accompanied by a union representative. The interview is crucial because in theory the Head of Department takes his decision as a result of the interview and during the BBC's appeal system (more accurately that system whereby senior management confirms or rejects, usually the former, lower management decisions; there is no neutral, non-BBC element involved) the recorded interview is used as source evidence for the offence and management's view of it.

In the background to the interview, but unmentioned by Mac-Shane, it goes on to say, were two important factors. First, Mac-Shane's allegation that the Manager of Radio London said 'We've got you at last, MacShane. You won't be able to get out of this one.' And secondly, the suppression of an article on racial violence by MacShane, based on two broadcast radio talks, which was supposed to appear in *The Listener*, but was dropped at the behest of the Director of Programmes, Radio. It was subsequently published in the July/August 1976 issue of *Broadcast*, the ABS house journal. The document says these points were not made during the interview because 'the NUJ side did not believe that the BBC would try to sack MacShane, so it seemed wise to avoid introducing evidence that raised the temperature'. It goes on to draw a lesson from this omission, arguing that as a general principle personnel undergoing disciplinary procedings should be sure to get all relevant points on the record.

The interview focused on MacShane's professional misconduct, or, as one NUJ source put it, his 'almighty bollock-dropping incident'. MacShane's main defences were that there had been no complaints from the public, that he had been 'requested' to make the call and therefore was not solely responsible for it, and that such calls were in any case established practice in BBC radio phone-ins. Central to the BBC's case against MacShane was that he had 'chosen to make political and personal remarks which he must have known as a professional journalist could be seriously embarrassing to the BBC. Additionally, it put the BBC in the position of broadcasting a remark which would be grossly offensive to a third party.'

It is hard to doubt that MacShane's troublesome past was *not* the key factor in deciding his treatment. At Television Centre, while there was little sympathy for him, the case did occasion a good deal of discussion. The NUJ's protest leaflet, distributed at Television Centre, summed up the sacking thus: 'The BBC says it is for a grave error of judgement. The NUJ says he's been victimized because he's deeply unpopular with BBC Management.' No one at Television Centre disputed the lack of professionalism in journalists ringing their own phone-ins. The argument that such faked phone calls were 'not an infrequent occurrence'[37] did not seem to weigh very heavily in discussion of the case.

As a trade-union issue, the central point of interest was the alleged victimization, since the man editorially responsible was not so harshly treated. The NUJ gave official support for any action taken by BBC journalists in support of their colleague, but the only chapel which did go on strike – for five days – was that of Radio London.

At Television News, there was no enthusiasm at all for industrial action. It was felt that the case did not merit it, and although many newsmen argued that victimization had indeed taken place, they thought MacShane deserved it for having been too awkward and unpolitic. Even those sympathetic to him personally, such as one reporter who took a leading role in the Television News chapel, argued that 'the bloody fool walked straight into it'. The Television News chapel called a meeting shortly after the dismissal had been announced, but it did not attract a high turn-out – some members who were normally active on issues such as pay and conditions confessing an indifference on this occasion. Those really hostile strongly resisted any suggestion of industrial action. For example, one sub in conversation in the newsroom exclaimed in outrage: 'And they were trying to get us to go on bloody strike about it!' The sole outcome was a chapel resolution asking for an official BBC enquiry into why differential treatment had occurred.

In general, BBC chapels were reluctant to take industrial action, and a meeting of FOCs in late July 1976 advised MacShane to appeal directly to the BBC's DG, Sir Charles Curran. According to NUJ sources, this advice followed a report to the FOCs by the NUJ's General Secretary, Mr Ken Morgan. Morgan had apparently been assured by Sir Charles, off the record, that there would be a job for MacShane. The union also advised this course of action because it had no faith in the BBC's appeal system.

The outcome of the appeal to Curran was an offer of six months' suspension of the dismissal notice. What this meant, in effect, was that MacShane could apply for other jobs during this period, but a failure to land one would result in a final dismissal. In the NUJ it was felt that six months was inadequate, since MacShane's previous experience indicated this was not enough time to find a new job. A further feature of the BBC's offer stipulated that MacShane was to work in the London newsrooms at Broadcasting House and Bush House in order to prove that he had the 'journalistic judgement of a BBC newsman'. When the offer was discussed at the National Executive Committee of the NUJ the General Secretary was instructed to point out the disparity between the formal, official offer and the off-the-record version. Since there was no alternative, the offer was accepted.

At the end of the six-month trial period MacShane was finally dismissed. The NUJ alleged that this was an act of victimization, basing this claim on three grounds. First, that the BBC had been involved in two other major libel cases, neither of which, although costly, had resulted in any dismissals. Secondly, that the BBC had not gone through the resettlement procedures as promised in August 1976. And lastly, that MacShane's work in the Broadcasting House and Bush House newsrooms had received no adverse criticism, but on the contrary had been praised. Despite favourable comments, and the existence of vacancies, he had not been offered a job.[38]

Two other cases which are also of interest concerned reporters who stood for public office. One in Radio News came from *The Times*. He held a seat as Labour Councillor for a London Borough and had successfully fought to retain his right to political activity. When he was offered a specialist post in education, he was told it would be unacceptable for him to remain a local councillor, and he subsequently resigned his seat. According to one source he did so because there was a Tory government in office at the time and with a row brewing over comprehensive education it would have proved embarrassing for the BBC to have an identifiable political opponent of Tory policy covering this area.

As mentioned earlier, another radio reporter, this time working as a freelance in current affairs, stood unsuccessfully as a Tory candidate in one of the 1974 General Elections. During this election, he took part in Conservative party political broadcasts. After the election although he experienced problems he was able to work once more in the current affairs area. Several newsmen in Radio News contrasted his position with the correspondent's, and interpreted this as a bias towards Toryism among BBC's higher management. The official reason for the difference in treatment was that one man was a staff correspondent and the other a free-lance, and therefore not contractually identifiable as a BBC voice (a fact which is probably lost on the general public). Additionally, one held office, and the other was unsuccessful.

CORPORATE IDEOLOGY AND PROFESSIONAL IDENTITY

I have dwelt on the above cases because they are so unusual – a newsman's criterion, if ever there was one. But here the exceptions genuinely do prove the rule. It can confidently be stated that impartiality, by which is meant an uncritical adherence to parliamentary forms of political behaviour, and an absence of political commitment, is the required ideological stance for the BBC newsman. It is a core component of the concept of corporate professionalism in a milieu in which political involvement is deprecated; for example, one left-wing woman sub was referred to as 'wearing her politics on her sleeve'. She had left and 'wasn't much good anyway'.

The Editor, Television News, told an instructive story. Some visiting European broadcasters were dining with BBC executives, and ENCA had pointed out to the guests that there were six top editors there at the table, and he just could not say how they voted. The Editor thought, as a rider to this observation, that inside the BBC discussion of politicians was more in terms of their *efficiency* than their ideology. This, I think, is a most succinct and apt summary of the BBC position. The legitimate arena, Parliament, is taken for granted: within that context there is a technical concern with how well things are done, rather than what groups stand for – until, of course, there is any threat to the maintenance of 'politics as usual': then the BBC's duty is to throw its weight behind the status quo.

This internally elaborated ideology is derived from the external conditions permitting 'independence'. Newsmen frequently point out that 'both sides' of every question are treated with equal detachment and scepticism, and all that is done is to *present* competing viewpoints, leaving the public to make up its own mind:

> . . . If broadcasting is to reflect the nation, we must include matters in dispute. We must communicate the views of others, however distasteful or embarrassing they may be to some. This is our duty as honest reporters. The public is entitled to the truth as interpreted by all sides – and so, on behalf of the public, we put probing, searching questions to Cabinet Ministers, railways chiefs, industrial bosses – all 'them who push us around'. The public have not the opportunity of putting the questions themselves. We do it for them.[39]

The official account, given here by a former Editor, News and Current Affairs, is almost invariably echoed within the News Departments. A Television News reporter observed of the Northern Ireland situation: 'The newsmen are the only people who know both sides. People know we're trying to do a fair job, and we'd never get hurt except by accident – except as far as the hooligan element is concerned. They recognize that we're doing a job for them.' Newsmen claim the ability to be impartial as part of their skill, and that *any one* of them would tell substantially the same story when confronted with the same set of facts. The personnel, as honest reporters, are a guarantee of the impartiality of the news output, the argument runs. And that is because they have absorbed the correct approach by meeting, through time, practical problems posed for the Corporation.

In the previous section, examples of what might be called intolerable deviance were considered. Clearly, newsmen *do* possess personal beliefs, which being controversial are potentially disruptive or embarrassing for the Corporation. But that in itself does not pose a problem, provided they do nothing, and to some extent say nothing, which will make their peers and superiors, and particularly influential outsiders, think that in some way their convictions contradict the accepted notion of professional impartiality.

Illustrating this, a number of newsmen went out of their way to cite occasions on which they experienced conflicts between personal beliefs and the dictates of impartiality. But they would stress that these could be resolved only by being professional in the accepted way. A television sub-editor, for example, said that he had been assigned to a story dealing with the indiscriminate killing of whales: 'I went and told it simply, despite the fact that I felt strongly about it. Let the public make up its own mind.' A correspondent observed:

I'm prejudiced because deep down I agree with comprehensive education rather than selective. I know the idealistic Labour solutions though they wouldn't work. Your basic ground-root attitude begins to infect you if you aren't careful.

He went on, however, to nullify this admission by saying 'I'm not taking an *a priori* position. I have attitudes but I'm traditional – I just want to tell the facts.' Another example is provided by a senior executive in Television News who noted:

On the crusade thing – we have a charter obligation not to express opinions. But people do hold opinions. If I could I'd start a crusade right now against the Common Market.

Sociologists studying news organizations have demonstrated a great deal of interest in this question of conformity of belief, and as indicated earlier the socialization and control of newsmen has been a pervasive theme in the literature. One test of successful socialization lies in the degree to which known (but harmless) deviant views can be tolerated. For instance, in Television News, a fairly senior intake executive variously described one reporter as 'a Bolshie' and another as 'a creeping fascist'. Yet, the executive said, he would have complete confidence in assigning either of them to controversial stories in which their own political sympathies might be expected to emerge. And he would do this because he knew they would be professional in their treatment of the news. He added:

In fact when we have an anti-police boy, we tend to put him on police demos. By Christ he's trying so hard to be impartial he's right. Put a fascist boy on say a Notting Hill community job. He really is objective – really gives them a hard time. But he comes up with an impartial approach.

There is, here, part of an answer to the problem of impartiality viewed from the perspective of the controllers: one man is as good as the next whatever his personal beliefs provided he acts according to the canons of impartial reportage. But to say this is not to say enough about what newsmen seem truly to believe. One of the two 'extremist' television reporters indicated his views in these words:

G

. . . I insist I am able, and I think it's one of the skills of a reporter, to be a complete schizophrenic. I can have strong political views, and do have, in some quarters. But when the camera is on they do not come into play. Sometimes in journalism you get someone who is unable to do that: it swiftly shows itself, and he very quickly becomes known as someone who is unreliable. . . .

'Schizophrenia' is a revealing term. There are, as it were, two co-existing structures of belief, even of identity: the personal and committed, and the corporate and detached. Furthermore, those who held committed views did not seem to feel that the Corporation's doctrines somehow violated their integrity. What was seen as honest and as authentic was the espousal of a professionalism partly defined in terms of impartiality. A startling indication of the way in which this bifurcation of belief is an integral part of newsmen's thought emerged in a related though distinct area of professional beliefs, that of news judgement. One reporter had a sophisticated awareness of organizational shortcomings as he saw them:

The problem is the degree to which any report can be fitted into some conceptual framework. The fundamental drive of news is to get there, and bring back a report on what happened. You have to report why ideally. . . .

This observation was made one morning over a drink in the BBC Club. Later that day, when the reporter was out on assignment, active rather than reflective, he went through a list of the questions which he would be asking people at the scene of the incident, and remarked: 'You learn these things through practice. It's difficult to teach people what news is: no one has a clear idea.' Professional intuitionism in the afternoon vies with the detached rationalism of the morning. Although not a strict analogy to reportorial schizophrenia regarding impartiality, this example does indicate the kind of oscillation which occurs between expressions of personal belief in private situations of an analytical kind, and the invocation of professional mystique necessary for a satisfactory performance of the job.

The mechanics of professional impartiality become as much a part of the fabric of everyday news production as making decisions on the basis of news values:

You have to form opinions, though you're not allowed to express them. I don't think they come out.

(Reporter, Television News)

*No one is ever biased or unfair . . . You unconsciously put the
pro's and con's – it's an unconscious technique.*

(Sub-editor, Television News)

A former BBC Current Affairs editor, Anthony Smith, has spoken of
this approach as 'the transmutation of balance into a kind of
allegory of life'.[40] Because newsmen know what constitutes an
impartially told story in just the same way as they know what is
newsworthy, on the whole they experience few practical difficulties.
Once the story has been identified the 'unconscious technique' is
applied to it. This does not, of course, mean that a neutral account
actually does result.

The implication of this interpretation is that while a few newsmen
may have strongly-held beliefs which they are not permitted to
express in the Corporation's outputs this does not in general pose a
problem either for them or for the controllers. For the potential
deviant here is an honourable way of excising his own convictions:
the stance of impartiality is construed as virtuous and therefore as
professional. And the self-regulating machinery of the editorial
system should take care of any loss of self-control. It must be said
that very few newsmen, very likely out of caution, did venture
strong political opinions to me during the course of fieldwork.

Indeed, some, extremely aware of corporate disapproval of
political stances, drew my attention to other possible styles of
behaviour which act, in some measure, as surrogates. One of these is
being an active member of the NUJ, but within definite limits, as the
MacShane case clearly indicates. In some ways to be an FOC, for
example, can be advantageous, as it demonstrates that you possess
managerial skills. Some activism, therefore, is not a bar to promotion,
provided it is 'responsible'. The Managing Editor, News, and the
Intake Editor, Radio News, for example, had both been FOC's and
this, given their senior rank, had evidently not harmed their prospects.
But there was general agreement among informants that too active
an involvement was damaging to careers. One source said that a
reporter had in his annual report the remark 'He will jeopardize
his career if he maintains his existing level of union commitment.'
This was not corroborated by anyone else, but such stories do the
rounds and express a mood.

The other major permissible style is what several called 'raffish-
ness'. Again, this is not without its ambiguities. For there is a sense
in which the amount of piss-artistry permitted oneself must not
interfere with basic competence. To be an affable drinking partner
is really important for good work relations in journalism. The bar is
the nexus of gossip, and there, in the atmosphere of camaraderie,

even the boss is, temporarily, just one of the lads. But to be a lush is dangerous. So, it was not surprising that there were a good many cautionary tales in the newsrooms. Of the duty editor finally sacked for incompetence. Of someone being 'pissed' on the air. Of the reporter who took a flight to Malta rather than Scotland and was 'busted'. I have touched on these modes of behaviour because they are acceptable where political activism is not.

Most newsmen seem genuinely to believe in the Corporation's formula for achieving impartiality, and that it thereby discharges its public duties. One trainee expressed his beliefs with some fervour:

> If it came to it, I wouldn't write about my views – it would be what happened rather than a conscious decision. I believe that people writing are doing it objectively and are proud of it.

Indeed, it is not the BBC's official theorists alone who elaborate corporate ideology. An unauthorized justifying account is sometimes mentioned. What it purports to explain, as does the doctrine of impartiality, is how the BBC's news emerges as a neutral construct. It is another way of saying 'all sides are presented', except that all the sides involved are *there*, in the newsroom, to make sure no *one* side prevails. 'Representative newsroom theory' is a vulgarized version of the theory of politico-social pluralism in liberal democracies. Because the newsrooms contain Labour, Conservative, and (so many assert) a disproportionately high number of Liberal voters, plus the odd proto-fascist and Marxist, the news *must* be neutral. Checks and balances see to that : the diversity of views among the personnel acts as a guarantee that no axe-grinding will take place. One assistant editor gave the following account:

> *In the newsroom there's a fair mixture of people from left and right on any given day.* If anyone tried to bend things he'd be out like a shot. It's more than the job's worth. It's easy to see if it's been slanted. I can't remember a case. It's so easy to spot, *it couldn't get through so many checks.* It could only get through at senior level – it would have to be the people at the top here.

What this quotation indicates is the way in which representative newsroom theory is anyway linked to the real safeguards of the editorial system. It has an important dramatic role, rather than a substantial one, for the checks only work as a failsafe: in fact actual political belief is unimportant, as it is corporate commitment which decides the conceptual orientation to news stories. Nevertheless, it is bad sociology to dismiss beliefs, even when they are not good explanations of action. So, to pursue another ramification of representative newsroom theory, we should take seriously the view expressed by yet another assistant editor that the newsroom contained many people with provincial newspaper experience who were therefore '*looking after the interests of all parts of the country*. It helps when people know the area – names, distances, people – when a story breaks.' We have in a nutshell the view that BBC News is, rather like Parliament, truly representative of the nation's diversity, and able to incorporate it, and encapsulate it in its productions.

So far I have shown how corporate ideology comes to constitute an integral part of the BBC newsman's professional identity. But there are, of course, differing degrees of commitment. At one extreme there was a resonance of Reithianism in the somewhat puritanical public service utterance of the Editor, Television News:

> There's something in all BBC newsmen. They work because they believe in the basic idea of a news *service*. We're trying to be the best and we're not sullied by other considerations than reporting what's going on.

The manner of expression here conveys an underlying sense of vocation.

Those most identified as 'BBC men' are News management and the more senior newsroom editors and correspondents. Their cognitive capture by the system is not surprising and perfectly consonant with the way in which editorial control is vested, in the last resort, in the safe men of the Corporation. It is true to say that to believe in the Corporation's mission, as the ultimate purveyor of truthful news in Britain, is at least a highly important condition for advancement.

The view identified above is one in which BBC News is seen as bearing 'the most fundamentally important of all the BBC's responsibilities'.[41] In other words, being the right sort of newsman is a way of discharging one's duty as a member of the *Corporation*.

Contrast this with those who do not see the BBC as a unique institution, or at least claim not to, and who tend to work with the idea of its being an organization which allows them to be professional newsmen. This view is particularly strongly-held among younger newsmen, and there are two main variants. In the first you are working for BBC News, and your loyalty does not extend beyond the boundaries of the Division. In the second you are a journalist first and foremost, the BBC's news is just like other media products, and the News Division gives you the facilities for exercising professional (or craft) skills: the pleasure derived from beating deadlines, or imposing order on the elements of a story.

Comments on commitment from this quarter have quite a different flavour from the one quoted above:

> At a pinch you'd subscribe to BBC ideals, but you don't really think in terms of commitment.
>
> (Radio Reporter)

> There's still a vague feeling that the BBC is at the pinnacle of the news media.
>
> (Chief sub, Radio News)

These comments are grudging; they do not have the smack of full-blown organizational commitment. In a sense, this does not matter. (Except perhaps to a management which, ideally, demands a sense of dedication. For in its view to be a BBC newsman is not to be *any* newsman.) It is not, of course, necessary to feel committed in order to do the right thing in terms of editorial policy. And, if the import of my account is accepted, it is not true that if members of the News Division were working for other organizations (with the possible exception of ITN) that they would produce this particular kind of news.

This is recognized by those most aware of the News Division's impact on their professional identities. They are able to point to a process of socialization into a definite and desired mould. One chief sub in Radio News put it this way:

> You're aware of entering a tradition with certain ideas about good taste. You do think the same way although all individuals are tackling their bits of copy separately.

A senior duty editor in Radio said the BBC attracted 'politically neutral people' and that 'you couldn't do the job otherwise'. Another sub-editor said that there were no basic ideological problems 'Because people self-select themselves for work in the BBC. You know the things the BBC does by having listened to it.' Both these explanations are recognizable as based on 'anticipatory socialization'.

There is also a kind of cynicism about newsmen which in the context of the BBC partly functions as a substitute for commitment. They've seen too much, heard too much, watched too many people fitting their performances to suit microphone and camera. To talk of commitment is something which is not quite consonant with this self-image.

To see politicians as they really are, as performers and manipulators, introduces a dissonance between *actual* politics and the *ideal* politics of a 'national genius' kind mentioned in the quotation cited earlier. This reinforces an existing sense of detachment from the unpleasant world of the greasy pole. This is, in turn, reinforced by being the only way in which the News is *allowed* to cope with it.

Paler versions of commitment focus on matters which are not ideologically central. For example, BBC newsmen are on the Corporation's staff, which is significant as it means they are working in what is a relatively safe haven, sheltered from the storms which currently afflict British journalism. In a very basic way, some point to economic security as the foundation-stone of loyalty. In particular, this was a point made by journalists recruited from Fleet Street, and the following remarks typify this view:

It's cosy and secure, with no fears about redundancy like Fleet Street. The BBC will keep going, like the government.

I had two newspapers fold under me – the *Daily Graphic* and the *Sunday Dispatch* at the age of 36; so I decided this was the time to find an organization which was not going to die under me. So . . . I joined the BBC.

Others focus on the paternalism of the BBC or some of the more obvious features of its organizational style. Thus, for example, of newsmen who had come in from Fleet Street, one observed that the BBC 'was like an insurance office, while the Street's more like a bookie's'. Another noted 'It's a soft job – genteel. I'd never seen a newsroom with carpets before.' Reporters tended to see the Corporation as status-conferring. To work for BBC News meant that you went 'for the big stories'. This is quite apparent in the following quotations from interviews with reporters:

We don't go chasing after vicars who've run off with choir boys. It's only big stories which demand the reporter's presence in TV terms.

It's an exaggeration, but your first story is the death of the prime minister or something, rather than the flower show.

The difference between radio and newspapers is that with a newspaper you've got to *fill* it with something. So you get lumbered with trivia. Here the story is worth doing. It's either newsworthy or significant in its own way. I've talked to more Cabinet ministers and Opposition leaders in seven months than I did in seven years at the *Mail*. You get fed up of ladies with pet dogs who're in trouble with their landlords.

Despite the fact that many played down the idea of commitment, it is clear that to survive in BBC News one needs more of an attachment to prevalent notions of corporate professionalism than gratitude for a job, or a vague awareness that the BBC is somehow big and important. To make the job into a career, that is, to move one step beyond survival, it is important to make the right noises and ultimately to entertain the right beliefs. Tom Burns, writing about the BBC in general almost a decade and a half ago, noted that the Corporation's 'management is everywhere conscious of the need to involve people in their work over and above the measure of their contractual engagement'.[42]

This seems just as true today. Although without doubt, since the sixties the idea of being a dedicated Corporation man may be both less fashionable and more ambiguous in character.

FRONT MEN

> Within the walls of a social establishment we find a team of performers who co-operate to present to an audience a given definition of the situation . . . We often find a division into back region, where the performance is prepared, and front region, where the performance is presented.
>
> (Erving Goffman)[43]

> Presenters, commentators, news correspondents, current affairs reporters and newsreaders have one thing in common. They are all in various ways the voice of the BBC. Within the BBC the differences between their roles are well understood, but to many of the audience these distinctions have little meaning – as can be illustrated by the fact that letter writers often describe William Hardcastle as a newsreader. *Each of them, for as long as he is on the screen or behind the microphone, is the BBC.*
>
> (*Principles and Practice*)[44]

Performances by news personnel are given in the context of a production so styled as to seem an impersonal and neutral recitation of the facts. The newsreader binds the programme together with his narrative, reports from the correspondents and reporters are presented as evidence about the real world, and are grounded in that world by supporting techniques such as actuality film or sound. The intention is to provide a news service which is perceived as impartial and authoritative by the bulk of its audience.

Current practice at the BBC preserves the anonymity of the processors. Unlike their current affairs and documentary counterparts they remain uncredited at the end of the programme. Although in autumn 1976 ITN began to credit the studio director and programme editor, for the BBC, the news is still not any man's news. The absence of credits confers an image of consistency. In terms of Goffman's observation, cited above, news production is so organized that the only visible vehicles of corporate integrity are the News Division's front men, the newsreaders and reporting staff who appear in sound and vision.

The BBC has always been concerned about how its personnel perform on the air. Krishan Kumar has convincingly argued that of late professional broadcasters have become even more important. He notes the tension between the BBC's standing as an 'independent' and distinctive institution in the national culture and the constant pressure for control from the state. Kumar argues that the growth and ascendancy of news and current affairs programming and the attendant dangers for autonomy, have forced the BBC to adopt a new strategy for survival. This originated in the early 1960s. Unlike the Reithian BBC the contemporary Corporation cannot seek to lead in times when to have an explicit sense of direction must be perilous. Thus, its current conception of broadcasting is one of 'the BBC as middleman, as honest broker, as manager and impresario. And one of the most important consequences has been a heightening of the significance of the professional broadcaster. . . . It is in their stance, through their style and presentation, that the BBC tries to keep its autonomy and ward off clutching embraces from all around.'[45]

The people who mediate the news and chair current affairs programmes have to be fashioned in the Corporation's image of itself as *above* the things that it reports. This is the BBC's *Luftmensch* ideology in action.

The newsreader, for long the object of a veritable cult of personality in the press is conceived of as incarnating the integrity and authoritativeness of the BBC's news output. One newsreader summed up the necessary style in response to a question:

P.S.: Presumably you have strong beliefs about various issues, and that some things are right or wrong? You nevertheless have to suppress these feelings. How do you cope with this sort of thing?

Television Newsreader: You don't show anything. You learn early on that if you're going to be accurate there's no room for allowing personal feelings to come into it. You tend not to take sides on major issues *either publicly or privately*. You get used to this. I've found no conflict. You have to keep a very high standard: you mustn't become associated with a given side,

The quotation again illustrates the way in which the demands made by the Corporation may come to dominate the individual's private life. It fully affirms the view that in order to be a credible performer one should not harbour any personal commitments. One radio newsreader felt he bore the Corporation's integrity in his person to such an extent that he argued it was illegitimate for him to have *any* political involvement or opinion 'outside'. And this is by no means an isolated example.

It is not surprising, moreover, that newsreaders should cease to distinguish between their public and private selves, for they would seem often to play an intimate part in many people's everyday lives, and it is hard for them to ignore this. One wartime newsreader has written: 'Thousands came to look upon us as belonging to the family, and wrote that they always answered aloud our final "Good night".'[46] This intimacy can, on occasion, assume strange characteristics. A television newsreader remarked in the newsroom: 'There's some nut who's convinced I can see what's in her living room. She wrote me a letter the other day asking whether I liked her new curtains and underwear.'

As Robin Day has pointed out, the emergence of ITN in 1955 introduced for the first time a conception of the news 'anchorman' as journalist rather than as 'a human reading machine, or a television equivalent of the printing press'.[47] But despite the difference of style, ITN shared the BBC's aim of winning confidence through authoritativeness.

BBC newsreaders tend still to have a somewhat traditional image – to be polished performers first and foremost. Although, from November 1972 to March 1976, the *Nine O'Clock News* was jointly presented by a former reporter and newsreader working in tandem, and for some time the BBC-2 news programmes tended to use former, and sometimes active, reporters as presenters. The public image of the BBC newsreader is crucial as a form of product identification, given competition with ITN.

Not surprisingly, therefore, the BBC's audience research has shown considerable concern with the public's image of newsreaders and presenters. Findings indicate a very high rate of recognition among the general public for both BBC and ITN newsreaders (the latter were included in the surveys) 'and the highest number of attributions of those adjectives which [there can be little doubt] were used in a complimentary sense'.

Similar concern is evident concerning perceptions of reporters' performances. A piece of research on thirty-three front men of various kinds reported that 'the adjective "biased" was not widely attributed to *any* of the individuals' and 'that "reliable" was commonly regarded as an attribute of most of the thirty-three individuals'.[48]

Naturally, reporters are very aware of their responsibility for managing the Corporation's image in their relationships with sources. By way of illustration one might note the views of one newsman who had reported or presented news for the BBC for the best part of two decades. He observed that when he was filming with a camera crew he always felt as though: 'I'm the nearest most people get to meeting the BBC. They'll probably never meet another BBC-man in their lives, so it's very important to make the right impression.'

One could hear many echoes of this view. Thus, the Economics Correspondent said, 'Being a BBC correspondent produces certain responses in people. I suppose it's bound to make you think of yourself as a BBC person.' Here, there is a sense of conforming to public expectations, of a specific persona which is necessary in social interaction. Others stressed that appropriate conduct was inculcated from the very beginning of their association with the Corporation. A news trainee while on reporting practice spoke of how 'when you're out and about there's some stress laid on the fact you're representing the BBC'.

In fact, in the corporate view, captured in the quotation from *Principles and Practice* at the head of this section, performers not only represent the BBC, but rather *are* the BBC for the duration of their performances. To establish the authoritativeness and impartiality of the Corporation's 'own men' in the public mind is a continuing managerial preoccupation. This goal emerged with considerable clarity, for example, during an interview with the Managing Editor, News. During the course of this he argued that sophisticated members of the public would get to know the work of foreign and home correspondents through specialized programmes such as *From Our Own Correspondent* and *In Britain Now*, and their television equivalents. On the basis of viewing or listening to more extended reports, and of accepting their authority, members of the audience would come to 'accept the snappy one-and-a-half-minute pieces in which seemingly off-the-cuff judgements are made'.

CONCLUSION

The concept of impartiality summarizes the practical and cognitive limits faced by the BBC's personnel in producing news and current affairs programmes.

Officially, the BBC's news output is value-free, which means that those who produce it, in their capacities as producers must somehow appear to be free from the influence of values concerning matters in dispute. This myth of value-freedom is essential for public consumption, and believed in by those who propagate it. Value-freedom, objectivity, impartiality are essential validating ideas for broadcast news production, which is perpetually exposed to critical appraisal. Such ideas have the same rhetorical function for news as they have had for sociology in its long-standing attempt to sell itself as a science.

The BBC's official stance, therefore, is that it practices 'neutral' journalism. This view is accepted in the Corporation as the most appropriate one (given the BBC's public service mission) and also more pragmatically recognized as the only possible one (given the actual socio-political constraints). As the role of broadcast news is therefore circumscribed, alternative postures of investigation or committed reporting are simply ruled out.

Such anchorage in the *status quo* makes imperative the need for the myth of a collective of neutral producers. Deviance from the model of professional impartiality poses a problem for the Corporation. When a newsman declares his convictions in some manner – even though these may be inside the political mainstream, and usually are – this contradicts the myth of neutrality. To have individuals with identifiable political postures in the Corporation gives outsiders a way of challenging the myth of neutrality, and opens the way to general criticisms of bias.

This chapter has illustrated the internal mediation of the practice of impartiality through the creation of a desired identity for newsmen, to which all, in different ways, conform. At its most basic, to adhere to this model is, as one newsman put it, 'a condition of employment'. In its fully developed form what it means is that some newsmen acquire what is virtually a sense of vocation.

Empirically, newsmen act impartially to their own satisfaction through achieving balance in the construction of stories. In this respect, impartiality is the internal label for the product of a set of organizational practices. To be impartial in this way, though it is routinized, does require continual personal effort. From the evidence, it is clear that some newsmen have potentially awkward views, although being in general well socialized they rarely allow these to surface at work. A neutral style is the corporately acceptable one, and it is this style which also suffuses the news output. The BBC needs its personnel to be socially perceived as credible neutral mediators and the front men bear this image in the context of a production whose whole tone is that it is giving us 'the facts' rather than articulating a perspective within which fact and value are inextricably interwoven.

8
The reporting of Northern Ireland

You operate within the going establishment view. You don't have to
be on the government of the day's side, but firmly on the side of the
law of the land. The Army's more okay than the IRA.

(Television Newsman)

In recent years, the social and political conflict in Northern Ireland
has illustrated the power of the state to circumscribe the broadcast
media's coverage of events, issues and points of view there. This has
been handled not through overt censorship, but rather through a
mediated intervention, in which spokesmen in the sphere of politics
have defined the permissible limits, and these conceptual orientations
have been picked up and reproduced within the media. The internal
mediation of the boundaries of the permissible has taken place pre-
eminently through a tightening of editorial controls within the
broadcasting organizations. In late 1971 and early 1972 some news
and current affairs broadcasters protested that censorship was
taking place. The debate which then arose rapidly subsided, and
coverage of Northern Ireland entered a routinely constrained phase.
In early 1977, the question of state control of Northern Ireland
coverage flickered briefly into life again.

In the previous chapter, it was shown how the concept of impartiality, and its related operational practices, are worked out
within a framework of socially endowed assumptions about consensus politics, national community and the parliamentary form of
conflict-resolution. The situation in Northern Ireland has been
defined in ways which take it out of the boundaries of consensus
politics. The dominant framework of analysis is one which makes
'law and order', 'violence' and 'terrorism' its key analytical terms.

The British state is not a neutral arbiter of events in Northern
Ireland, but rather, through its administrative apparatus and security
forces, it is a direct party to the conflict there, and its principal
official enemy is the Provisional IRA. This has entailed difficulties for
the broadcasting media, as their place in the political domain
constrains them into taking a patriotic stance and supporting the
'national interest'. 'Extremist' violence, therefore, becomes the
object of moral repugnance, whereas the legitimate violence of the
security forces is handled within a framework which emphasizes its
regrettable necessity.

Northern Ireland's crisis is not one which can anyway be handled in terms of consensus politics. Where, to put it in over-simple terms, one substantial group is for the Crown and the maintenance of links with the rest of the United Kingdom, and another for an all-Ireland Republic, no consensual assumptions about a single community of interests may be made. For broadcasting to be genuinely impartial, it would have to pose questions seriously and continuously about the persistence of British rule in one part of the United Kingdom. And this would entail consideration of the political plans of the two IRA factions.

I shall not attempt to explore the complexities of Northern Irish politics, but only some of the ways in which they have affected broadcasting's reporting of them. Fieldwork for this book began in February 1972, at a moment when the BBC and commercial television had just been subjected to extreme pressure from the British Government to be more responsible in their coverage of Northern Ireland. My first day of fieldwork, at Radio News, was on Wednesday, 2nd February, a day on which the funerals of thirteen people shot by British troops on 'Bloody Sunday' in Londonderry were being held. The BBC had just emerged from a severe pummelling over its screening of a programme entitled *The Question of Ulster* (which is discussed below), and there was an air of tension in the newsroom, and among news executives. One could not be unaware, then, as later, that Northern Ireland raised central questions of editorial policy and control.

This theme was difficult to investigate, however, in the earlier stage of research, 1972–73, when there was great reticence on the part of newsmen and executives concerning the BBC's policy on Northern Ireland. It was hard to discuss it in a way which went beyond the BBC's official positions and which gave much critical insight into the actual operation of the policy. During the next major phase of fieldwork, in 1975–76, the issue was no longer a hot one, although it was still problematical. The system of editorial control had been stabilized, and criticism was now muted. Northern Ireland had become a routine story. Tragic certainly, but now somewhat boring. The sense of crisis encountered earlier was now absent and, indeed, many newsmen wondered why I should want to discuss the matter. Although this time the official rationalizations and explanations of BBC practice were once again forthcoming, more were prepared to talk about specific incidents which troubled them, and which they saw as raising questions about the reality of the BBC's independence from the state.

There are definite phases in the history of the BBC's Northern Ireland coverage. Broadly speaking, until 1968 the situation in the

Province was ignored by the national BBC, as indeed it was by all the other British news media. Next, as the civil rights campaign got off the ground with violent clashes between Catholics and Protestants, and the involvement of the police, the attention both of British and other news media became focused on Northern Ireland. At this time the BBC built up its resources there, and operated a rota system for television and radio personnel covering the 'Troubles'. More recently, since 1975 especially, news coverage has been largely handled by the regional BBC, material being sent over to London in packages for networking, and the scope of coverage has diminished. These phases need to be considered more closely.

DEVELOPMENTS UNTIL 1972

Until 1959 British broadcasting in Northern Ireland was entirely in the hands of the BBC. In that year ITV finally reached the Province in the shape of Ulster Television (UTV). The creation of Northern Ireland by Act of Parliament in 1920 instituted a partition which has since remained a central issue in Irish political life. Broadcasting came to the new Protestant-dominated statelet in 1924. From the first, as indicated by the testimony of Sir Gerald Beadle, formerly Director of BBC Television, the BBC's hierarchy was tied into the sectarian regime:

> mine was a task of consolidation, which meant building the BBC into the lives of the people of the province and making it one of their public institutions. . . . I was invited to become a member of the Ulster Club; the Governor, the Duke of Abercorn, was immensely helpful and friendly, and Lord Craigavon, the Prime Minister, was a keen supporter of our work. In effect I was made a member of the Establishment of a province which has most of the paraphernalia of a sovereign state and a population no bigger than a moderate sized English city.[1]

Such candour would have been unwelcome in 1969 (Sir Gerald was writing in 1963) when the links between the Northern Ireland BBC and the Unionist establishment were coming under closer scrutiny. The BBC from the first was subjected to pressure from the Unionists to broadcast in a manner which supported the *status quo*. It was considered disloyal to raise the question of the border's permanence, and so, effectively, one central strand of local politics was excluded from discussion.

Anthony Smith has provided the most detailed account to date of the BBC's involvement in Northern Ireland politics. In 1926, he notes, there were protests from Unionists when the BBC, then under Beadle, celebrated St Patrick's Day. In the 1930s and 1940s, when G. L. Marshall was Director, Northern Ireland, the policy was 'to keep an iron grip on all local news and allow nothing to go out which suggested that anything in Northern Ireland could or would ever change'. During this period, and this was to prove of much importance, the powers of the chief BBC official in Belfast were established so that 'he came to act as a kind of censor over the whole of the BBC's output from London (concerning Irish matters) both in its domestic and overseas services, and naturally this tended to to give a Unionist tinge to anything that came out'.[2]

Cathcart too has argued that BBC broadcasting was generally supportive of the Unionist regime, and that it 'effectively ignored the existence of the Catholic community and the nationalist opposition'. He quotes the Controller, BBC Northern Ireland as saying, in 1947, that 'BBC programme policy in Northern Ireland is not to admit any attack on the constitutional position of Northern Ireland'.[3]

After the Second World War, there was some liberalization of policy when Roman Catholics began to be represented on the Northern Ireland BBC's religious advisory committee and its regional council. During the 1950s there were a 'number of spectacular contests', as Smith puts it, between Lord Brookeborough, the Northern Ireland premier, and the regional BBC. One well-known incident concerned a *Tonight* programme dealing with the Border question, another an interview with the actress Siobhan McKenna in which she expressed sympathy for IRA internees in the Republic. Both items were dropped in Northern Ireland.[4]

The coming of commercial television in 1959 brought some change of approach. As it had an audience-seeking rationale in order to attract advertising, it could not, despite its Unionist ownership, afford to alienate one entire segment of the public. UTV was also constrained by the Television Act of 1954, and later that of 1964, to pursue a balanced and impartial approach. And in its early years particularly it moved ahead of the BBC, giving Republican views some play in the news programmes it began to produce after 1961. The liberalization of commercial television pushed the BBC in the same direction. A new Controller, Northern Ireland, Waldo Maguire, took over in 1966. He had previously edited Television News in London and began to extend more help to visiting reporters from London.

Ironically, the process of easing controls in Northern Ireland was developing just prior to the outbreak of the violent social conflict which made the Province such a newsworthy location. Violence has been the dominant theme of news from the Province since then, as Philip Elliott has pointed out in a recent analysis of media coverage.[5]

For the BBC, as for ITV, confronting the problems of reporting civil disorder was to produce a progressive tightening of editorial control. Because it was his patch, and because of the precedents, the role of Controller, Northern Ireland, came into greater prominence as news coverage increased. Smith remarks: 'as the political crisis deepened, reporters from news and current affairs, sound and vision, working out of London were expected to work from his office under a high degree of supervision'.[6] The BBC's policy is to transmit all programmes nationally if it can. It therefore sought not to produce material for the UK which was so inflammatory that the Controller in Northern Ireland decided that the region ought to opt out. In effect, editorial control over Irish matters moved upwards from the programme level to that of the Controller. Editors and producers were encouraged not to create situations where 'opt outs' became necessary. Although they could appeal against the Controller to the DG or ENCA concerning Northern Ireland, this was a major step, challenging the judgement of a very senior BBC official.

According to Desmond Taylor, a turning point in the BBC's coverage came in mid-August 1969. At this time the 'public order' question became most pressing:

> We managed without too much trouble until enraged mobs were on the streets, and the serious killings started. Then a new and frightening consideration made itself plain: what if our broad-casting what we did was to increase the killing? There was no existing case law to go on, so a special meeting of senior news and current affairs staff was called. . . . In the end we agreed to use reported speech rather than actuality for statements of sectarian opinion. The next day the Army moved in.[7]

This initial limitation on the use of 'sectarian voices' lasted a day and a half.[8] The following year, BBC Northern Ireland opted out of a *Panorama* report thought likely to provoke violence.

During the course of 1971, the BBC began to develop in greater detail policy guidelines for dealing with conflict in Northern Ireland. By this time British troops, who had for a while been welcomed by the Northern Ireland Catholics, were regarded by them as the arm of the Unionist regime. Another significant development had been the entry of the IRA into conflict with the British army in 1970. The IRA (Provisionals and Officials alike) had become the primary 'enemy' in Northern Ireland. It is in this light that one should consider this passage in *Principles and Practice in News and Current Affairs*:

In February 1971 the BBC considered and rejected a suggestion that there should be total ban in interviews with *Republican extremists* in Northern Ireland. But the present Director-General, and his Editor, News and Current Affairs (then Mr Crawley), insisted that such interviews should only be filmed and transmitted after the most serious consideration, and that the BBC *should be seen to be clearly opposed to the indiscriminate methods of the extremists.*[9]

The notion of a principal enemy is embodied in this memorandum. It is not without significance that in a document issued for guidance *Republican* extremists alone are singled out. There is no mention of Unionist extremism – already well-established by that time in the shape of the UVF, formed in 1966. This group, declared illegal in that year, pursued a campaign of violence against civil rights activists, and was in direct conflict with British troops until 1970.

The BBC's position on Northern Ireland coverage continued to be worked out during the course of 1971, and involved the highest managerial and editorial levels of the Corporation. Lord Hill has noted that the Board of Governors 'discussed some aspect of programmes about this unhappy province at almost every meeting'.[10]

The next major developments occurred after the introduction of internment without trial for IRA suspects by the Northern Ireland government. A series of News and Current Affairs minutes were leaked to *Private Eye* which printed extracts from them.[11] These give a picture of successive tightenings of control. A meeting on 13 August 1971, four days after the introduction of internment, notes the desire of the Controller, Northern Ireland, that 'the controversial broadcasting rule – that each item or programme should be self-balancing – should be reintroduced'. There was resistance from several editors to the idea of *24 Hours* doing an in-depth programme on the IRA. There was also a complaint from the Editor, Television News (foreshadowing protests), that 'Reporters in Northern Ireland were saying it was now difficult to take statements by army PR at their face value'. These several themes were pointers to the future approach of more obviously balanced (i.e. cautious) coverage, of less substantial investigative reporting, and of mounting frustration on the part of some producers and reporters at 'taking the army line'.

On 3 September, a press conference featuring Joe Cahill, an IRA leader, on *The World at One* was criticized for being 'broadcast in the aftermath of the lunchtime bombings'. This was the last occasion on which an 'IRA voice' was broadcast in 1971. On 10 September *24 Hours* was criticized for interviewing the Irish Prime Minister, Mr Lynch, without balancing the interview with a Unionist government speaker. The Director-General is quoted on this occasion as saying he was aware that 'the editorial staff did not relish being interfered with'. He was responding to an observation by the Editors of Radio News and Radio Current Affairs that 'one risked creating an atmosphere in which editors would be so inhibited that they would cease to be able to make sensible decisions about stories concerning Northern Ireland'. The Editor, Current Affairs Promotions, said at this meeting that 'there was a suspicion, no doubt quite unjustified, that an element of censorship was coming into play'. This was to prove prophetic, given the accusations of censorship levelled later in the year.

On 17 September, the minutes noted a further criticism of *24 Hours* for interviewing Mr Lynch without balancing. By 22 October, when the BBC came to examine allegations of torture against people detained under the internment provisions, the need for balance in each programme had become a firm dogma. The minutes noted that 'ENCA had been glad to see that editors and producers had observed the policy of providing immediate balance in all current affairs items when contentious material had been sought out by the BBC, just as Controller, Northern Ireland, had recommended in the previous spate of allegations'.

In October 1971, however, it was not the BBC alone which was being cautious. In that month, the ITA banned the screening of a documentary on Irish politics called *South of the Border*. Since the proposed programme, made by Granada TV's *World in Action* team, contained footage of interviews with IRA leaders (although these were balanced by critics of their views) it was judged sensitive by the ITA. The ITA did not see the documentary and ignored the advice of its Northern Ireland Regional Officer that it should be shown. Lord Aylestone, the ITA's Chairman and a former Labour Party chief whip, was reported as saying the programme was 'aiding and abetting the enemy'.[12]

Also of considerable significance was a speech by Mr Christopher Chataway, the Minister of Posts and Telecommunications (then accountable to Parliament for broadcasting), which was delivered on 20 November. In this speech, Chataway said that broadcasters were not required to strike an even balance between the IRA and the Ulster government, or between the army and the 'terrorists'. The broadcasting authorities were urged to exercise their editorial judgement 'within the context of the values and the objectives of the society they are there to serve'. This was a clear reminder that broadcasting stood within the consensus, and that the IRA were outside the bounds of toleration. Chataway went on to say: 'Nobody wants propaganda substituted for truthful reporting. At the other extreme, it would be just as obnoxious to have the soldier and murderer treated like the employer and the trade unionist – as if they were moral equals.'[13]

This statement was a dispensation from the normal rules of balance. More truly, it was a clear warning that they should be suspended. If it was intended to affect the output of the BBC it came late. Within the BBC it had already been decided to forbid interviews with any member of the IRA without permission from the Director-General, and this had not been granted since April 1971. On 23 November, just after Chataway's speech, Lord Hill wrote to Mr Maudling, the Home Secretary, in terms which accorded with the state's definition of the situation:

> We see it as our over-riding responsibility to report the scene as it is, in all its tragedy, to all the people of the United Kingdom. We do not side with the Catholics or the Protestants. The BBC and its staff abhor the terrorism of the IRA and report their campaign of murder with revulsion. . . .
>
> In short, as between the government and the opposition, as between the two communities in Northern Ireland, the BBC has a duty to be impartial no less than in the rest of the United Kingdom. But, as between the British Army and the gunmen the BBC is not and cannot be impartial.[14]

Hill also defended the BBC's editorial practice to Mr Maudling, informing him that the 'BBC already undertakes a scrupulous editorial watch on all levels'. In his book, Hill argues that the abandonment of impartiality was 'a fairly self-evident proposition for anyone with a sense of responsibility'. He goes on to advance an argument which is strikingly akin to that of Reith's at the time of the General Strike: 'What they [the BBC's critics] don't seem to see is that we are fighting a battle against censorship, control, regulation, intervention from outside. The claim of programme makers in news, current affairs or in any other field that they should decide what goes on the screen or emerges from the microphone without guidance or instruction from above, is just the sort of claim that brings external control nearer.'[15]

Hill's argument, advanced by other top BBC men, was that if the BBC did not limit its coverage (in effect, censor itself) then this would provoke outside intervention. By being 'responsible', therefore, the BBC (and the ITA) were able to sustain their formal independence. While Hill may have been satisfied that responsibility was *not* censorship, this was not the case with all those working in news and current affairs departments in the BBC and ITV.

On 22 November a well-attended meeting of media people con-cerned with Northern Ireland coverage met at the Institute of Contemporary Arts in London to protest against the increasing closeness of editorial control. From reports of this meeting it would seem that the restrictions were felt more acutely by those working in the current affairs fields than those working in 'hard' news.[16] This is not surprising as news attends to the immediate, the instant facts about the situation, whereas current affairs has more of a contextual-izing drive, putting more effort into researching background and trying to provide a perspective, an approach more prone to ask awkward questions, and therefore the more apt to be discouraged in an atmosphere of caution.

An anonymous article in the *New Statesman* the following month gave detailed instances of censored stories, some of which had been mentioned at the ICA meeting. The article argued that 'Lord Hill's questionable principle of support for the army against "the gun-men" has degenerated into support for the army against the minority; and for the representatives of the majority against the representatives of the minority'.[17]

These themes were also taken up in the shape of a lengthy letter to Lord Hill and Lord Aylestone from the Federation of Broad-casting Unions (FBU) disclosed in *Open Secret*, the journal of the short-lived Free Communications Group. In its general argument, the letter challenged Hill's view that intensified control led only to greater responsibility:

> The BBC's interpretation of its function in regard to Northern Ireland leads to distortion rather than to censorship. However, from evidence we accept from our members it is clear that the checks and balances introduced to underpin this interpretation are becoming as effective as censorship, probably more effective because they are not much known outside the circles immediately involved, are superficially not more than an intensification of normal safeguards, and are too vague and distant a target for public criticism.[18]

The FBU letter continued by arguing that the BBC erred in favour of the established order in Ulster, and that it assumed a community in which violence would be universally deprecated. It claimed that broadcasting staff were not supported in clashes with authority, and sought assurances that those who disagreed with the news judgements of senior editors would not be adversely affected, given evidence of a blacklist against certain reporters. Most significant ideologically was the appeal to principle made in the letter which drew on the positive liberalism of the BBC's ideal of commitment to impartiality. The move away from this ideal was condemned:

> Its [the BBC's] contribution is to describe it [the crisis] so well that everyone who has any responsibility for solving it fully understands its causes, course, and potentialities.[19]

In spirit this recalls the remarks made by Sir Charles Curran in his elaboration of the BBC's information policy in 'a mature democracy'. It met with little constructive response. Hill would not discuss the letter because one of the FBU unions, the ACTT, was not recognized by the BBC. Aylestone considered the ITA to be 'without fault or blemish'.

Much attention was also given at the ICA meeting to the rules which inhibited reporting. These had been fully worked out during 1971, and by May 1972 appeared in codified form in the revised version of the BBC's *News Guide*. It is a measure of the importance of the Northern Ireland situation that its handling should warrant, for the first time, a section of its own in the *Guide*. In the previous edition, that of 1967, Northern Ireland did not figure at all. The rules are as follows:

1. News staff sent to Northern Ireland work through Controller Northern Ireland and News Editor Northern Ireland; they must be consulted.
2. No news agency report from Northern Ireland should be used without checking with Belfast newsroom first.
3. The IRA must not be interviewed without prior authority from ENCA. There can be no question of doing the interview first and seeking permission for broadcast afterwards.
4. Recordings of broadcasts by illegal radios must not be used without reference to ENCA. (This applies to any illegal radio, not just those in Northern Ireland.)
5. We should not report bomb scares concerning BBC buildings for the obvious reason that such reports would encourage hoaxers or people who wished to disrupt BBC output. (This too does not apply only to Northern Ireland.)[20]

Rules 1 to 4 set Northern Ireland coverage into a special category, one in which reference upwards is a *routine* part of news producing practice. There is no other area of output which has similar constraints. Rule 1 establishes the key role of the controllers on the spot for newsmen working in Northern Ireland. The *New Statesman* article described the hampering effects of this rule:

Any current affairs editor who wants to do an item on Northern Ireland now has to submit the idea both to the News Editor in Belfast and the Editors of Current Affairs for television or radio in London. On approval, the items are recorded and then once again submitted for inspection to London and Belfast, and frequently as well to the Editor of News and Current Affairs for final approbation.[21]

By the beginning of 1972, however, the argument about the impact of the BBC's editorial system on reporting had been overshadowed by a blatant attempt at intervention by the government in the BBC's programming. This event is a key one in the history of the BBC's coverage of Northern Ireland, because the BBC has argued that its resistance to pressure on that occasion proved its independence from the State. The row concerned a television programme, *The Question of Ulster*, which the then Conservative government pressured the BBC not to screen. The issue was a major controversy about broadcasting's relationship to the state. It arose at a time when the BBC, through Lord Hill's letter of November 1971, had just made clear its unequivocal support of the security forces' efforts in Northern Ireland.

At the beginning of December 1971, however, the BBC's proposal to mount a two-and-a-half-hour current affairs programme on the Irish problem caused a good deal of indignation in Conservative and Unionist circles. The programme was variously termed a 'tribunal' or 'inquisition' and modelled on the US Senate hearings; it was to take place under a 'neutral and judicial president'. One could read this entire exercise as an attempt to seek out the 'rational middle ground' in Northern Ireland politics. In the words of Desmond Taylor, the BBC's Editor, News and Current Affairs: 'It was designed to give the British public a very cool look at what the various parties in the Ulster dispute were saying about how to end the violence in Northern Ireland.'[22]

The programme was to consist of a forum of eight politicians, drawn 'from a very wide spectrum of Irish views', each of whom was to be questioned by the 'tribunal' of three eminent establishment figures, Lord Devlin, Lord Caradon and Sir John Foster. The British government were also to contribute their views, and a minister from the Northern Ireland Parliament at Stormont was to be one of the eight Irish politicians. In the words of Lord Hill, who, as the BBC's Chairman at the time, was at the centre of the row, 'There would then be eight Irish speakers – two from the Republic and the rest from Ulster, giving four each to these antitheses;

Protestant/Catholic; Loyalist/Republican; Right/Left; Moderate/ Extreme'.[23]

On 9 December 1971, Mr Brian Faulkner, then Northern Ireland premier, expressed reservations about the format and the idea itself. Next, Mr Maudling, the Home Secretary, became involved, and sent for Hill, who was accompanied to a meeting by the BBC's Director-General, Charles Curran. According to Hill's account, Maudling described the programme as 'potentially dangerous, quite apart from the view that it had a built-in bias. Of the eight Irish participants in the main part of the programme, only one would represent the Ulster Unionists, with seven expressing dissenting views. Only one favoured internment.' This discussion with Maudling, says Hill, resulted in a 'better' reflection of the 'special position of the majority party in Ulster'.[24] But even this concession to Conservative pressure to restructure the programme proved unsatisfactory.

The next step came with a letter from Maudling to Hill which said that 'the programme in the form in which it had been devised could do no good, and could do serious harm'.[25] The BBC was subjected to a campaign of hostility from the government, Tory backbenchers, and *The Daily Telegraph*. However, it justified its persistence with the programme in terms of a statement of the ideals of impartiality and balance:

> The basic aim is not to reach conclusions but to place before the British public fairly and fully the issues in dispute and the conflicting views on the various possible solutions. The BBC believes such a programme to be in the public interest, and that the suppression of views, however unpopular, would be both unwise and dangerous.[26]

It should be recalled, however, that in the Hill letter of November 1971, the BBC accepted limitations on the degree of impartiality with which it could now present views emanating from the IRA. No representative of the IRA appeared in the programme. Further, the programme was boycotted by Maudling and Faulkner, who tried out what Hill called the 'technique of veto by abstention'. To counter this, however, the BBC used filmed extracts of interviews and speeches to flesh out their positions.

The importance of the programme, and the eventual screening, should not be underestimated, for the incident is seen as one which established the BBC's independence over Northern Ireland coverage. There was a high investment of prestige in the programme: Hill notes how the most senior levels of the BBC were involved in the arrangements, which is indicative of the tightness of editorial control.[27] It was impossible for the BBC not to resist such overt and dramatic pressure, for it would have lost credibility quite irretrievably. That it did pose a crisis internally cannot be doubted. Desmond Taylor observed 'this programme was the subject of the most sustained attempt to keep it off the air that any of us had ever experienced'.[28] John Crawley, then in the top post of Chief Assistant to the Director General, and therefore privy to the dealings between the Conservative government and the Corporation, subsequently wrote of the controversy:

> since the matter was one of high policy, in which lives were at stake, why did the Home Secretary not seek to invoke the right of veto, which is clearly vested in the Government? There is evidence that he gave some consideration to the possibility of doing so. Yet he stopped short of that sanction, limiting himself to putting public pressure on the BBC more heavily than it has ever been done before. . . . It is to be supposed that what stayed the hand of the Prime Minister on various occasions was the realization that once the veto has been used, the independence of the BBC or ITV has gone for ever.[29]

Crawley goes on to observe that the day before the programme was broadcast the Home Secretary took the unprecedented step of sending the BBC's Chairman an open letter. The message from this account, as from the others, is clear: *The Question of Ulster* is seen as a firm vindication of the BBC's refusal to knuckle under. It was clear from interviews with the Editor, News and Current Affairs, and his Chief Assistant that broadcasting the programme was seen as being almost as important as the BBC's stance during Suez. Sir Charles Curran described it as 'the central example in my time of the BBC's insistence on editorial independence'.[30] In a similar vein, in a lunchtime lecture, the Editor, News and Current Affairs, talked of the controversy as a turning point: 'Complaints continued, but in diminishing volume and eventually died away.'[31] His Chief Assistant put a gloss on this: 'We were told of a horrible stinging nettle. We grasped it, and found it didn't sting at all. After the programme we became more confident.' In the BBC, the fact that the programme did not cause wholesale disturbances is seen, quite rightly, as giving the lie to Maudling's view that it could only have devastating consequences.

The ideological importance of *The Question of Ulster* is therefore of prime importance. That the BBC did not bow to pressure by axing the programme is incontrovertible. But whether one ought to accept its own account of the significance of the event is another matter. The BBC presents its resistance on that occasion as a paradigm instance of its relations with the government.

More important than this, it seems, is to scrutinize the long-term effect on daily news and current affairs coverage of an acceptance of the state's definition of the situation, and the waiving of impartiality in Northern Ireland coverage. This has involved defining some views as illegitimate, which, coupled with an ahistorical approach concentrating on violence, has made much reporting from Ireland largely incomprehensible. It is this tendency which is over-shadowed by a concentration on that one, dramatic occasion of successful resistance in 1972, as will be argued later.

A plausible interpretation of why the government did not step in is that it probably concluded that to have the BBC (and ITV) producing a *generally* constrained coverage – though certainly not one which was externally censored – far outweighed the immediate irritation caused by the BBC on this one occasion. Why Maudling should have openly pushed things so far is open to conjecture (although he was apparently under considerable right-wing pressure), but what remained intact, and would have otherwise been threatened, was the legitimating ideology of BBC 'independence'. This had already been circumscribed by Chataway's prescription, and by Hill's acceptance of it. But this constraint was considerably different from the government actually *openly* saying the BBC *must* follow a certain line in its reporting. The style of the thing – getting the BBC to act 'responsibly' on its own initiative – bespeaks a much more subtle way of reaching the desired outcome.

The relative subtlety of the British state's intervention may be contrasted with events in the Irish Republic around the same time. Radio Telefís Eireann (RTE), the Irish state broadcasting authority, has long been more closely supervised than the BBC. Under Section 31 of the Broadcasting Authority Act, 1960, the Minister is given veto powers over particular items of broadcasting, a residual power similar to that which exists in Britain. Section 31 was activated in October 1971 through a government directive aimed against publicizing the aims and activities of the IRA (although that organization was not explicitly mentioned). Inside RTE, according to Golding and Elliott, the view taken by the Director-General and the Head of News was that 'the actions of illegal organizations are a necessary part of the news and must be reported. . . . The one clear proscription was against allowing a member of an illegal organization to put his point of view directly.'[32] This position was virtually the same as that obtaining in Britain. In November 1972, RTE broadcast an interview with the then Provisional IRA Chief of Staff, Sean MacStiofain, which resulted in the government's dismissal of the entire RTE authority. The reporter who conducted the interview was jailed. This quite unambiguous intervention by the Irish state was a sharp contrast with the British approach. Since then, RTE has pursued a very low-key, 'factual' approach to reporting matters concerning the conflict in the North, and has stressed its obligation to maintain public order.

DEVELOPMENTS SINCE 1972

Since the debate over censorship, and the row over *The Question of Ulster* in 1971–72, the question of broadcasting's coverage of Northern Ireland has sporadically occasioned public debate. This is evident from heated exchanges during a television discussion in September 1976 and a short-lived row in early 1977. Moreover, official concern has been repeatedly evident. One may read this concern as a way of periodically reminding the media of desired directions for coverage.

Quite recently, the Gardiner Report suggested that 'The Governors of the British Broadcasting Corporation and the Independent Broadcasting Authority should re-examine the guidance they give to programme controllers or companies about contact with terrorist organizations and the reporting of their views and activities'.[33] The report warns newspapers and the broadcasting media about providing 'propaganda platforms for those whose aim is the violent overthrow of lawful government'. The media are also warned not to glamorize and sensationalize acts of violence.

Such points read oddly after discussions with BBC newsmen, and observation in the newsrooms. From such a vantage-point it would seem that the lessons of low-profile reporting of Northern Ireland were learned a long time ago and that they hardly need restating. It was evident, for instance, just after *The Question of Ulster* row, that an attitude of safety-first prevailed concerning coverage of Northern Ireland. Indeed, one might take the careful construction of that programme itself as a token of how gingerly the BBC was treading.

Since 1972, there have been no major shifts in the BBC's policy on Northern Ireland coverage. In effect, therefore, the controversies at an early stage of the crisis have had lasting impact on its reporting since then. In general, there has been a tendency over time for the Troubles to become less prominent as a news story. This fact is reflected in a shift of resources away from Northern Ireland.

In 1972, when fieldwork began, there was a heavy commitment of London-based personnel to manning the news service out of Belfast. Television News would, as a matter of course, have a film crew stationed in Belfast. Until 1974, the level of senior duty editor and above in the Belfast newsroom had been manned by shifts coming out from London. It was also quite common for London newsroom staff to work in Belfast on editing and production. Television reporters worked in Belfast and Londonderry on rota, as a routine part of their activity. A similar commitment obtained in the case of Radio News, which at the peak of its involvement had a reporter on rota in Londonderry, as well as one in Belfast, where it also had a news organizer and would send editorial staff. It was the Troubles which resulted in the BBC establishing a full-time correspondent in Dublin. There were frequent complaints, particularly between 1972–74, that the rotas were overburdened by this commitment.

By 1975, the picture had changed. London-based resources had been withdrawn from Northern Ireland, although reporters, notably from Radio News, were still being sent there. It was not surprising that a newish sub could say, in 1976, that he felt like 'the man who'd missed the war'.

Discussions with newsmen produced three main reasons for this change in policy. First, it was argued that there was public *ennui* with all the bombs and death, and so nothing more than routine reporting was needed. One assistant editor said in 1976 that there had been a shift in news policy. Violence in Northern Ireland was the norm, so they were now looking for something unusual in the context of this normality, namely good news stories. Examples he gave were new industrial projects which would create jobs, or community projects which would benefit people. This attitude might in part explain the coverage which the BBC, in common with the rest of the media, have given the women's peace movement. Secondly, a related news judgement, it was argued that after 1974 Northern Ireland was less crisis-ridden, and therefore there was not such a need for coverage. This view was expressed by the Editor, News and Current Affairs, in an interview with the *Irish Times*: the phrase used was that 'the main heat was now out of the story'.[34] In an interview with me, Mr Taylor said, 'Now there's not so much news, it doesn't require crews in the streets.' He also said that since the British government had taken over once again with the demise of the power-sharing Executive there was 'no political situation there, where parties are seeking advantage'. These views are certainly open to question. A political vacuum deriving from an absence of government policy does not by any means abolish the crisis in Northern Ireland's social order. Nor indeed, by the standards of conventional news value – bombs and death – has there been any the less of a story.

But the reduction of London's commitment was not solely an

editorial judgement. This brings us to the third reason: financial considerations. Mr Taylor said that it had been cheaper to reinforce staffing in Belfast, rather than send out crews and editors from England. 'It's a double-benefit: we're saving money and we've got twenty-four-hour coverage.' The financial argument was also cited by other newsmen. Another point made by Mr Taylor is interesting. He argued that having Northern Ireland covered by people permanently stationed in Belfast was preferable to having outside 'firemen' coming in, as 'the people there understand the situation a lot more'.

This opinion of the expertise of the Northern Ireland newsroom is one which also marks a shift. It will be recalled that this newsroom has a strategic role in Northern Ireland coverage: according to ground-rule 2, cited above, all news agency reports have to be checked with it for accuracy. Proposals for stories to be shot or recorded in Northern Ireland still have to pass through the Controller in Belfast.

The view of the Belfast BBC encountered in 1976 is very different from that which was given when the commitment of London personnel was great. According to an assistant editor in Television News the Belfast newsroom was totally Protestant in 1969 with the exception of one Catholic who 'found things difficult outside rather than inside'. Without apparent irony he said 'the newsroom wasn't biased – they just couldn't see the situation from anything other than an establishment angle'. He went on to say that the BBC had been vulnerable over the composition of the newsroom staff, and that was why they had to import personnel from London. This view was widely supported by statements made by other newsmen, when there was still a heavy commitment from London:

We take as a fact stuff from Belfast: it's thoroughly checked. The local newsroom is full of violent Protestants. We send over the Englishmen to get unbiased reporting.

The Belfast newsroom is full of Orangemen. It needed people from this side of the water to counter in-bred prejudice.

The argument here, of course, is that the untarnished professionalism of the imported personnel will act as a guarantee of impartiality. But even this ameliorative account (things were bad, but are now improved) functions within an overall exclusion clause concerning the extremists. A radio reporter commented that when the Unionist government was still operating at Stormont (until it was suspended in March 1972) newsmen were required to regard it in the same way as the British establishment. He also expressed the view that Belfast personnel were inclined towards Loyalism, and pointed to the very different atmosphere in the BBC there: while there were several Catholics working there, he said, everyone knew everyone else's religion, something which would *not* be the case in the London newsroom.

A number of newsmen sought to explain the BBC's Northern Ireland policy by drawing my attention to what was variously termed the 'Ulster mafia' or 'masonry' in senior positions in News and Current Affairs. Newsmen, pursuing this line of argument – it was often presented in a whimsical or joking way – pointed to Northern Ireland Protestants occupying the following positions: the Editor, News and Current Affairs, a former Controller, Northern Ireland, a former Editor, Television News, the Head of Current Affairs Group Radio, the Head of Journalists' Training, formerly an assistant editor in Radio News, an assistant editor in Television News, and the Northern Ireland Political Correspondent. All of these, it was argued by those who took this view, were bound to be sensitive or committed to one side because sectarian divisions in Northern Ireland were so extreme such commitment could not be doubted.

Such a crude personal bias theory should not be taken seriously, especially as no substantial evidence was produced to support the view. But the story is not without sociological importance as all newsmen know of it, and some certainly *do* think that it holds true and act accordingly.

THE PUBLIC ORDER APPROACH

An explanation of the BBC's news policy should not be sought in theories of personal bias, but rather in the way in which the Corporation defines itself as 'an organization within the constitution' and hence as one upholding the legitimate established order. This means that the BBC is essentially for order as it is defined by the state. The system of devolved power in Northern Ireland collapsed in 1972, despite subsequent, but relatively short-lived, attempts to revive it, notably through 'power-sharing' between Protestants and Catholics. The definition of order has therefore been principally in the hands of the British government, and its maintenance in the hands of the security forces, particularly the British army.

There are three particularly important elements in what may be called the 'public order' approach to news taken by the BBC. First, there is general support for the British army and its role in law-enforcement in Northern Ireland. Secondly, and related to this, there is a negative evaluation of extremism and terrorism, and of the Provisional IRA in particular, generally considered the army's principal enemy. And lastly, there is a view of the nature of responsible media coverage of the Troubles which is especially sensitive to criticisms of the inflammatory effects of broadcasting. There will be no attempt here to present these themes in a detailed chronological account. Rather, I will draw on the public statements of BBC spokesmen and points made in the newsrooms, as well as some observations made during fieldwork.

The view of the army

The Northern Ireland conflict, particularly since 1972, has tended to be represented in most of the national media as a struggle between the British army and the Provisional IRA. The instability of political life there in the conventional terms of electoral party politics has meant that most news coverage – even when formal political activity is at its peak, as during election periods – has tended to centre on violence and law-enforcement.[35]

The reporting of Northern Ireland is a form of war reporting, and in such a context it is not surprising that there has been a considerable effort by parties to the conflict to secure propaganda victories. To report on matters adverse to the army is particularly difficult for the broadcast media given their relationship to the state. The pressures of 1971 which produced Lord Hill's declaration of non-impartiality concerning the army and the gunmen are an indication of this. The BBC's Editor, News and Current Affairs, has referred to the political sensitivity of the BBC's having reported allegations against the army in what he calls 'the propaganda war', and he has noted pressures on the BBC from backbenchers and the Ministry of Defence over the publicity given these allegations.[36]

The allegations in question concerned the use of torture by the British army against internees at the interrogation centre at Ballykinler. These were later borne out by the Compton Report of 1971 instituted by the British government, and subsequently by the European Commission of Human Rights in 1976. Looking back on this period, one newsman in Radio News observed that the BBC had been very uncritical, and that he was convinced that this was a policy matter, and that there was 'guidance'. A similar charge was levelled by the anonymous writer of the *New Statesman* article who argued that 'it was made quite clear that all interviews with ex-internees were to be presented in as sceptical a manner as possible.

Quite clearly until the Compton Report bore out much of what had been alleged, the BBC's intention was to discredit the allegations and those who made them.'[37]

There is incidental evidence to support this view in an extract from the News and Current Affairs minutes quoted in *Private Eye*. There, the Chief Assistant to the Editor, News and Current Affairs, explains why he did not use an interview with an internee in September 1971:

> After weighing up all the factors, taking into account the fact that it had not been possible to make the item's treatment defensible as a whole on the grounds of fairness, he had decided that the item was expendable. It had in any case been an item of marginal importance, being a description by an admitted extremist of conditions in the Crumlin Road prison.

The internee in question was Michael Farrell, a leader of the left-wing People's Democracy. It is quite clear from this account that his political affiliations made him suspect as a source of testimony. The People's Democracy is described in an internal BBC briefing document on 'Political and Activist Groups in Northern Ireland' as 'Left-wing Trotskyist group. Mainly concerned with agitation.'[38]

The view presented of the army, and of the government's security policy, has remained a matter of considerable concern within the BBC. Desmond Taylor has recently specified the BBC's view of the place of the army's version of events in the output:

> I certainly feel that the Army, as the lawful and useful arm of the state, must be given a right to speak its voice and version of things to the people of the state through the public broadcasting system.[39]

He has also indicated how the developments in the army's public relations effort came as a relief to the BBC when the army 'initiated a policy of putting up spokesmen to give its side of the story which sustained public belief in our fairness and impartiality and did the Army a good deal of good in the process'.[40]

Various British journalists have commented on the increasing effectiveness of the army's PR operation, among them Simon Hoggart and Simon Winchester, both of *The Guardian*, and Andrew Stephen of *The Observer*.[41] Apart from both observing that the army on occasion 'plant' anti-IRA stories, Hoggart and Stephen both comment significantly on the rapidity with which information about incidents is passed to the media, which has a tactical advantage. As

Hoggart points out: 'the first account is always the unchecked word of the soldier on the spot'. Quickly establishing a version of events is particularly important where broadcasting is concerned, as radio and television pursue immediacy in reporting.

It is the BBC's stated policy to make sure the army's version of events always gets a hearing, and in the newsrooms this tends to be interpreted in a particular way. One television sub described it thus: 'I've always assumed the official line is we put the army's version first and then any other.' A radio news organizer observed: 'You don't always have time to check out the army's account, especially when an incident has occurred in border areas. After all, it is the British army, and we are on their side.' These remarks were passed in 1975 and 1976. It was during this later period of fieldwork that a number of newsmen in Radio News, severally, and off the record, talked about a low-key and silent 'revolt' against the policy on reporting the army's statements.

What this amounted to was that a small group of people had simultaneously concluded they were 'taking the army line'. They knew what was going to be acceptable and worked within these limits. Changes were brought about, it was claimed, by tacit use of attributions which conveyed doubt about army statements – a practice which could hardly be faulted. Thus for example they introduced the phrase 'the army *says*'. This established a precedent which became common usage. There was no direct confrontation with management. There are some indications that something similar had happened in Television News. One newsman, spoken to in 1976, said there had been a tendency to take 'the army line', but 'we quickly scotched that'. He went on to say that they now gave 'both sides of the story – the army and the Republicans'.

This concern was limited to quite a small number of newsmen. One news organizer said he thought only one or two people considered the policy wrong, and the general approach was, 'You take what the army and the police say, and then you make independent enquiries'.

A number of newsmen gave examples which supported the view that the British army is supposed to have relatively uncritical treatment. One reporter said he had been labelled a 'lefty' for arguing with editorial judgements on Northern Ireland. He had used the term 'army sniper' in one of his reports, and was told by the editor of the day that this was quite unacceptable, and that it must be rephrased as 'army marksman'. The editor of the day had insisted that members of the British army simply could not be called 'snipers'.

One newsman, who had worked as a trainee in Belfast, gave an example of how he felt the BBC had assisted the army's PR effort:

H

We had a programme on BBC Belfast on how army families were spending Christmas. But we weren't allowed to cover the way the internees' families were spending Christmas. I suppose they think it's dangerous of the BBC to give publicity. My personal view is to disagree with this. There's no suppression as such. But this should have been broadcast on human grounds.

Another reporter told of a story about the army shooting an unarmed man in a field. The man had had no known IRA connection. He had been taken away from a meal with his parents. The editor of the day had not liked this story, he said, and had tried to shake him on the detail. He had asked whether the reporter was sure the army had been involved, and not impersonators. The general point the reporter wished to make was that although the story was broadcast he had been made to defend it more than usual.

Some observations made in the newsroom support the view that stories concerning the army or security policy are handled with especial care. In July 1976 a story came in from Belfast that a 65-year-old man had been beaten up by two soldiers who were now missing from their unit. The story was run in the 5.45 p.m. bulletin on BBC-1. During the post-mortem after transmission, the editor of of the day said: 'It's a dubious one. We don't know whether the soldiers were pissed, whether it's political or what. We'd better wait and see what else comes through.' The sub handling the story said 'We'll leave it then.' The editor of the day was concerned about the story's interpretation. When asked why he was being so cautious, he replied: 'I'm keeping an open mind on it. It depends entirely on how our Belfast newsroom interprets it. . . . We could jump at it as though the world's coming to an end. We don't know its significance. Is it a breach of discipline? Soldiers' loss of nerve? It falls into the category of if a Catholic's been found killed, it must be a Protestant who's to blame.' Obviously, this meant he did not want an automatic assignment of blame to the army. The story was dropped from the running order of the next bulletin.

The handling of another story illustrates the same cautious approach, this time in relation to the government's security policy.

One morning in June 1973 two minutes after the 7.00 a.m. news bulletin had been transmitted the newsroom received a complaint about the content of the bulletin. It came from the Public Relations Officer of the then Secretary of State for Northern Ireland, Mr William Whitelaw. The reporter's contribution from Belfast had contained a reference to an explosion at a public house 'a few miles beyond Belfast airport'. The PRO suggested that as the airport was a well-known target and a sensitive area that the report could be rephrased to give the location more exactly. The night editor became concerned that the report might be dragging in the airport unnecessarily. From an editing point of view, he observed, 'We can't take it out without doing the whole piece again.' In discussion, the night editor and the news organizer, who was very familiar with Belfast, decided that the reporter had not given a clear enough location of the bombing. The news organizer estimated that the pub was about 14 miles outside Belfast. There had been two separate bombing incidents, one of which had been in the city centre. This therefore provided a point of contrast with the other bomb. The night editor said: 'I should have seen that before it went out.' The chief sub added: 'It's important to the story that people are going to pubs outside Belfast.' The night editor concurred, saying, 'It makes it [the story] seem silly. People [there] know where Crumlin is.' The chief sub set the incident in context for my benefit: 'We must have gospel-like accuracy; every detail must be right if possible.' At 7.53 a.m. a request went to the reporter to 'do a re-write' with more detail concerning the exact location of the two pubs; Belfast airport was not to be mentioned.

In effect, the content of a news story was altered at the request of an official acting for the British government. The way in which the alteration took place was rationalized in terms of the very genuine BBC commitment to accuracy. The underlying issue here, though, is the impression which the government wanted fostered about its grip on security. The newsmen accepted without question the sensitivity of the area, and that since there had previously been attacks on Aldergrove Airport that it ought, therefore, to be quite clear the IRA were not getting near it now. All of this was implicit in the handling of the story, and the alterations were made with alacrity and without question. It is quite true that the report was inaccurate. But the question of its inaccuracy was a question of the relevance of Belfast airport, a target-area, whose security was a matter of prestige to the government. Conceivably, without the conflict it would be relevant enough to say 'a few miles from Belfast airport'. The night editor, however, felt constrained to accept the redefinition of relevance. This seems a clear case of pressure at work, and one can see how it was accommodated without challenging such basic journalistic values as speed and accuracy.

The 'extremists' policy

As the account of developments until 1972 showed, the BBC's policy on the interviewing of 'extremists' was initiated at an early stage of reporting the current troubles. The censorship debate, since 1972, has been largely a dead letter, and the interviews policy has persisted. It was in force during the entire fieldwork period, and from discussions with newsmen, it is clear it was widely accepted as the correct approach.

The main change in the interviews rule has been its extension, as the Editor, News and Current Affairs, put it, to 'all illegal organizations'. As paramilitary activities on the part of Protestant (loyalist) organizations became more important – the main ones being the UDA, UVF and UFF – the rule evolved for dealing with the IRA was applied to them. In an interview in 1973, the Deputy Editor, Radio News, justified the restrictions in terms of preserving public order: 'There's the same ground rule that the reporter must get permission if he's going to tape an interview. To have the chap talking is liable to stir up the other community.' During 1972, the rule concerning interviews with the IRA was eased. Reporters had to obtain permission in advance from the Director-General if they wanted to record an interview with IRA men. 'Otherwise', Desmond Taylor has said, 'journalists were free to talk to the IRA and use reported speech to convey the results.'[42] There was a good deal of sensitivity about the way this restriction ought to be interpreted. During an interview in 1974, the Editor, Radio News, was at great pains to stress there was not a *ban* on extremists' voices, but it had to be remembered that they were simply propagandists, and the BBC had to be careful that it was not used by them.

The notion of restricting the opportunity for enemy propaganda has been prominent in the periodic justifications of BBC Northern Irish policy offered by its Director-General, Sir Charles Curran. In 1974, for example, he noted that he had given 'prior permission for two such interviews', both of which were with David O'Connell, the Provisional IRA's chief of staff. One was in 1974, when the power-sharing Executive collapsed, leading to a vacuum in constitutional politics. The other was in 1972, a year in which the then Secretary of State for Northern Ireland, Mr Whitelaw, was having secret conversations with the Provisional IRA, and a brief truce was negotiated with them. By 1977, the number of IRA interviews was still two. From an editorial point of view, Curran has said, 'the question which I have to consider is whether the undeniable wish of the IRA to make propaganda through such interviews will be balanced by the value of the information which will be brought to the attention of the British public'.[43]

In a subsequent elaboration of this 'national interest' argument in 1976, Curran once again made it clear that the BBC saw members of illegal organizations as the enemy but that 'If you have an enemy –

and the organizations are illegal precisely because they are the enemies of democracy – it seems to me necessary you should understand the enemy.'[44] This later policy statement came about a month after the Irish government had entirely banned the broadcasting of interviews with the Provisional IRA and Provisional Sinn Fein on RTE. The BBC rejected this option, although Curran's statements contain the main concepts in terms of which any statements issuing from the IRA are evaluated in the BBC: namely, as 'undemocratic enemy propaganda'.

The approach to the IRA and other illegal organizations in Northern Ireland is one which has exercised the BBC's editorial hierarchy a good deal. The question of whether the BBC can properly interview people who are outside the law and not turn them in to the security forces is one problem which emerged as especially important during a discussion with the Editor, Television News, in 1974. This problem first arose for the BBC at an early stage of the Troubles when a BBC Television Current Affairs reporter was jailed for four days for refusing to identify an IRA-man on the grounds of professional ethics.[45] Nothing like this has since happened, but there have been continual pressures from politicians and the army which have ensured that letting 'the enemy' speak has been a rare occurrence. Sir Charles Curran has recently made it clear that 'when such meetings take place, the IRA must be entirely responsible for protecting their own secrets' – notably, the location of the meeting.[46]

This entire approach to illegal organizations is predicated upon notions of consensus and legitimacy. By identifying them as outside the bounds of tolerance, broadcasting reproduces decisions and definitions which are initiated by the state. The BBC has had to produce criteria for categorizing the actions of illegal organizations, which then become the basis for framing the approach to stories, and hence structure the content of the news. A particularly interesting memorandum on this subject, dated 17 January 1974, was to be found in the television newsroom log:

GUERRILLAS AND TERRORISTS[47]

ENCA's meeting has been discussing the proper use of the terms 'GUERRILLA' and 'TERRORIST', when we report acts of politically motivated violence.

'TERRORIST' is the appropriate description for people who engage in acts of terrorism, and in particular, in acts of violence against civilians, that is operations not directed at military targets or military personnel.

'GUERRILLA' is acceptable for leaders and members of the various

Palestine organizations of this kind, but they too become 'terrorists' when they engage in terrorist acts (unless 'raiders', 'hijackers', 'gunmen' is more accurate).

There will be occasions when we will wish to quote, or use as actuality, statements describing as 'guerrillas' people whom we would actually call 'terrorists'. In such cases we should use a 'back credit' to clarify that we are quoting, e.g.,

'That was a spokesman for the Palestine Liberation Front, commenting on the terrorist attack at Rome airport.'

We should, in a common sense way, treat other guerrilla/terrorist groups in much the same way. We should remember that these people shoot, throw bombs and kill and maim, and often such straightforward and unequivocal phrases as 'the men who killed' may be the best description of all. We should be particularly wary of the word 'commando', which, to our audience, retains its wartime flavour.

In coverage of Ireland, the term 'terrorist' is the one pre-eminently used, rather than 'guerrilla'. The latter term suggests a greater degree of respectability, and a more legitimate quasi-military status for the insurgent side. The memorandum makes it very clear that the BBC should avoid as much as possible any conferring of legitimacy on the spokesmen of insurgent groups, and the condemnation of insurgency as an instance of illegitimate violence is also very apparent. There are therefore clear prescriptions for handling stories in the newsrooms which approximate closely to the public position taken by the BBC.

Elliott in his content analysis of British media output has noted that during the periods he studied, 1974 and 1975, the Provisional IRA received most attributions of responsibility for violence. This group was identified as the principal source of a terrorist violence, which, he argues, comes across as 'the result of inexplicable, asocial forces'.[48] Elliott also notes that 'the British media did tend to use the ambiguous label "sectarian" to identify those incidents in which Protestant extremists were involved and to couple reports of murders by such groups with explanations in terms of loyalist anger, reprisals or a Protestant backlash'.[49] These findings square broadly with the impression gained during fieldwork that the IRA was perceived as the major disruptive agency in Northern Ireland, and that newsmen had far less clearly formulated views on loyalist groups as key initiators of terrorist activity. There was little questioning, on the whole, of the policy lines for handling *all* 'extremist' groups. The following remarks are representative of most reporters' thinking:

You don't do an interview with anybody representing one side or the other without clearing it first. You may go and talk to someone for an hour, and then you're told that you can't use it. It causes far more trouble if it's done and not used, because then you're accused of suppression or censorship: 'The bloody BBC came round here, and I gave them an hour, and then they didn't use a minute of it.' You'd get trouble from the UVF or the IRA. *You can see there's an actual need for it.*

(Reporter, Television News)

We're not explicitly or specifically told to stay off a story. BBC policy varies with the situation. It's a standing rule that we do not interview the IRA on tape without prior reference to the ENCA who probably gets in touch with DG. This now extends to the UDA – that's rough justice. There are not really instructions. Occasionally you're told to handle with care, to check out the facts. It's a hot potato politically. You balance by getting the views of so-and-so. It's a precaution so you can't be attacked in Parliament or the press for presenting a one-sided picture of the situation.

(Reporter, Television News)

These accounts accept the reasoning offered by the BBC's controllers, and are careful of how the Corporation might look to outsiders. The first justifies the exclusion of recordings on the ground that were they to be made and *then* excluded, that this would smack of censorship, so they are therefore not made, and so far as the newsman was concerned the issue of censorship did not arise. The second brings into play the key ideological concept of impartiality between extremes to justify the BBC's policy. A radio reporter gave a slightly different account:

BBC policy is against interviewing IRA men in Belfast because of its illegal status there. You'd be an accessory after the fact. There's no bar in Dublin. But you have to make sure they don't make political capital. . . . It's an organization pledged to kill British soldiers. They are waging war. You have to think who's near the the law and who's a long way away.

In this statement is encapsulated a specific concept of the reporter's role. He is seen as a war correspondent, reporting on an internal war in which the legal definitions produced by the state have to be respected, and in which they define, for the purposes of reporting, who is the enemy. A similar point was made by one television reporter who disagreed with the BBC's policy:

As far as the IRA goes we're fighting a war, and they never get representation except by ENCA's special order. You need a prior permit for an interview. You don't put it up, obviously, or you're a trendy lefty backing the IRA; so you don't bother without a cast-iron excuse. That's the centralization. If they released the IRA for interview they would show their true colours one way or another. *The mechanism is such they'd say there was no ban, but that you just need to get permission.*

The same conception of the IRA as primary enemy is embodied in the above quotation. There is no sense in which support is urged for its cause, but rather it is argued that the IRA ought to be heard in order to discredit itself, to show itself as propagandist. A similar line was to be heard among some very senior editors in the News Departments who had reservations about the interviews policy. They too argued in terms which were succinctly expressed by one newsman who had worked as a trainee in Belfast:

In a free and democratic country you ought to give them a chance to air their views. It starts off with 'not this faction' and then 'not these Catholics', and you end up by taking a Protestant position, but saying 'that's a Catholic view', and we'll have to be careful.

This view was echoed by one seasoned newsman, whose commitment to the BBC's ideals was striking, and any criticism therefore the more significant. He argued (in 1975) that 'There was, is, the view that the IRA are the baddies; to that extent there's an unwillingness to report Prod terrorism'.

Most newsmen offered no such criticisms of the Corporation's record or policy. But relatively few were in any case prepared to engage in extensive discussions of this area. Most typical responses were on the lines of the reporter who had reported on sectarian fighting in the streets. There were, he said, thirty-two complaints from either side, and Controller, Northern Ireland, had said to him 'You've done a good job.' In general, there was considerable sensitivity about critics' accusations of bias, and it was argued that while extremists were given short shrift, the two communities in Northern Ireland received balanced treatment.

The general newsroom position may be found in two articles by Martin Bell, an experienced television reporter, much respected in BBC News. In *The Listener*, the BBC's weekly magazine, Bell argued that he had not found himself 'overwhelmed by any sense of a corporate doctrine of what it might be permissible to report. Events press far too urgently for that.' Bell's argument was that all the reporter did was 'talk to both sides, record their versions of the event, and leave the viewing public to judge'.[50] In a later article, Bell produced a further endorsement of the BBC's line and argued that in the unique circumstances of covering Northern Ireland, reporting had rightly become subject 'to a tightening of editorial control: that means in practice that editors edit, which one has always understood was what they were paid to do'.[51]

The attitude towards complaints of partiality was instructively illustrated on one occasion in the radio newsroom. A duty editor who had just received a telephone call approached the editor of the day in a state of great annoyance:

> Some bloody woman rang up and accused us of being biased towards the RC's. So I told her you were an Ulster Protestant.

The editor of the day gestured towards the senior duty editor and added:

> And a Welsh Presbyterian!

In this way impartiality was made flesh. The editors were asserting that the personnel were the guarantors of even-handedness. For if a Protestant could produce news seeming to favour Catholics, how could there possibly be anything in what the critic said?

To conclude this section, two separate observed incidents illustrate different aspects of the policy on extremists' voices. On one occasion in the radio newsroom in March 1973, the editor of the day put a note aside for the incoming editor due to take over the night shift. It read: 'O'Connell interview. Not to be used until you've contacted [the Editor].' He proffered an explanation of this action. 'We don't carry IRA interviews. We must check to clear it. We do use it if it's newsworthy. We can't do it on our own initiative: it's a protection for ourselves. We don't get that many.' The Provisional IRA had called off their cease-fire and were going to explain why at a news conference in Dublin due that night. The Dublin correspondent had requested permission to tape-record it. In fact the correspondent did not tape an interview, and the following day there was a straight radio report on the news conference. The editor of the day made it clear that 'If it was an extreme UDA story I would ring up the Editor and say that I plan to run this'. He said of extremist organizations 'There's no embargo as such; we don't chase them. They don't tell us not to if it's newsworthy. It's not for us to give them a platform.

As long as it's not propaganda.' One could see operating in this explanation the criteria set out by the Director-General.

On another occasion, in July 1976, the television news prospects noted that Tomas MacGiolla, the President of Official Sinn Fein, was due to visit Britain from the Irish Republic, and that he had been invited by Joan Maynard, a Tribunite Labour MP, to speak on solutions to the conflict in the North. MacGiolla had explicitly condemned violence and sectarianism, and the official IRA, whose political wing he represented, had for some time eschewed terrorism. At the morning meeting on the 14th July, it was noted that there would be 'a bit of Brenard's' (news agency arrival film). MacGiolla was described in discussion as 'a Marxist character', and the editorial decision was that he should be watched to 'see if there's any chance of expulsion by the Home Secretary'. The story was thus defined in televisual – potential action – terms rather than in terms of a possible interview concerning Sinn Fein policy. At the meeting on the following day, the diary ran thus:

> Controversial visit to England by the President of Sinn Fein, the political wing of the IRA, Tomas MacGiolla. He is expected to have discussions with MPs and Trade Union leaders. WATCH.

The news organizer said that there was agency film 'but there's no point in pursuing it further. The arrival was covered by radio. He's coming to address MPs and he's already talked to the Special Branch. There's the predictable Tory uproar.' The Editor, Television News, came in here with a clear editorial prescription: 'Somebody will react. I'm not proposing to activate it.' This meant that unless something happened – for example, violence at a meeting – Mac-Giolla's visit should not be covered by Television News. On the following day MacGiolla was down in the diary as having a press conference in London, but the story was not considered at the meeting. Over the sound link, Radio News said they were 'watching the Irishman'. The outcome of this editorial decision was that the Sinn Fein position did not get covered on television, partly, it seemed, because of the controversial nature of those views, partly because there was little in the way of a good action story there.

The 'responsibility of broadcasting' argument

The main effect of pressure from the government on broadcasting since the public rows of 1971 and 1972 has been to produce a shift in the nature of coverage to that of a low-key style; 'objective' rather than investigative. Philip Elliott has recently argued that this approach to coverage, with its emphasis on the 'who, what, where and when' of immediate, usually violent incidents, is one which excludes the necessary information and contextualization for a wider understanding. This is an argument with which I would agree. The particular notion of 'responsible journalism' implied by this approach is internally justified by a specific view of the role of the media – and the BBC in particular – in the Northern Ireland conflict.

From the outset, fears were expressed by the broadcasting organizations that the appearance on the streets of television cameras or the broadcasting of sectarian views might exacerbate the situation. The recent Troubles began at a time when TV 'demo' journalism was a particularly fashionable genre, and accusations were levelled in the 'sixties, which have since persisted, that television caused the events which it reported. There are no empirical foundations for this view, but it is one which has not failed to strike home.

The official BBC standpoint was very fully elaborated during an interview with a senior editor in Television News:

> Our problems in Northern Ireland are often compared to Vietnam and there is a similarity in the sense that both we and the American networks are bringing home the reality of war. But for us there is something additional which makes it totally novel: for the first time in BBC history we are confronted with a situation very close to urban guerrilla war, *and not in some colonial area but on home British soil.* We have a situation in which British, English-speaking soldiers are facing British, English-speaking inhabitants, even if a lot of them aren't too happy about being British. Our situation is a shade worse than that of the US. The Vietnam war is literally brought home, whereas in Northern Ireland we are not only telling the domestic audience what's going on but are also broadcasting back to the participants their activities, on the same day. So the soldier in his barracks can see the action he was involved in during the day, and people at home who took part in a riot can see themselves there on the screen. Obviously one thing which we cannot do is tell people where and when these things are going on at the time. There is no more certain way of bringing reinforcements out on the streets. . . . *We have to control the basis on which the protagonists see each other,* and that is a very novel situation. However objective and impartial you try to make it you can't fail to be in trouble with both sides – especially now that views have polarized so much – since neither will admit the other's point of view.

This viewpoint contains some important conceptual orientations to Northern Irish coverage. First, it expresses the view that Northern Ireland is part of the home country rather than a colonial possession. In terms of contending views of the struggle there this does rather beg the question which would be posed by an impartial approach. The above résumé of the position was given in 1972, when the commitment of London-based resources was high. At that time reporters spoke of Northern Ireland 'as the biggest home news story since the war'. As the possibility of British withdrawal entered the political agenda, newsmen tended to talk about it less as a home news story. Certainly, in broadcasting's output 'Northern Ireland' is very much a story category which stands apart from the rest of British coverage. It comes over as at best only ambiguously British, as violence is thought to be an un-British way of solving political problems.

Second is the argument about the effects of the media. The view expressed conveys the fundamental and settled conviction that a socially responsible broadcasting service stands against disorder, that it ought to be for order on the streets, and in politics. This takes us back to the conception of the BBC's role in the democratic process expressed by the Director-General:

> We have a responsibility to provide a rationally based and balanced service of news which enables adult people to make basic judgements about public policy in their capacity as voting citizens of a democracy.[52]

The yardstick of rationality in this account is the extent to which a people finds solutions to its political problems by democratic, i.e. parliamentary, means. By this criterion, the social and political conflict in Northern Ireland is judged as fundamentally irrational. The 'media effects' argument is premised on this view. This is strikingly illustrated in Desmond Taylor's Lunchtime Lecture, where he discusses the initial formulation of a viewpoint on reporting Northern Ireland:

> My own first view was that, while the BBC's normal policy assumed the existence of a rational audience, the Northern Ireland audience at that moment was *not* rational, and any reporting of opinion, however carefully balanced, would have an inflammatory effect.[53]

While extreme sectarian views have since then been given an airing, this argument has tended to persist as part of the rationale for keeping paramilitary figures away from the microphone. It has been linked with the other argument, considered above, that they are anyway propagandists and should therefore be rationed in their appearances.

In the newsroom, it was often asserted that news bulletins could arouse strong passions. For this reason the BBC had to be especially accurate, and therefore the Northern Ireland newsroom needed to be consulted. One editor of the day elaborated on the importance of avoiding the 'careless word'. A mistake had been made one day in a news summary: Protestants were holding a rally in Londonderry, and instead of writing that they were marching *alongside* the Catholic Bogside, the chief sub had written they were marching *into* the Bogside. This had produced a street fight between Catholics and Protestants.

Whether this actually happened or whether it is a piece of newsroom folklore is difficult to discover. A news organizer gave the same example some two years later. He said he had no personal knowledge of media reports having actually produced violence. Concerning the above example, he observed: 'It was said to have caused rioting – and anyway, you make the assumption people are tanked up.' The fact the same example reappeared could mean the event occurred and that it was used as a routine way of producing evidence for a general belief.

Another example given in the newsrooms is quite independently cited by Robert Fisk as originating in public concern about the role of broadcasting in Northern Ireland. Interestingly, no one could specify its origins in the newsrooms. Fisk says: 'Back in 1969, it [the BBC] was blamed for helping to foment a riot outside the Catholic Unity Flats at the bottom of the Shankill Road by broadcasting an account of stones being thrown at a Junior Orange procession there.'[54] Fisk goes on to say that according to the Scarman report of 1972 no such specific charge was sustained. Those who told the story did not however cast doubt on it.

A news organizer commented that 'these things probably happen' and that once you had been to Northern Ireland you could safely assume people there were listening to, or watching, news broadcasts, and that they would react. Martin Bell has described the broadcasting newsman's sense of being under continual scrutiny: 'Roman Catholics and Protestants alike are avid newswatchers. They could never be accused of indifference to the image of themselves that appears almost nightly on their screens. Often, I believe, they switch channels keenly in pursuit of it. They share especially in television's immediacy – being often the witnesses of an event itself and shortly afterwards of television's account of it.'[55]

This awareness of broadcasting's potential for the creation of disorder, whether well-founded or not, is important in the internal legitimation of the present notion of responsibility which governs the BBC's news approach. While in its general effect it is supportive of the state, it has, on one important occasion, proved quite the opposite.

Robert Fisk has analysed in detail the role and performance of the Northern Ireland BBC during the loyalist Ulster Workers' Council (UWC) strike of May 1974 which brought down the power-sharing Executive, and led to the present political deadlock. He argues that the BBC handled a political and insurrectionary strike as though it were simply an industrial one. The crucial factor was the failure of the British government to intervene effectively against the strike. In this context, because the BBC broadcast the strike call, put UWC spokesmen on the air as authoritative spokesmen, and passed on UWC communiqués it 'seemed to be acknowledging the authority of the strikers, perhaps even giving them the stamp of approval'.[56] While Merlyn Rees, then Northern Ireland Secretary, described the strike as political, the Northern Ireland office did not mount an effective publicity campaign against it, refusing for some time even to provide spokesmen. The fundamental weapon held by the UWC was its threat to discontinue the electricity supply, and its line that this was on the point of breakdown. This, Fisk argues, was untrue 'but it proved the most potent symbol of the strike: the inevitability of catastrophe if the executive remained in office'.[57] This line was not countered. The way the BBC interpreted its public order role was to go in for informational news dealing with public statements concerning the availability of food and services and the electricity supply, but it did not analyse 'the causes of the strike or the intentions of the men behind it'.[58]

An internal report from Mr Richard Francis, the Controller, Northern Ireland, argued: 'As an independent institution, we had a duty to reflect significant bodies of opinion – however arrived at – as much as to support institutions of democracy not widely accepted.'[59] It is apparent from this that public order – in the context of Northern Ireland at that time – was best served in the BBC's view by recognizing the *de facto* control of the UWC

The next major confrontation between the BBC and the state over Northern Ireland occurred in 1977. In January of that year, views attributed to Mr Roy Mason, the Northern Ireland Secretary, became public and once again illustrated how broadcasting is reminded of its limitations. Apparently, in November 1976, during a private dinner with the BBC's Chairman, Sir Michael Swann, held at the Culloden Hotel in Belfast, Mason is reputed to have accused the BBC of disloyalty, support for rebels, and of acting as the purveyor of enemy propaganda. He is also said to have suggested that the IRA would have been defeated if the Northern Ireland office had been in control of BBC policy, and to have proposed a three-month news ban on the reporting of terrorism.[60] If seriously meant, such views are absurdly uninformed. Yet, despite their crassness, they are important because of the quarter from which they derive, and the circumstances in which they were delivered. Evidently, Sir Michael Swann retained some scars from the encounter, for he referred to it later, in public, as 'the second Battle of Culloden'.[61]

Towards the end of February, the BBC responded to Mr Mason's call for censorship. Mr Richard Francis, its Controller, Northern Ireland, made an outspoken speech which generally reaffirmed the liberal arguments presented at the time of the *Question of Ulster* row.[62] Much of the speech covered familiar ground. However, there were one or two new emphases which merit comment.

For instance, Francis observed that the Northern Ireland conflict 'throws a light on the problems of impartially reflecting significant forces in society, of whatever origin, as much as supporting democratic institutions not widely accepted'. This sentence is virtually identical to the one quoted above from the confidential report on the UWC strike. Its recurrence suggests that the BBC's experience of defining its own approach in 1974 was of lasting importance. What Francis was saying amounted to a clear-cut rejection of the state's right to determine which views should be reflected in the Northern Ireland output. He indicated the problems raised by the view that 'in a situation lacking consensus the BBC should stand by the Government "in the national interest". But which Government? Which national interest? Often the Government at Westminster has been at odds with Stormont. Often the Westminster Government's point of view has been opposed, not only by undemocratic and violent organizations, but also by a majority of elected politicians in the Province.'

Francis went on to argue that since there was not a state of emergency or a state of war in Northern Ireland, the media ought to function as a fourth estate. He rejected the view that 'managing' the news would solve the problem. Rather: 'A thorough and reliable knowledge of society's ills and of the other man's "unpalatable" views are essential for any realistic evaluation. . . . If the violent activities of terrorists go unreported, there must be a danger that they may escalate their actions to make their point.' Later on, he made the related observation that, 'Maybe we have been guilty of under-representing the forces which have had the most profound effect on everyday life in the Province?'

While emphasizing that the BBC needed the greatest possible

scope to define its approach, Francis was careful to echo Lord Hill's principle of 1971: 'we are not impartial as between democratic and undemocratic means. We do not give equal time to right and wrong, there has never been any question of that. . . .' This underlined the BBC's commitment to constitutionality.

Yet, a definite note of exasperation is detectable when the army's information policy is considered: 'Quite frequently in this propaganda war, the army have put themselves at a disadvantage.' The point is also made that propaganda 'doesn't stem only from paramilitaries and illegal organizations – neither are they always wrong. It stems too from Government, political parties and the security forces. . . .'

The issue did not lie dormant after this speech. On 2 March, the BBC broadcast a report on the *Tonight* programme alleging the use of brutal interrogation methods by the Royal Ulster Constabulary. The story was based on the testimony of an Enniskillen schoolmaster picked up as an IRA suspect. Apart from the immediate background of the row just outlined, the *Tonight* report came at an inopportune moment for the British government, which was then defending itself at the European Court of Human Rights against charges of torture used against detainees in 1971.[63]

The *Tonight* programme was duly condemned by Mr Mason's office. According to press reports he had earlier threatened the use of regional D-notices against stories considered helpful to 'terrorists', and on this occasion a civil servant was 'understood to have telephoned the BBC to try and convince executives that one of the subjects in the *Tonight* programme was a prominent Provisional IRA organizer'.[64] Mr Mason shortly after said that he had dropped the idea of a D-notice system when it was made clear that the Dublin press could not be made to toe the line.

It was not only the Northern Ireland office which pressured the BBC. In a full-scale attack on 12 March, Mr Airey Neave, the Tory spokesman on Northern Ireland, accused the Corporation of irresponsibility.[65] In his strictures he received the full backing of the Conservative leadership. Neave's main theme was 'We are losing the propaganda battle in Northern Ireland', and he pressed the BBC's Governors to review their policy guidelines. His speech had two targets. First, Francis's response to Mason; and secondly, the *Tonight* programme. The BBC's position, Neave stated, was one of 'portentous unreality': far from not being in a 'state of war', Northern Ireland was actually 'on the brink of civil war'. Neave rejected the idea of the media operating as a fourth estate in Northern Ireland, and argued the well-worn view that publicity assisted 'terrorist' recruitment. It was not, therefore, responsible to report

IRA statements on their news value alone. Furthermore, the BBC's reporting of the allegations against the RUC was seen as undermining the credibility of the police, and as damaging to their morale, particularly as the allegations were uncorroborated.

Neave's attack coincided with the publication of an extensive *Sunday Times* report alleging that the British army had gone in for numerous dirty tricks between 1972 and 1976, amongst which were attempts to discredit Ulster politicians, the use of false information to influence government policy, and the setting off of explosions which were then attributed to the IRA. Relations between the state and some of the British media were, therefore, somewhat strained.[66]

The tenor of Neave's remarks was endorsed by Mr Alan Wright of the Police Federation of Northern Ireland, who blamed the *Tonight* programme for the killing of a policeman in County Fermanagh by the Provisional IRA on 13 March. Mr Francis stood by the veracity of the programme, and was supported by Sir Charles Curran, who rejected the view that it had caused the policeman's death. Curran reaffirmed the central principle that 'the BBC has to remain credible to both sides in Northern Ireland. That's very important – both sides.' He also pointed out that the BBC had not sought the information concerning alleged police brutality, but that once it had been made available it could not be suppressed.[67]

This latest incident simply confirms the consistency of the state's attempt to affect BBC coverage without going in for direct censorship. It also illustrates the consistency of the Corporation's responses to such attempts. Its institutional need to retain some credibility forces the BBC to define the public interest in ways which necessarily contradict state policy at certain moments.

The intractable nature of this clash is reflected in the Annan committee's observations on broadcasting's reporting of Northern Ireland. At first one is left unsure about which way the committee is going to jump:

Broadcasters cannot be impartial about activities of illicit organizations. Nevertheless, these organizations are a political force in Northern Ireland; and it would be unrealistic for the broadcasters not to take account of them. This does not mean, however, that the proponents of illicit organizations should be allowed to appear regularly on the screen, in the mid-seventies, still less to appear in order to argue their case. Terrorism feeds off publicity; publicity is its main hope of intimidating government and the public; publicity gives it a further chance for recruitment.[68]

One need search no further for a passage which embodies the cliché of 'having it both ways'. Both Mr Francis and Mr Mason could find comfort in some of these lines. After confessing its inability to make an 'unequivocal ruling' the committee opts for the *status quo*, and endorses broadcasting policy: 'we think that the decision whether to permit such appearances (i.e. by members of illegal organizations) must remain with the broadcasting organizations, and should not rest on the *fiat* of a British Government. We would expect these difficult decisions to be taken at the highest levels in the BBC and in the IBA.'[69] And so, presumably, it will continue.[70]

CONCLUSION

The argument of this chapter challenges two erroneous views of the relationship between the BBC and the state. One is the view that the BBC is simply a subservient tool which uncomplicatedly 'takes the army line'. The other is the myth that the Corporation is completely independent and proved this by resisting over *The Question of Ulster*.

The latter view, that the BBC is independent, is principally pre-mised on its refusal to drop *The Question of Ulster*. Far from being exemplary this is, rather, a success story in the midst of general defeat. The government, while not invoking the crude tactic of a ministerial ban, temporarily abandoned the much more subtle approach of issuing guidance. *The Question of Ulster* row therefore posed a quite unambiguous challenge to the BBC's independence in a way that insistence on greater responsibility resulting in tighter editorial control did not. But by the BBC's own lights it was being as responsible as possible, and was still accused of producing a potentially inflammatory programme.

The incident illustrates how a public order approach to broad-casting, which is elaborated by *broadcasters*, may diverge from that of the state. The BBC's guiding idea at the time was that of providing a forum for all relevant constitutional views on the Irish question. This approach reflected its genuine liberal belief that a hearing of these positions would contribute to a solution. So far as the BBC, and many others, were concerned this posed no challenge to public order as defined by the state. The programme could not be dropped at Maudling's insistence as no one could then have ducked the fact that the BBC *was* being censored, and its public legitimacy would have disappeared. The state, by its handling of the situation, made it impossible for the BBC not to pursue both its institutional interests and its quite genuinely liberal view of its social responsibility.

The handling of the UWC strike also provides evidence of the BBC's relative autonomy from the state, and the imperfection of control when direct censorship is not applied. Again, the BBC pursued an interpretation of public order broadcasting which was sharply at variance with the desires of the state. Legitimacy was officially deemed to be vested in the power-sharing Executive. But the situation on the ground – where the UWC was in effective control of much of the province's social and economic life – made that view untenable. In a provincial context, where the overall integrity of the British state and social order were not deemed under threat (as during the General Strike for example), the BBC had some room for manoeuvre.

It is such deviant acts which make the BBC–state relationship so complex, and support the myth of its general independence. The imperfection of state control obviously provokes frustration. Hence the role of Mason's and Neave's diatribes, like the earlier, more subdued prescription by Chataway, is to mark out boundaries. Such ministerial guidance has had a considerable reinforcing effect on the formation of broadcasting policy. The Chataway formulation has proved to be of enduring significance in its insistence that the BBC show itself to be anti-IRA and pro-army. Hill's letter in response constituted an undertaking that the BBC would construct a particular version of reality in reporting Northern Ireland. Such exchanges are not in general perceived as censorship, and therefore the BBC's detractors have been faced with a problem. Ministerial intervention has been elusive, and there was nothing in the BBC's approach to editorial control which approximated to popular imagery of classic totalitarian censorship, with its directives and specially planted supervisory personnel. The FBU letter to Hill and Aylestone recognized the problem when it pointed out that increased editorial controls are 'superficially merely an intensification of normal safeguards, and are too vague and distant a target for public concern'. Given this, the debate has largely foundered.

The absence of debate, and the powerful myth of *The Question of Ulster*, have obscured the long-term effects of the state's intervention and its partial, indirect control of broadcasting through its specification of the appropriate terms of reference. In general, broadcasting presents us with a series of decontextualized reports of violence, and fails to analyse and re-analyse the historical roots of the Irish conflict. Such an approach is largely shared by the rest of the British media, and this cannot but contribute to the dominant public view of Northern Ireland's present troubles as largely incomprehensible and irrational. It is not surprising that many see 'terrorism' as the cause of the conflict there rather than as one of its symptoms.

9

The limits of change

Changes in the organization of television and radio news production invariably come with the advent of a new Editor. Such changes are planned, and it is generally accepted that new Editors appear on the scene because higher management outside the News Departments want certain policy guidelines put into effect, and that to have such changes associated with the person of an innovator – even if by some the innovations are thought to be retrograde – is the best way of effecting them. Importantly, then, the conditions which permit major change lie *outside* the immediate context of the News Departments themselves.

The observations which I have to make are given a certain sharpness by reference to the debate which has been going on amongst media practitioners about the best direction for news broadcasting. At the centre of controversy in 1975 were three articles by Messrs Birt and Jay.[1] I will not comment extensively here on the substance of their proposed reforms for television news and current affairs structures. Suffice it to say that they have argued that the present structures of factual programming in television create a 'bias against understanding'. They consider that reforms in television journalism are necessary to overcome this, and demand a rejection of traditional news and visual values and practices, an abolition of the distinction between news and current affairs, and a reorganization of journalistic specialisms. There is little which is original or novel in this *potpourri*. But the impact of their articles on broadcasting circles has been considerable, which is doubtless more than one can say for the efforts of most media sociologists. One point by Birt and Jay is especially relevant to what follows:

> The BBC, being capable in principle of a strategic command decision, is on the face of things better able to undertake a radical change, which will offend many entrenched interests, than is independent television with its convention of unanimous consent.[2]

Whether the BBC's centralized command structure is likely to move in an innovative direction, to produce a comprehensive type of news broadcasting governed by a goal of serious enlightenment, remains to be seen. The BBC has already made its stand clear on this in a resoundingly conservative document which reaffirmed that it stood by its doctrine of 'the reporting of unadorned fact'.[3]

The dangers of pursuing the path of highly contextualized news have been discussed on the basis of Finnish experience, which Birt and Jay seem to be unaware of. Innovative moves in Finland (between 1965–70) bore some similarity to those now suggested by Birt and Jay. Although there, those supporting the changes showed an explicit realization that informational mass communication necessarily challenged the *status quo*, conventional wisdoms, and 'bourgeois hegemony'. Traditional notions of impartiality and balance had to go, as did their empiricist underpinnings. (One can understand the BBC directorate's reluctance to depart from unadorned fact when such cherished nostrums are under threat.) The Finnish informational policy was designed to engage the audience, and create a demand for further background information. While pluralistic in spirit it was interpreted by established forces – the conservative press, the church, commerce and industry, and educational institutions – as left-wing, and eventually, after a shift to the right in Finnish politics, axed.

In their discussions of highly contextualized news, Birt and Jay naïvely forget to consider the context within which television news is itself produced. This is, despite genuine public service features, a pre-eminently commercial one. Intelligent news does not meet mass commercial criteria too well. Nor can such news be divorced from the political economy of the society and state in which it is produced. The organization of broadcast journalism is not so independent a variable as Birt and Jay would like to believe, and radical change is likely to meet resistance. It is worth noting at this point a general implication of the Finnish attempt to broadcast informational news:

any ideology of mass communication stressing the transmission of a wide and versatile spectrum of information, when honestly applied, *is bound to be partial in favour of the suppressed interests of society.*[4]

A news organization wedded to a policy of corporate caution, which directly derives from the consensualist political constraints facing the BBC, is unlikely to initiate travel along such potentially dangerous paths. Possibly, if ITN were to innovate, the BBC might follow as it did in the past.

What then is the kind of change which is most permissible? The argument of this chapter is that it is *primarily* cosmetic. There are changes in news content of a more fundamental kind which reflect the changing social and moral climate. Such changes over time are common to all organizations in their general outlines. Specific interpretations of good taste will differ between news organizations. But these are largely matters of emphasis. Self-consciously to pioneer changes in content, to redefine news values themselves – these are matters the News Departments of the BBC are unable to undertake, and the BBC's directorate, I should guess, exceedingly unwilling.

Much of this book so far has been about the limited room for manoeuvre in the production of broadcast news. Here I wish to draw attention to the rather limited kinds of change introduced by new Departmental Editors, and the ways in which these were interpreted within the newsrooms.

What we find is that such changes throw into relief *the scope of variation* in the system of broadcast news production.

To understand the basic limitations on the form and content of broadcast news we have to situate its production in relation to the state, and notably to a definition of 'impartiality' which constrains it into a posture of overall endorsement for the established social order. To experiment is dangerous politically. This has most recently been shown by Tracey in his study of the row over the programme about the defeated Labour administration of 1970, *Yesterday's Men*. Essentially, his argument is that such satirical programmes about politicians are unacceptable. The political pressure which ensued, he contends, has pushed political television back into the routine practice of deference: 'The effect was a restoration of conventionality, a return to known assured formats.'[5] Dearlove, in an analysis taking a similar line, has argued that at the present time top BBC personnel act rather to defend politicians than the independence of their own programme makers.[6] In other words, there are powerful pressures to conformity, which are articulated through the points of contact between elements within the state and the broadcasting system.

The news is seen by the Corporation's theorists as an output of signal importance. It is often described, using a newspaper analogy, as the BBC's 'front page'.[7]

For News, therefore, to be reconstructed in a manner likely to invite severe reprimand would be highly unusual to say the least. As I have so far argued, given its centrepiece role as the embodiment of orthodox, safe, and definitive broadcasting practice, it cannot afford to slip out of the anchorage of an essentially conservative form and content. This chapter is a further illustration of this argument.

THE SOCIAL REALITY OF 'NEWS' AND 'CURRENT AFFAIRS'

Any discussion of the limits of change in the form and content of news, must confront the present structure of broadcast journalism in the BBC and elsewhere. Current affairs programming has been mentioned at various points in this book, and in Chapter 2 some observations were made about its development. To write about the news/current affairs distinction in 1977 is to consider a well-established orthodoxy regarding the division of journalistic labour in broadcasting. Indeed, it is not just in Britain where the distinction is utilized. As Golding and Elliott point out, it is widely adopted in countries where the BBC model prevails; they observe:

> broadcasting journalism had to come to terms with the highly regulated distinction between fact and comment which it was constrained to observe by its centrality, close relationship with government, and constitutional position . . . the distinction between fact and comment was institutionalized in organizational form by the separation of 'news' and 'current affairs'.[8]

While an absolute distinction between fact and comment is philosophically dubious, its institutional reality in the BBC is inescapable. The outsider entering the world of BBC journalism cannot fail to be schooled in its significance by those he encounters. Ernest Gellner has made the relevant observation that 'to understand the *working* of the concepts of a society is to understand its institutions'.[9] This view may be explored in relation to the 'reality' and 'necessity' of the news/current affairs distinction and its institutional manifestations.

Before this is done, it is pertinent to note an internal contradiction in the BBC's theory of the separation of fact from value. This emerges when we consider the role of the news correspondent. News is supposedly about fact alone, current affairs coverage providing the forum for explicit evaluation, commentary, contextualization, informed speculation. The *news* correspondent, however, has an official brief as a kind of analyst/commentator, albeit of a very low-key *style*. While the public image sought in such news evaluation is neutral, and the correspondents are generally low on personal charisma (unlike current affairs 'stars'), it is clear that the role itself, even in the BBC's questionable terms, is one which mixes the retailing of fact with evaluation. The overall justifying account underlying the news/current affairs distinction is therefore weak, undermined by *internal* organizational arrangements themselves. Newsmen seem largely unaware of this point, however.

From the newsman's perspective then, the output most closely related to his own is daily current affairs, which is discriminated from 'hard news' by a number of rough and ready criteria, tabulated on the next page. While it is admitted that, at the margin, the two kinds of product shade into each other, the fact that the separation is not simply conceptual, but one institutionalized in the form of distinctive production teams, creates a social reality which cannot be ignored. In sociological terms, a reification has taken place. Just how much this is so was brought home during fieldwork: in the course of a discussion with News trainees learning how to produce programmes, there were remarks passed about 'trying to abolish the news/current affairs distinction'. They had found it very difficult to do this. The very fact that such failed revisionist thinking should be admitted is an indication of the persuasive power of present arrangements within the Corporation.

The newsman's occupational culture is one within which competition is esteemed. There are two linked ways in which newsmen in broadcasting, as in print, compete with each other: speed and exclusiveness. The news and current affairs producers of the BBC are not only pitted in competition with their formal rivals the commercial companies, but also compete amongst themselves.

Burns has noted that after the war such internal competition was adopted as a cardinal principle.[10] In the present organization of news and current affairs production one sees its continued application. Such competition at times looks rather bizarre to the outsider.

The Radio News perspective

Radio News has to be discussed separately from Television News because its relationship to current affairs production is somewhat different. In the News Department the bulletins on Radio 4 are seen as the most significant. Under the BBC's scheme *Broadcasting in the Seventies*, published in 1969, the Radio 4 channel was organized in terms of 'four main news and magazine periods – breakfast time, lunchtime, early evening, and late evening'.[11] From the News Department's point of view the crucial phrase is 'news *and* magazine'. Many of the news outputs are slotted into current affairs programmes or sequences, as they are known. Thus, the early morning bulletins at 7 a.m. and at 8 a.m. are a distinct part of the *Today* programme, the main lunchtime bulletin at 1 p.m. runs for the first ten minutes of *The World at One*; the bulletin at 10 p.m. fits into the first thirteen or so minutes of *The World Tonight*. This leaves the News Department with long – and therefore prestigious – bulletins of its 'own' only at 6 p.m. and 11.30 p.m.

ATTRIBUTES OF NEWS AND CURRENT AFFAIRS
IN NEWSROOM THINKING

News	*Current Affairs*
is presented in bulletin form, notably in radio, and in those TV broadcasts of 15 minutes or less.	is presented in programme form or in sequences (radio).
is 'hard'; it gives you the facts (only).	picks up, or follows, a news story; it assumes the facts are known by the public.
is like the front page of a newspaper; it has to give all the big stories of the day.	is more like a magazine, or feature page articles; it provides interpretation, gives background.
is objective, impartial, 'straight', factual.	is more prone to comment or opinionated, seeks out angles.
tells you simply *what* happened.	tells you *how* and *why* something happened.
is immediate and highly topical.	is topical, but not necessarily tied to *today's* events.
is concise, short of space because obliged to give the day's news.	has more time (space), is less concise, expands.
is the most purely informative.	is more entertaining, (possibly) educative.

There is a conflict implicit in this situation; it takes the form of a politics of the time slot:

On *The World Tonight* we're getting twelve minutes, and we're pushing for fifteen, and it looks as though it will stay frozen at thirteen. The programme tends to resent the encroachment of the news part. So we have two bulletins a day which are *just* news: otherwise we're just grace and favour creatures – we're *allowed* part of the programmes.

(Editor of the day, Radio News)

The degree of competition was illustrated on one occasion when the presenter of *The World Tonight* came into the newsroom for a brief, informal chat with the editor of the day. When he had left the senior duty editor remarked:

> 'Do you know what Edwin did last night? Got an extra minute out of them, and ran to 14.50!' Editor of the day: 'That's the way to do it.'

While pushing for extra seconds is one aspect of internal rivalry, a more prevalent form of one-upmanship is the hoarding of interviews. As one old-hand radio current affairs man said: 'We are in competition, pursuing the same kind of stuff, and hold each other in utter contempt.'

While this utterance is more extreme than most, the operational separation does in fact force this kind of outlook on the various production teams. There is a curious practice in the newsroom: whenever the news bulletin part of a programme has been transmitted and the current affairs section begins the newsroom loudspeakers are turned off and the broadcast ignored. On one occasion a current affairs man asked: 'Do they still switch off the sequence after they've heard the bulletin?' When told that they did he shook his head wisely and said: 'It's done at their own risk and peril – *The World at One* will create news at its best.' On the other hand a *World at One* producer observed that if they ever discovered that the news bulletin's 'leads' had changed then it was 'only accidental'.

The news and current affairs teams work separately under their own editorial direction. During fieldwork virtually no apparent operational liaison could be observed. In 1973 *The World at One* began to send a representative to the morning meeting, after having no formal contact at all. This practice lapsed, however, after a few months. All the sequences are aware of the priorities sketched out by the news prospects, and the editor of each one normally has a brief discussion with the News' editor of the day; this is not seen, however, as a formal obligatory consultation. There is a good pragmatic reason why little overt consultation occurs: the various programme teams can *listen* to each other. And although the sequence is so ostentatiously switched off in the newsroom, one or other sub-editor is normally detailed to listen for any interesting interviews.

Inside the newsroom, Radio 4 bulletins are thought of as having a quite independent identity; one sub-editor summed up this perspective: 'We think of it as a bulletin always – not as a programme. We don't think at all about *The World at One*. Half the time we don't know what they're going to do until we hear it. We do our bit and they do theirs quite separately.'

Lack of co-ordination in production leads to routine duplication in reporting arrangements. Radio News controls the pool of 20 general reporters, out of which about half are attached to the daily current affairs programmes. However, once a reporter is attached he comes under the instructions of the individual programme's own editor. A Radio News reporter described the result of this: 'You often find that there's a *World at One* reporter on the scene when you get there. Neither of you knows the other's going to be there; nor does the desk.'

On the other hand where this duplication is absent, there is another source of tension:

> Reporters have various customers to satisfy. We've got one in Dublin covering the Dáil, but since the next bulletin is at 6 o'clock he sees to [the] *PM* [programme at five o'clock] first. This puts a lot of pressure on reporters who have to write separate pieces for the sequences and the news bulletins.
>
> (Editor of the day, Radio News)

Of the various daily current affairs sequences *The World at One–PM* team is identified as the News' main rival, and described in grandiloquent terms, typical in the BBC, though more suited to feudal times, as 'a group of robber barons' or a 'powerful empire'. One senior sub talked of battles to control the sound circuits through which reports are fed in for editing:

> You get trouble between us and the sequences. It's a tussle as to who comes first. I suppose it's a matter of which is harder. News is more important and should come up first. Sometimes we're beaten by *The World at One*. It can get very sticky – we had a flaming row after.

The Radio News Department is, however, assured of its place in the BBC's scheme of things. As one radio Talks producer, far away from the scenes of battle, observed quite accurately, 'the news is the most continuous output, and the [audience] figures show that listening falls off from the end of the bulletin part of the programme as it moves into the current affairs section'.

Given that the news is conceived of as providing the nation's basic and most reliable diet of information, newsmen are apt to see the current affairs role as rather residual:

We see the sequences as reacting to the news. If we play something
big on occasion they might not follow up. They mightn't react, and
they might say 'That's complete as it is.'

(Deputy Editor, Radio News)

If current affairs programmes tend to follow up or give a
longer examination in depth, it would be reasonable to expect them
to define the newsworthy stories very much in relation to each day's
news output. This is broadly what happens. Fieldwork in *The World
at One, Newsdesk* and *Newsbeat* offices indicated that the production
teams began the newsday with the same agenda, the News Prospects,
as the newsroom editors. Each editorial conference draws up its
guidelines in relation to the anticipated news output and also that of
other current affairs sequences. Each programme has its own
distinctive formula or production concept, on the basis of which the
programme is built and through these nuances of style and treatment
they proclaim their separate identities.

In the *World at One* office, quite unlike the newsroom just a few
yards away down the corridor, the news/current affairs distinction
was *raised* as problematic. An editor of the day in the newsroom
while admitting there were difficulties did not see these as very central:

The distinction exists in the mind of the BBC and not *in fact*; it's
the way the media does the thing. Heath getting up in the House of
Commons – that's news, what's comment? At the extremes the
distinction holds. I suppose it varies. It's a question of suiting the
customer – giving him ten minutes of hard news without the chat.
People don't want to wait all that time for the information – half
an hour for their football scores. They don't want all the ins and
outs.

This representative newsroom view indicates why the newsmen do
not worry unduly about the distinction between news and current
affairs. They feel they have a stable audience, and though they are
not so unsophisticated as to see themselves as absolutely divided in
kind from the sequences they are in the strategically advantageous
position of defining the hard news stories of the day. The sequences
have to take these stories and embellish them, or find entirely different stories or possibly new angles not explored by the reports in
the news. The strategic power of definition in the newsroom presents
current affairs programmes with the problem of carving out an
identity. The production team in *The World at One* office, for example,
seemed quite aware of the way in which the arbitrary institutional
distinction between news and current affairs affected the character

of work. The key figures in the programme team, including the Editor and main presenter felt that the distinction was just conventional, the latter musing hopefully. 'If you blew up the BBC and started afresh . . .'

The Television News Perspective

Television News is not linked to the various current affairs groups. Unlike their radio counterparts they have quite separate facilities and are 'totally divorced' as one correspondent put it. Television news bulletins, or programmes, are products of the News Department alone; on a normal newsday there is considerable uncertainty about what the current affairs units are doing:

> We only have the vaguest idea of what *Panorama* and *24 Hours* are going to do. There's an element, with a daily programme, of competition.
>
> (Senior duty editor, Television News)

> They [outsiders] don't realize what a big organization this is, and that so many people are doing their own thing. You can ring up and say 'This is the BBC' and they'll say 'We've just spoken to the BBC' – and you find out it was *Panorama* or *24 Hours*.
>
> (Foreign duty editor, Television News)

According to one news organizer at Television News, current affairs programmes are always eager to get the news diary. *24 Hours* (now defunct), he said, used to go to the lengths of sending a taxi from Lime Grove, where the current affairs group works, to Television Centre. The television newsman's concept of the role played by current affairs in relation to news is the same as that of his radio counterpart:

> Basically the distinction is this: our job in news is providing the public with a service of factual information about the day's events, with such explanation as is required to understand and make use of the factual information. *The job of current affairs is to amplify this service,* but more importantly to offer a range of information and informed opinion on current events.
>
> (Chief Assistant to the Editor, TV News)

Current affairs journalists seem to share this view of their role. Commenting on the coverage of the 1966 General Election campaign, Jay Blumler has noted that 'There was a strong feeling that

the obligation to report campaign events, as such fell principally on
the News Division and that the task of current affairs programming
was to go forward from the news, not to repeat it. In addition, a fear
was expressed that the compilers of the news bulletins were in a
position to "pinch the best OB material", leaving only more dull
passages for *24 Hours* to present later.'[12] Tracey, in a more recent
study has noted that 'The bulk of political television programmes
operate not news values but a number of programme values which are
in part extractions from and elaborations of events as determined by
the news division. . . .'[13]

Television newsmen, like their radio counterparts, do monitor the
current affairs outputs. Their desire for exclusivity is manifestly
serious as the following two incidents illustrate. A duty editor on the
BBC-2 desk unsuccessfully attempted to arrange an exclusive interview by the BBC's Washington Correspondent with some of the
leading actors in the Watergate Affair. The following day the
foreign news editor came over to the BBC-2 desk to tell the editor of
the day that the correspondent had conducted the interview but that
it had been snapped up by the current affairs programme, *Midweek*.
There was great annoyance at this: the correspondent should have
sought permission, it was argued, and they had put up the ideas
anyway. The foreign news editor successfully negotiated for free
access to the videotape in question. On the same occasion, the
editor of the day decided to drop an item about an Indian boy guru
from his bulletin because the news magazine *Nationwide* had covered
it. Manifesting this competitive spirit, news organizers tell of successfully keeping sources from current affairs programmes, and of other
times when they have been at the receiving end of this treatment.

The news/current affairs distinction has two major implications.
First, its acceptance and persistence within the Corporation provides
an important source of orientation for the News Departments. If the
news is the 'front page' then it clearly has high priority. The residual
status accorded current affairs is an index to newsmen's thinking
about their own status within the Corporation. Secondly, there is a
cultural implication: the two groups of journalists are provided with
different rationales for their work. Distinctive contents, formats and
styles are associated with the different classes of output. As Bernstein
has noted, in a different context, a strong classification implies a high
degree of *control* over the organization, selection, and transmission
of knowledge.[14] The newsmen draw their boundaries in practice by
a stress upon immediacy as against topicality, upon hardness as
against softness, upon brevity as against elaboration, and so forth.
The present conceptual distinction has an impressively firm social
reality in terms of established production routines. It is not surprising,

therefore, that changes in news have taken place largely *within* existing terms of reference, for these pose definite limits to change.

CHANGE AT TELEVISION NEWS

Here, I shall consider changes made by two different Editors, Mr Derrick Amoore and Mr Andrew Todd. I have departed from the normal practice of anonimity because Editors' decisions fall into the public domain, and besides, they could be easily identified simply by reading the relevant BBC handbooks. Apart from this, to identify changes with particular editorial regimes makes for a more comprehensible narrative.

The first major change during fieldwork was in the format of the BBC-1 *Nine O'Clock News*. This bulletin was extended from 20 to 25 minutes, and it was presented by two newsreaders instead of one. A further innovative stroke was the use of a projection of the newsroom as background to the newsreaders at the beginning and end of the bulletin. The veil was stripped from behind the scenes: no longer was the public to be allowed the delusion that the bulletin was the sole authorship of the newsreader. In fact, this inside look at the production-line caused confusion, irritation, distraction among the audience, and no little opposition within the newsroom.

It might be thought that approval for such extensive changes, which had internal implications of extra work and the learning of new techniques, were widely canvassed in the Television News Department. It might also be thought that to give an old-established news vehicle such a drastic facelift would also be a matter for audience research, since there were potential effects on audience size. Neither of these courses of action was taken.

Discussions with newsmen prior to the change in November 1972 indicated considerable vagueness about the date on which the 'new bulletin' would commence. Rumour and speculation were current at least six months before the date of the change. It was known beforehand that there were to be two newsreaders and that the projection of the newsroom would be used. But it is indicative of the way in which the changes were introduced that the plans were described by newsmen as 'cloaked in total secrecy'.[15] According to the Audience Research Department no research whatsoever is normally conducted in respect of format changes, which are 'generated by individual departments: they'd have very strong ideas about this'. Consequently, no research on the likely audience reaction to the new format was conducted. It was pointed out that when ITN began to use two-man presentation in 1967 'we knew the figures went up soon after they started using them'.

According to senior editors the new format was very much the Editor's idea. Mr Amoore confirmed this, saying that he had been 'bored with studio sets' and that the new format had seemed 'the only appropriate thing'. He had held discussions with only the most senior newsroom editors and the engineers as the change was 'a bit irrelevant to the rest [of the staff]'. It is apparently expected that new Editors will 'shake things up' but there were mixed feelings about the value of this particular change. The plan was put into effect about one and a half years after the Editor took the chair. The Deputy Editor, Television News, confirmed the Audience Research Department's account: 'As far as the new format goes we didn't *seek* the audience. We never even rationalized our thinking here. The old format had outlived its usefulness and needed loosening up. It was Derrick's [the Editor's] idea – he was determined. There was resistance to it in TV News – some Assistant Editors didn't like the thought.' Enlarging on the thinking behind the changes, the Deputy Editor said:

> We felt we needed a facelift anyway. There's the BBC image of the old maiden Aunt who'd bought good clothes at one time and can't afford to buy up-to-date gear. We wanted to go away from the straight-forward and factual approach. The audience is much more sophisticated.

Clearly the format change was an innovative gesture made in conditions of surprising uncertainty about the audience's reactions. Internally, there was a lack of consultation about the changes – which, when we come to examine the next two cases, can be seen to be the basic style of innovation in News.

Having said this, it is worth noting the overall loyalty of the television staff to their production, whatever their reservations. In conversation many were anxious to scotch the myth that by introducing two-man presentation they were thereby aping ITN's *News at Ten*. Rather, they appealed to history: the BBC-2 programme *Newsroom* had used the technique in the mid-sixties, with one presenter reading the foreign news, the other the home news, but none, they lamented, remembered that now.

This change – one which was purely cosmetic – was an exercise of editorial power, based on the assumption that if the new format would not attract viewers, it would nonetheless not lose any. According to Mr Amoore there was initially a heavy body of complaint from viewers which had eventually slackened. The changes did not quite end there. There were various tinkerings with the new format. The newsroom backdrop was eventually discarded. And instead of a view of the newsroom in the introductory titles, there was a satellite's eye view of the earth, which attracted its own share of opprobrium.

The editorial regime in question lasted until early 1976. During this time, there was a sharp change of mood in Television News. This must be related to the general retrenchment taking place in the BBC as its finances entered a rather precarious phase. While in 1972 and 1973, when the earlier fieldwork was conducted, there was a mood of great self-confidence in Television News, and about the assured place of news in the Corporation's output, by 1975, this had quite disappeared. The main symptom of the News Department's loss of prestige was the axing of the BBC-2 late-night programme, *News Extra*.

According to informants this came about because the programme, the most sophisticated news output of the Department, was extremely vulnerable at a time when the BBC was looking for cuts.

News Extra was axed for several reasons. The most fundamental would seem to be its failure to attract high audience ratings, at a time when outputs had increasingly to be justified in those terms – even those on the 'minority channel', BBC-2. In the world of commercially competitive broadcasting, not even a public service Corporation can escape the *ultima ratio*. While *News Extra*'s defenders argued that it was being transmitted on a channel where audiences were anyway not high, this proved to be no defence. Generally to attract no more than half a million viewers is disastrous in television terms.

There were background factors. One, which for informants in News Division was particularly important, was the known dislike of the Controller, BBC-2, for News outputs on his channel. When new schedules were being organized in 1975, the Controller said that he did not want a long news programme on his channel which was competing with the new *Tonight* current affairs programme on BBC-1. In the anodyne words of a BBC publication:

> There was some controversy in 1975 when a re-arrangement of the complementary schedules for BBC-1 and BBC-2, making way for a new current affairs programme, brought about the demise of the long BBC-2 bulletin. The time devoted to news on BBC-2 was not greatly reduced, but the total was henceforward divided between *Newsday* and *Newsnight*.[16]

According to one source, *News Extra* had not been 'sold', while the current affairs interview on *Newsday* had been 'useful PR' among prominent and influential people. Apart from this the pro-

I

gramme's producer was on good terms with the Controller, BBC-2 and made a case for his programme. For these reasons the die was cast. The Controller made it clear he wanted only a short news bulletin late at night, and, as one senior newsroom editor described it, 'The decision was handed down from on high'.

To lose a major programme, even if the airtime is more or less compensated for by other expanded or replacement outputs, was a severe blow to the Television News Department. It reflected a decline in its power and prestige at Television Centre.

Apart from this, such a loss had a deep effect on morale. During a subsequent period of fieldwork in 1976, it was clear there had been a significant decline in job satisfaction in the newsroom, notably amongst the former *News Extra* team. The measure of this can be gauged by the fact that the NUJ chapel called for an enquiry, and asked for newsmen to send in written evidence which

> largely concerned the level of job satisfaction, the involvement of all staff in the planning and treatment of coverage, and the degree of communication between those engaged on a particular story.
>
> (TV News Chapel Notice, July 1976)

One senior duty editor summed up feelings on the shop-floor rather well when he said that 'When we had *News Extra* we showed that we weren't just bulletin producers. We showed that we had intelligence and it brought us professional esteem outside. It was eccentric and stimulating and it kept open the possibilities.' There was, for the production team, a sense of pushing at the traditional bulletin form and creating more of a programme.

The situation of July–August 1976 just described needs to be set against the context of yet further changes. While the atmosphere changed after the loss of *News Extra* in September 1975, the sense of trimming back and concentrating on BBC-1 news outputs was reinforced by another change of Editor in February 1976.

The incoming Editor, Mr Andrew Todd, had formerly been Managing Editor, News, and had in this role controlled the purse-strings of News Division. He was reputed, as one newsman put it, 'to have a talent for financial management'. It was widely felt that higher management thought him to be the right man for a period of cut-backs.

In his turn, he fulfilled the role of innovator. His impact on the News Department was as follows: he reinforced the existing trend of putting increasing emphasis on BBC-1 outputs, making the *Nine O'Clock News* even more emphatically the flagship programme;

he introduced various cosmetic changes into the format of the news outputs; and lastly, he brought in distinctive ideas on the use of language and good taste.

Under the new Editor, the *Nine O'Clock News* was very clearly given more prominence in terms of internal working arrangements. The team working for the *Nine O'Clock* became more of an élite. Mr Todd made it clear, for example, that correspondents' main efforts were to be directed towards the 'flagship' programme: they were to brief writers on stories for the 5.45 p.m. bulletin, and to reserve their studio spots for the later programme. The new policy drew acid comments, particularly from the BBC-2 production team; one chief sub observed, 'I don't know why we're running a Department if all we do is concentrate on one programme'.

A further consequence of the emphasis on the *Nine O'Clock* was a spate of industrial conflict between the Television News chapel and the management over a new rota which the Editor wanted introduced. The Editor, doubtless transmitting demands for economy, wanted newsroom staff to work a seven-day rather than a six-day fortnight (the days in question being 'newsdays'). This was strongly resented, as was a new proposal to create a *Nine O'Clock* team, and a 'newsroom team' which would produce the rest of the output.

All these observations have to do with the *internal* impact of a change of Editor. More significant for the audience, because of their visibility, were format changes introduced by the new Editor. One senior duty editor saw these changes as a move back into the fifties. This expresses a mood rather than stating something historically accurate.

The main change was the move from dual presentation back to *one* newsreader. In an interview, the Editor said he felt the alternation from one man to another fragmented the output. He felt there was a need for simplicity where 'One man tells you the story'. Other format changes included a different map of the world, and new uniform titles for the series of programmes on BBC-1: *Midday News, Evening News* and *Nine O'Clock News*.

These changes were *not*, nor were the earlier ones under the previous Amoore regime, the product of audience research. Mr Todd said in an interview, 'I have to admit that the changes were almost entirely intuitive.' He made the point, however, that he had personally dealt with some 300 letters approving the changes, and, that in general there was 'an enormous amount of approval, and an insignificant amount of disapproval'.

When he had last been in Television News, one-man presentation had been the norm, and his reversion to this practice was experienced in the Department as expressive of a generally conservative shift.

Certainly, the Editor did have a strong sense of the special place of
BBC News in Britain and stressed vis-à-vis ITN that 'BBC's news must
be as good, if not better, than its competitors. It has to be better in
news information terms, rather than being a show. I'm in the information business. With ITN you feel to some extent they're there
to do an act, you get into the Morecambe and Wise area.'

Apart from these cosmetic changes, which are, it would seem, the
characteristic establishing statement of incoming Editors, the new
Editor had some decided views on news content, and linguistic style.
To take the latter first, in the newsroom Mr Todd was identified
with a 'war on cliché'. This drive for linguistic purity, which has
resonances of Reithianism, was fully codified in a document prepared
by a senior duty editor, who also happened to be a novelist, which
set out a number of linguistic do's and don'ts.

In the newsroom, this script report was primarily assessed in terms
of its PR implications. The new Editor, it was said, had to impress his
superiors, and also make a splash in the press (which he did), with
the underlying intention, perhaps, of swaying the Annan Committee on Broadcasting. While internal and external consumption
were therefore thought to provide the rationale, it was widely
realized that the document expressed a conservative mood. The
spirit of the enterprise is encapsulated in a quotation from the BBC's
News Guide which it cites approvingly.

> English is a living, changing language. There is no standard
> English to be found embalmed in the books of grammar. We
> must be ready to accept and assimilate new words and phrases.
> *But it is not for the BBC to set trends. Our rule must be to follow,
> not to pioneer.* And we must have a respect for the language and for
> the many listeners who will be genuinely offended when it is
> misused and abused.[17]

There is here an idea of the linguistic place of the BBC in the
national culture, one which harks back to the Corporation's long-
standing obsession with correct usage, and this expresses the shift in
mood occasioned by the new editorial regime.

What is particularly interesting to an outsider is the manner in
which the document entirely restricts its attention and scope to a
criticism of what it terms 'the quality of the language'. While it
dwells upon colloquialisms, grammatical errors, misused words and
phrases, jargon, cliché and so on, it nowhere in its twelve pages
seeks to offer a critique of *television* news as a type of communication.
There is no consideration of whether visual techniques – which are
obviously of paramount importance in production – are effectively

and meaningfully combined with words. Clearly, this attempt to reform practice was bound to be marginal. Indeed, the report's author saw its main effect as 'an increased consciousness of the importance of style'.[18] That is hardly a fundamental reorientation in the practices of television news production. The entire exercise is an instructive illustration of the limitations of internal critiques.

The other changes concern news judgements and their effects on content. It was widely felt that Television News had become more cautious in subtle but evident ways. The Editor, for example, was not over-fond of covering demonstrations. According to one chief sub, he had asked of one demonstration involving about 25,000 demonstrators, 'Are they respectable?' and had needed convincing about the value of coverage. In an interview, the Editor said that he felt demonstrations were covered far too automatically; he had to consider whether they were worth reporting when it was possible that the issues they concerned had themselves already been adequately dealt with.

A change of Editor is not an accident. He is seen as the vehicle through which a Department might be pushed in the desired direction. The new Editor, Mr Todd, was, in his words, 'close to ENCA' and he observed: 'Decisions about change are made *before* your appointment. The implication of your being asked to take on the job is that change is in the air, necessary, desired.'

One assistant editor evaluated the format changes as 'readily visible, easily produced, and with an immediate PR effect'. The really significant changes, he felt, concerned the use of words and the general approach: 'there's less adventurousness, they're playing safe'. One example he gave was some coverage of the Duke of Edinburgh which had not been very good 'and normally we would have junked it'. However, there was 'a strong encouragement to use it'. Another example concerned a story about British mercenaries in Angola. 'There was a definite feeling we should not have very much to do with with mercenaries' families. The story was the mercenaries and we weren't to look beyond it.' He observed there had been a shift in the line on what constituted good taste. The way he described it is characteristic in style:

There wasn't a directive, such as 'We will eschew interviews with hospital survivors of accidents'. Rather, there's a suggestion that this kind of thing is just going over the line which marks good taste. What seems to be going on is 'We've had a period of adventure, now let's be responsible'. You can sense a climate: the bosses will be at the back of your mind as you're working at the desk. If you covered an aircrash there'll be protests in the

newspapers about ghoulishness, and you've got to be sensitive
to this.

In the newsroom, the view of the new regime as a cautious one
was widespread. One senior duty editor observed that there was less
willingness to spend money. He gave as an example a story about
the effects of poison gas pollution in Seveso, Northern Italy. In
former days, a reporter would have been sent out there as soon as
the story broke. Now, they had waited for two weeks, relying on
predictable agency film, before deciding to send a man out.

CHANGE AT RADIO NEWS

As the special Audience Research Department reports indicate,
Radio News has suffered a considerable decline in its pulling power.
This is consistent with the general decline of radio audience sizes
since the introduction of television. By 1970 to retrieve sagging
fortunes radio programming had been thoroughly changed following
the plan set out in *Broadcasting in the Seventies*.

In 1970 Radio News acquired a new Editor, Mr Peter Woon, and
the changes introduced by him were, in several ways, far-reaching.
Two years later when the fieldwork began they were still a matter for
heated dispute in the newsroom. The core of the dispute was about
the role of 'voice' in the major news bulletins on Radio 4. A 'voice
piece' is a 'live' or tape-recorded report spoken by a reporter or
correspondent. The words spoken by the newsreader do not fall into
this category. The voices of people 'in the news' are categorized as
'actuality', not 'voice'; 'natural sounds' such as gunfire, explosions,
heckling, and so forth, are also classed as 'actuality'. In the 'voice'
dispute the use of both 'actuality' and 'voice' in news bulletins was
at issue.

BBC Radio News has traditionally given a key role to the newsreader. A former newsreader, Alvar Lidell, has written of the long-
standing view that 'the newsreader was not meant to obtrude: his
brief was to be the vocal equivalent of newspaper print leaving the
listener (like a man reading his *Times*) to form his own impressions.'[19]

At the time the new Editor, Mr Peter Woon, came into the Radio
News Department a slight departure had already been made from
this tradition with an occasional inclusion of voice or actuality in the
news bulletins. Voice reports had for some time been used experi-
mentally on the 1 p.m. Saturday bulletins.

Mr Woon decided to make a final break with the notion of 'vocal
print' and to use more 'voice pieces' in the news bulletin which he

regarded as 'anyway moving in that direction'. The newsreader therefore ceased to read the entire bulletin and became an anchorman linking together discrete reporter-spoken pieces. In radio terms the news bulletin moved towards what had traditionally been a current affairs format, long practised in programmes such as *Radio Newsreel* and *From Our Own Correspondent*. These programmes, together with the pioneering radio current affairs programme, *The World At One*, provided the basic stylistic models for the revamped news.

The Editor pointed out in an interview that the idea was not in fact 'all that new-fangled'; actuality had occasionally been used in news bulletins in the 1930s and *War Report* had also made extensive use of the technique.

The change implied not just an alteration in overall news presentation and the newsreader's role, but also a different style of work for the sub-editors. Until then the job had involved a good deal of writing; a new emphasis was now placed on editing magnetic tapes.

One sub, commenting in writing on an earlier draft of this case study, noted: 'The role of the sub has changed since the advent of Peter Woon. From being a writer of stories he/she has become a compiler of cues without the need of skilful writing. Boredom often results.' This view was echoed by many others, especially old hands who had been in the newsroom prior to the changes. There was a lament for the loss of craft skills; as one news organizer put it, 'We're losing the art of writing'. He went on to disparage what he saw as the obsession with technique at the expense of content: 'There used to be a lot more tight writing, and just two or three voice pieces. Now you get one minute of voice on a minor item – a ship going aground – which in the old days would have got five lines in the bulletins, which is about all it would have deserved.'

Those who supported the changes, such as the intake editor, did not see things this way. They rather argued that a new professionalism was in the making, that of the sub-cum-producer, and that a static technology had begun to move.

Clearly, though, reporters, being given prominence, became more prestigious: from being a subs' bulletin the output had become a reporters' bulletin. In the newsroom, this was seen as a direct consequence of the new Editor's having been a reporter himself. The Editor confirmed that this was a significant element in his thinking.

The changes were resisted but unsuccessfully. Various early retirements resulted, and also a number of leap-frogging promotions for younger sub-editors who endorsed the theories of the new regime. The new orthodoxy is summed up in an internal history written in 1970:

And so into the Seventies under a new Editor Radio News. . . .
With his advent, a new emphasis was quickly put in bulletins on
'live' and recorded on-the-spot coverage – *which to radio, he felt
strongly, was as pictures are to Television News, and often more
vivid and authoritative than the conventional sub-edited story.* The
number of 'inserts' has varied, naturally, according to the day's
events; the average for a 15-minute bulletin is put at six. Change is
always resisted, but on this occasion some listeners had a legitimate
complaint – that editors did not always take intelligibility into
account in putting on the air, say, a voice piece from a distant part
of the world. The point was taken and suitable instruction given.[20]

While during the fieldwork the new format was an established part
of routine practice, resentments were still strong.

One radio newsreader described the situation before the fall from
grace: 'Formerly bulletins were carefully prepared, and written in
good English. They were very well laid out a half-hour before and
the copy taster refused to accept additional copy for inclusion into
bulletins.' There is, in this comment, a sense of having departed from
traditional linguistic standards, and of order. To be immediate
rather than considered was but a further suggestion of decline. It
hankers back to an earlier definition of professionalism, when the
BBC stood as unequivocal guardian of middle-class linguistic usage.

The 'voice' *coup* was seen as so extreme that even outside the
immediately interested context of the newsroom it had become a
BBC talking point. One Radio Talks producer said in conversation
that when the new Editor, Radio News, had taken his chair he had
ordered 'an immediate quota of five voice pieces per bulletin
irrespective of content'. According to another source, the Editor's
first memo had read: 'I badly want more voice pieces in the News'.
Mr Woon's version was that he *had* issued an instruction along these
lines: it seemed to him that radio had to demonstrate its particular
abilities, namely its speed, and its capacity for using voices. He had
therefore notified his staff that he would regard 3 or 4 reports or
actuality inserts as the norm in a ten-minute bulletin. He had
made the proviso, however, that the material had to be good enough
for broadcasting. It was widely thought that the Editor had been
abrasive in his dealings with the newsroom staff. He had been
regarded as very successful in building up the BBC-2 Television News
programme *Newsroom*, and had been brought in to effect change.

The voice issue can be interpreted in part as a dispute over competing definitions of professionalism. The time-honoured ways of
presenting (and producing) news were overthrown. Identification
with the programme concepts of the new regime became essential

for those who wanted self-advancement: these, therefore, became the professional ways of producing news. One editor of the day who, as a promotee was a beneficiary of the change, observed:

> One time news was what the newsreader told you; he *told* you what X was saying. I'm in favour of voice. It takes longer but you can actually *hear* X saying whatever it is. You want sounds, voices, people. It's more honest. It's the reporting business of taking the listener or reader as close to the event as you can get. Ideally you want to let people witness the riots with him. You send, as it were, a representative. It seems meaningless to transpose a reader between the representative and his audience. There are too many hands to pass through. This way it's only second-hand, and you get the atmosphere and spirit.

The audience is used in this argument as a stick with which to beat opponents. Detractors in their turn argued that the new-style news was incomprehensible. The use of voice was talked of as 'debased coinage', 'conning the public', 'garbled mush'. Mr Woon, taking up this point, noted that he had received many letters complaining about the use of voices, although he could not be sure what proportion of the public was represented by these. He had, as a matter of policy, retained the newsreader-read bulletin on Radio 3 in order to provide an alternative service, and he referred complainants to this facility.

There was, though, a good deal of cynicism about the way the changed policy ought to be pursued in practice. As one news organizer put it: 'voice-pieces are just conning the public if you're not really at the scene'. The official line, presented above in the extract from the internal history, is that the use of voice had to be justified on journalistic grounds. Some two years after the changes, in an official memorandum, the Editor, Radio News, stressed that there was no quota of inserts into bulletins: 'our only standards are journalistic, broadcasting ones. Ask yourself "Is this the best way to tell the story?"' [21]

Obviously, this reflected a realization that the ritual use of voice and actuality had gone too far. Their correct use was explained by the intake editor:

> We try to get to someone very important who's saying something important in his own voice, if possible. We may have to do this at his doorstep, at dinners, at an airport. It's better to get the Employment Minister actually talking about the strike rather than having someone else telling us what he said – you can get the intonation better.

By this account the use of voice or actuality ought to be sparing, and subordinate to the news judgements which define stories as important. In the newsroom the use of actuality was linked to the idea of bringing stories to life. Thus, for example, a Welsh reporter's voice at a pit disaster was said to produce a better atmosphere. It was often said that American reports were acceptable from Vietnam because it 'brought things home' (a view which I also heard expressed in Television News).

There was some evidence that the new approach had become formularistic, that the means had become the end. Editors felt that they *had* to use voice pieces or they were failing in their professionalism. For example, on one occasion an editor of the day remarked that he only had 'three voice pieces. For a 15-minute bulletin we need about nine.' Another editor of the day bluntly said that the use of 'actuality clips is now a formula'.

When covering a story about the French exploding a bomb at Muroroa Atoll, the editor of the day was pleased to receive a report from the New Zealand Broadcasting Corporation, even though the sound quality was poor: 'We'll use twenty or thirty seconds when it (the bomb) goes off. All those pips (over the telephone line) add something.' He explicitly referred to it as 'decoration according to the Woon theory'.

By the end of my fieldwork the issue had certainly become far less potent. A Radio News reporter observed: 'Initially, there was a strong inclination to use voices because that was the policy: I feel it was overdone. We've begun to find a better balance.' A sub summed up the experience, ending on a similar note:

> It was a big thing when Woon came in. Everyone went mad trying to please him. There was a tremendous upheaval. A lot of pedantic old-style people were retired early or received paper promotions. It was mostly a good thing. We went mad at the beginning – everything was on tapes. There were reports from radio cars you couldn't understand. They're much stricter about voice now, and it sounds better.

It is instructive to see how the change was largely attributed to one man's whim. In fact, looking beyond the immediate power politics of the radio newsroom, it is clear that the change, while implemented by the new Editor, was consonant with the general policy of creating a new-look radio news and current affairs, sketched out in *Broadcasting in the Seventies*. Moreover, as Mr Woon himself pointed out, the change was not totally without precedent. One can see the entire voice episode as a period in which innovation was *accelerated*, possibly in anticipation of commercial competition. Television news had had to face this problem fifteen years previously, but had reacted rather than anticipated.

Nevertheless, the introduction of voice as the dominant stylistic feature of radio news did affect the subsequent power structure of the newsroom, produce a need for recruiting more reporters, and turn the bulletins into reporters' rather than writers' outputs. It also provoked a re-definition of sub-editorial skills. This Great Change, or the Woon Era, as it was variously called in true dramatic headline style, was internally debated in terms of professionalism, and the impact of format changes on the public.

Curiously though, given the claim of the new regime to be able to communicate more clearly, no audience research was carried out to establish whether its production techniques would actually achieve this. Mr Woon said that there had been no such research, as he had not felt that it was necessary. Having come into Radio News from television he was keenly aware that 'radio's distinct advantage, sound' was not being used in the same way as television's advantage, pictures. He thought that sound was interesting, and that to 'engage a person's ear you have to vary the sound'. You could not take a cavalier attitude and say that what was being done would suffice, and that it was of no interest whether or not people listened. There was a duty to make sure that people did listen and become better informed. The new, professional notion of how radio news ought to be broadcast was justified by fusing both a pragmatic, audience-interest argument, and a sacerdotal public-service one.

SCOPE AND LIMITS OF INTERNAL CRITIQUES

The changes discussed above were initiated by Editors, who acted as instruments for the views of higher management. One other possible source of change in the News Division is the journalistic workforce itself, and it is illuminating to consider the range of ideas presented to me in discussions during fieldwork about the defects of the system.

What is most striking is the almost entire absence of a *radical critique*. If this book's message has been clear there should be no great surprise in this. I have dealt at length with the creation of a concept of professional identity which suits the constraints of a state-defined impartiality. One need simply note the example of the newsman who delivered himself of criticisms of the BBC's efficiency vis-à-vis ITN, identified himself as a left-winger, and said that I should have to find someone with equally forceful but opposite opinions to check whether or not he was right!

A few pages ago I referred to the state of dissatisfaction in Television News in 1976 which produced an NUJ 'editorial enquiry'. The request for members' views by the TV News Chapel met with no response at all. While one active unionist expressed the hope that the collection of the membership's opinions would result in a demand for greater workers' control, this was a quite atypical sentiment. Rather, the observations and criticisms made by members of the News Division rarely went beyond the typical products of a mild trade union consciousness. In this connexion, it is perhaps not without significance that, so far as can be ascertained, no more than at most a handful of News Division journalists ever joined the short-lived Free Communications Group, which had a radical programme of workers' control for the communications industry.

As pointed out in Chapter 7, the legitimacy of the Corporation's power-structure is rarely questioned. Even over Northern Ireland, disquiet resolved itself into routine. Consequently, authorized initiatives concerning significant change are *expected* to issue from above, and only those concerning pay and conditions to be the serious subject of union negotiation. If the presentational style of news, a relatively superficial matter, is not itself subject to debate, it is scarcely to be expected that the very ideology and practice of news production itself will be subjected to fundamental criticism at shop-floor level.

These points are best illustrated by considering concrete instances of criticism encountered.

One of the most frequent objections was levelled against the intrusiveness and breadth of the editor of the day's brief, and mainly came from sub-editors. The editor is seen as too overbearing, as one who limits creativity and autonomy, as too involved in the flow of paper and the shaping of visual packages. While such criticisms do show an awareness of the structural role of the editor, they tend to be couched in terms of personal style, of one or other person being 'on a short fuse', 'a right bastard', or someone 'who can't bear to lose control of the details'. The emphasis on personality tends to obscure recognition of the way in which the editorial role is part of a system. Newsmen reading the study often expressed surprise that the editor of the day's intrusiveness could be explained in relation to an ideology of extra-safe news and the needs of centralized bureaucratic control, rather than a slight tendency to megalomania.

Other criticisms concern matters of efficiency. A frequent grouse which derives from the organizational separation between news and current affairs, and between the radio and television departments, is the duplication of coverage. A typical observation is the following one, a written comment on an earlier draft of this study:

Part of the news organizer's job, as I see it, is to co-ordinate the effort of covering a given story and one of my constant complaints is the number of BBC reporters who turn up at any given spot to do just that. One recent example: the return of the mercenaries to Heathrow. Representing the BBC were two reporters from TV News, two from BBC Radio (pool), one from Radio London, one from *World at One*, one from *Newsbeat*, one from *Newsdesk*, eight in all.

This criticism concerns the absence of a centralized newsdesk in the BBC. To give just another example: one radio reporter complained about a lack of help from a television reporter, who like him was covering a bomb-scare at Heathrow airport, saying, 'We might as well have been from separate organizations.'

Sometimes observations are made containing criticisms of the logic of the news/current affairs division of functions, but they are posed at the level of organizational practice, not at the level of theorizing about the structure and objectives of an optimal broadcast news. That is not to say that *all* newsmen do accept the news/current affairs distinction as holy writ. There were numerous detractors, and there seemed, after the Birt/Jay critique, to have been more who had given the matter some thought, rather than simply taking refuge in the BBC's standard explanatory formula. One television newsman, for example, favoured a news–current affairs link, and a direct career line from news into current affairs and vice-versa. An assistant editor in Radio News argued that the present system was 'just one of the Beeb's extravagances' and that there was 'nothing fundamental in it'. He went on to argue for a particular version of 'greater flexibility': 'If there's a major story then the news ought to get more time.'

Newsmen in Radio News often pointed to the anomalous arrangement whereby the Radio 4 bulletins which drew the largest audiences – those at 7 a.m. and 8 a.m. – were produced by a weary overnight skeleton team presided over by only a senior duty editor. Daytime bulletins, by contrast, had an assistant editor in charge, and a larger production team. Again, this comes under a general rubric of efficiency. Indeed, one of the expectations of those who read this study was that it would have a good deal to say on this theme, and make recommendations in that direction. Such manpower dispositions are objects of discussion within a system which is already taken for granted.

Other views concerned the use of time-slots. Some argued that stories were 'not run for long enough' and that it was assumed that the audience was watching or listening to all the outputs, so that newsmen projected their own *ennui*. Another such argument, advanced by a radio reporter was that the fifteen-minute bulletins should be used for 'two and a half minute pieces by correspondents, and not filled with rubbish'.

There were also reservations about the effects of working with the media of radio and television. Quite a number of television newsmen felt themselves to be 'captives of the technology', and too often using pictures for their own sakes rather than for the intrinsic merit of the story. One senior duty editor, for example, argued that television ought not to shy away from 'talking heads' if they were the best means of explaining complex topics. In radio, as this chapter has shown, there were residual doubts (even in 1975) about the cosmetic uses of voice reports.

In general, criticisms of the output were of a professional kind, rather than expressing reservations about the BBC's overall news policy. Thus, any slips in the smoothness of a production would be talking points. Poor deliveries by newsreaders or reporters occasions for bitchiness. Bad news judgement – leading with the wrong story – occasions for deprecation. Criticism of the political staff's slowness in breaking stories occurred quite often. An example cited by one senior newsroom editor was that over the 'Lambton callgirls' scandal, the political staff had to be urged to do things, 'rather than volunteering their services like a shot'. He went on to observe:

> The business of keeping the middle line inhibits investigatory reporting. There has to be some medium people can rely on. *We* shouldn't go too fast on a story which is later proved false. You know: responsibility is all.

This remark is analytical; it expresses a hankering after what the occupational mythology tells us journalism is *really* about; but it also counterpoises this with a well-founded realism about the limitations which face the BBC, and which, moreover, 'ought' to face it.

CONCLUSION

This chapter illustrates the scope and limits of change in production practice at Departmental level. Thoroughgoing change, which reconceptualizes and reorganizes the present institutionalized division between news and current affairs could not realistically be expected to develop at this level. It would have to be initiated at the top of the BBC's hierarchy.

Presumably, this was recognized in the Annan committee's report which suggested that the scope of news needed redefining in the direction of a 'news analysis' approach: 'The reporting of an event, the reporting of comments on that event, and an accompanying analysis of the background to that event are all the proper task of a news programme.'[22] This recommendation certainly entails a rejection of the BBC's doctrine of the 'reporting of unadorned fact'. Whether change will result remains to be seen.

However, Annan's proposals are clearer at first glance than on closer examination. While it broadens out the concept of news, it retains one of current affairs which is not logically quite distinct: 'opinionated comment on matters of general public interest is not, in our view, part of a news programme. That is properly the preserve of current affairs programmes, and we should like to see such programmes called more accurately public affairs programmes.'[23]

There is something of a contradiction here. Is 'opinionated comment on matters of general public interest' really so different from 'reporting comments on events'? Aren't all comments opinionated in some sense? In effect, Annan's retention of a news/current affairs distinction, however modified, has led it into a familiar *impasse*. How can it justify the acceptability of its distinction as opposed to the BBC's?

Annan's recommendations amount, *in toto*, to a slight broadening of the concept of news. The committee retains, however, that familiar fear that the public will not be able to tell facts from values if all the signposts are taken away. Hence its view that news and current affairs programmes do need to be firmly distinguished at the point of *consumption*, although in the course of *production* the complete separation of personnel need not be retained. The charade is therefore to continue. Annan's critique must be reformist rather than radical (and that is better than nothing) because it fails to take on board an acceptance of the view that news in *all* its forms is the product of a value-laden perspective. Different labels – even 'public affairs' – simply obscure this reality.

The Annan report also called for more experimentation in the presentation of news. In considering this point, it suggested the creation of new formats which are 'comprehensible and interesting to the nation as a whole'.[24] This point is linked to the broader definition of news. Although Annan does not specifically consider them, new formats have been devised by the BBC, as this chapter has shown, but these have hardly been far-reaching.

One striking feature of the changes documented here is the absence of audience research in all three cases. A change in the packaging in which news appears is not thought to be a matter on which the audience needs to be consulted. We are in the realm of 'professional gut feelings', and these feelings are limited to Editors. As one Editor put it: 'The news wasn't telling me in comprehensible form *what I ought to be knowing*. The audience ought to know about other things, and so the system had to be changed to meet the demands.' Clearly, the quickest and easiest way for a new Editor to assert himself is to change the format more or less dramatically, and normally without consulting the full range of news staff.

The changes considered here were not arbitrary. Taking the general thesis that each Editor is a vehicle for higher managerial policy, we can see Television News going through a period of relative licence under a 'current affairs whizz kid' to reach a period of relative conservatism under a long-serving 'hard newsman'. In Radio News, reflecting the recognition that a new-look news was needed, the new Editor sharply accelerated changes which had already begun.

In Television News, the original shift to two-man presentation occurred at a time when there was evidently some anxiety about the BBC's competitive position in relation to ITN.[25] Also, up to that point the Editor had not made any striking break with the past. The later retrenchment in News, culminating in the loss of *News Extra* brought in an Editor who pushed further the emphasis on one channel and one programme on that channel. He also brought with him a traditionalist conception of BBC News, and a move to more purist standards.

Editors can obviously effect change within certain limits. A news bulletin can move from being a sub's to a reporter's bulletin. A particular programme can be favoured, and its format changed. The most far-reaching changes concerned the use of language and the redefinition of good taste. But these, too, are of marginal effect. They might make newsmen more cautious, but they do not change the basic definition of the news as things which happen today set into a sequence, and given a minimum of background.

Changes such as these, while they might be internally contested, have no profoundly political ramifications *outside* the broadcasting organization. Whereas a switch from deference and the doctrine of corporate caution, to one of political satire and tough investigative-ness would be certain to bring a sharp backlash.

I have argued that far-reaching changes cannot be generated from within at a Departmental managerial level. Nor is there any likeli-hood that they will issue from the working journalists themselves. For such a direction to be pursued there would have to be changes in the BBC's current relationship to the state, and that could only occur through a restructuring of the place of broadcasting in British society.

Notes and references

Chapter 1 Introduction

1. Examples of British studies are Blumler, 1969; Burns, 1969; Halloran *et al.*, 1970; Elliott, 1972; Burns, 1972; Tracey, 1975. American broadcasting is covered by Gans, 1966; Tuchman, 1969; Warner, 1971; Epstein, 1973; Cantor, 1971. A rare insider study of French television is Cayrol, 1974. Golding and Elliott, 1976, have studied news production in Ireland, Nigeria and Sweden.

   Another American text which reaches me just before this book goes to press is David Altheide's *Creating reality*, 1976. That we should quite independently have arrived at such similar titles is obviously no mere accident, but dictated by the subject-matter itself. Altheide's study concerns itself with (mainly) local television news in the USA, and differs from mine in interpretation on a number of counts. He greatly overrates, in my view, the power of the news, and particularly in his analysis of Watergate tends to take an extremely voluntaristic line about the success of the media in toppling Nixon. Woodstein rides again. His notion of *the* 'news perspective' is too undifferentiated. For instance, were *no* media *for* Nixon? More generally, while I would agree that news is indeed the product of a cultural perspective, we need to be alive to nuances and distinctions between media which an undifferentiated conception of such a perspective obscures. It is precisely relatively minor differences which support the idea of a fully free press. Moreover, I cannot agree with Altheide's view that the 'news perspective' is a 'more troublesome' source of bias than 'values and ideology' (1976: 177). This is a false distinction as the 'news perspective' *is* a form of ideology. I would also disagree with Altheide's pluralism, and his consequent over-emphasis on news as *the* key cultural integrator. Having said this, I would nonetheless consider his book to be a useful addition to work in this area, and fully sympathize with its demystificatory intent, and its urgings to news consumers to be more critical of what they see, hear, and read.
2. Cf. Golding and Elliott, 1976: Ch. 1, which reviews some of the contemporary debate between newsmen and media sociologists.
3. This book is long enough as it is, so I will not develop any points about method and the problems of ethnography here. Cf. a forthcoming paper 'Urbane sociology and the Beeb: On studying an exposed organization'.

Chapter 2 The formation of BBC news

1. Briggs, 1961: Ch. 3 *passim*.
2. Cf. Erik Barnouw, 1968: 18–22; Golding and Elliott, 1976: Ch. 2.
3. Briggs, 1961: 130–4; Paulu, 1961: 86; Paulu, 1956: 155.
4. Carey in Halmos, 1969: 32.
5. Harris, 1976.
6. Briggs, 1961: 168.
7. Ibid: 172–4.
8. Ibid: 265; cf. also 262–3.
9. Gorham, 1952: 44.
10. Briggs, 1961; Boyle, 1972; Tracey, 1975.
11. Cf. his account in Ch. 5 sect. 3 *passim*. For a recent assessment by the BBC's DG supporting Reith's actions, given the constraints, see Curran, 1976a.
12. Quoted in Briggs, 1961: 376.
13. Tracey, 1975: 359.
14. Boyle, 1972: 194; Briggs, 1961: 367.
15. Tracey, 1975: 354–5 for the full quotation and the attribution to Gainford.
16. Briggs, 1961: 364–6.
17. Ibid: 373.
18. Ibid: 366.
19. Ibid: 374.
20. Ibid: 369.
21. Ibid: 266.
22. Ibid: 229–49.
23. Brown in Halmos (ed), 1969.
24. Williams, 1971: 117.
25. Scannell and Cardiff, 1976: 6.
26. Williams, 1968; cf. Burrage, 1969.
27. The publication of his Diary, however, was for many a case of Reith cutting himself down to size through self-exposure.
28. Burrage, 1973.
29. Cardiff and Scannell, 1976: 8–10.
30. So says G. H. G. Strutt, then prominent in news, to various top BBC executives. Quoted by Briggs, 1961: 267.
31. Briggs, 1965: 153.
32. Ibid: 153–4; Paulu dates the 6 p.m. arrangement as being made in 1927.
33. Quoted in Briggs, 1965: 154.
34. Ibid: 152; 155.
35. Ibid: 155.
36. Ibid: 156.
37. Miall, 1966: 12.
38. This is suggested by Dimbleby's former associate, Charles Gardner, in Miall, 1966: 13.

39. Howarth in Miall, 1966: 18; cf. Briggs, 1965: 157–8.
40. Briggs, 1965: 138; Howarth in Miall, 1966: 19.
41. Miall, 1966: 21; cf. Dimbleby, 1975: Ch. 3 for a detailed account.
42. Briggs, 1965: 501.
43. Paulu, 1956: 155.
44. Ibid: 156; Briggs, 1965: 159.
45. Quoted in Briggs, 1965: 128.
46. Ibid: 131.
47. Ibid: 133–6; 146–7.
48. Coatman, 1951: 292.
49. Barnouw, 1968: 22.
50. Dimbleby, 1975: 83–4.
51. Briggs, 1965: 389.
52. Ibid: 394; 392.
53. Ibid: 625–6.
54. Quoted in ibid: 628.
55. Ibid: 646; 648; 650–2.
56. Barnouw, 1968: 80–3.
57. Quoted in Briggs, 1965: 656–7.
58. Briggs, 1970: 31.
59. Coatman, 1951: 293.
60. Gorham, 1952: 172.
61. Briggs, 1970: 34.
62. Ibid: 31.
63. Quoted in ibid: 163.
64. Quoted in ibid: 308.
65. Scannell and Cardiff, 1976.
66. McInnes, 1970: 2.
67. Briggs, 1970: 80.
68. Ibid: 101–2.
69. Briggs, 1970: 49; cf. Gorham, 1952: 213.
70. Barnouw, 1968: 149.
71. McInnes, 1970: 4–5.
72. Briggs, 1970: 48; 155.
73. Gorham, 1952: 172.
74. Quoted in McInnes, 1970: 6; emphasis added.
75. Quoted in ibid: 7.
76. Cf. MacLeod, 1947, for a superb portrait of the wartime BBC, and the devious internal politics of getting rid of a 'red' announcer.
77. Briggs, 1970: 49.
78. Ibid: 120; Dimbleby, 1975: 94–5.
79. McInnes, 1970: 5.
80. Briggs, 1970: 656–60.
81. Dimbleby, 1975: 174–5.
82. Briggs, 1970: 121; 179–80.
83. Ibid: 543–7.
84. Dimbleby, 1975: 204.
85. Simon, 1953: 113.
86. Ibid: 203.

87. Haley, *The Responsibilities of Broadcasting*, 1946: 10–11; quoted in Paulu, 1961: 149.
88. Fairlie, 1959: 208.
89. BBC AR, 1957, 1962.
90. Grisewood, 1968: 201.
91. MacKenzie, 1969: 841–3.
92. BBC News Inf., 1969: 4; Gorham, 1952: 153; 156.
93. Cox, 1956: 88–94.
94. BBC News Inf., 1969: 5.
96. Dougall, 1973: 202.
97. BBC AR, 1953.
98. Black, 1972a: 22; cf. also Hood, 1967.
99. Dougall, 1973: 238, attributes the phrase to Hugh Greene.
100. Paulu, 1956: 160–2.
101. Ibid: 159.
102. Stuart, 1970: 35; 102–3.
103. Paulu, 1956: 293.
104. BBC News Inf., 1969: 5.
105. BBC AR, 1954.
106. Hood, 1967: 107; cf. also BBC News Inf., 1969: 5.
107. Stuart, 1970: 86.
108. Barnouw, 1970: 40; cf. Day, 1961.
109. Wilson, 1961: 13; 213.
110. Burrage, 1969: 250.
111. Cf. Williams, 1968: 118–19.
112. Hood, 1967: 106.
113. Day, 1961: 10.
114. Ibid: 49; emphasis added.
115. Ibid: 64.
116. Ibid: 72.
117. Ibid: 69, 70, 72; cf. Paulu, 1961: 93.
118. Quoted in Paulu, 1961: 89.
119. Ibid: 89.
120. Dimbleby, 1975: 267–9. (The concept 'current affairs' as referent of a distinctive form of programming first appears in the *BBC Handbook*, 1960: 44, shortly after Greene's appointment as DG in 1959. Current affairs programmes are labelled 'the wide range of topical programmes' which are 'in some sense complementary to the news bulletins'.)
121. Ibid: 271.
122. Smith, 1973: 77–80.
123. Tracey, 1975: 273; 519.
124. McInnes, 1970: 9.
125. Hill, 1974: Ch. 3; Smith, 1973: 82–4. The BBC had, however, been running an extended news programme, *Newsroom*, on the minority channel, BBC-2, since the mid-1960s. It took ITN to show that it could be 'marketed' as a *popular* programme.
126. Thomas, 1962: 54.
127. Swallow, 1966: 27.
128. Paulu, 1961: 93.

129. *The Times*, 30 November 1965.
130. Glasgow Media Group, 1976.

Chapter 3 *The production of radio and television news*

1. Glasgow media group, 1976: Ch. 3. It could be argued in defence that being restricted to two weeks' fieldwork in one newsroom, and sneaking five days in another, is hardly time enough to produce an adequate account. It depends. For an example of what *can* be done to describe and analyse the news production process in just one week see Halloran, Elliott, and Murdock, 1970: Ch. 5.
2. Golding and Elliott, 1976.
3. These were the outputs on the last occasion I did fieldwork, namely July/August 1976.
4. At weekends, when the outputs are more restricted, the editor of the day is generally in telephone contact with either the Editor or his deputy for routine consultations.
5. There are slight variations in name – News *Diary*, News *Prospects* – at Television Centre and Broadcasting House respectively. These don't indicate any distinction in purpose or content. At the BBC's External Services News, based in Bush House, London, the document in question is called the *Morning* Dairy.
6. At Television Centre, there are five Assistant Editors who man the two desks, generally working a shift consisting of one planning day and two days on the desk. At Broadcasting House, there are two Assistant Editors acting as editor of the day, working three-day shifts.
7. This gives too neat a picture; there are, in fact, 'late' stories which have to be dealt with *after* this point in the production cycle.
8. Cf. Golding and Elliott, 1976, on the dependence of smaller broadcast news organizations – in Sweden, Nigeria and Ireland – on agency material. See also the interesting analysis of Eurovision news exchanges by Collins, 1976: 11–16.
9. The sources for these figures were: the Editor, Television News, the Chief Assistant to the Editor, Television News, the Foreign News Editor (Television) and the Head of Home and Foreign Correspondents. They were given during interviews in 1974 and 1976.
10. Cf. Golding and Elliott, 1976: on their evidence, only the Swedish broadcasting organization, SR, with fourteen foreign correspondents, can be usefully compared with the BBC. Epstein, 1973: 100, says that NBC News has nine TV crews abroad.
11. *News Guide*, 1972: 61.
12. Glasgow Media group, 1976: Ch. 3; Day, 1961: Ch. 6; Tyrrell, 1972: Ch. 1; *Sunday Times Magazine*, 26.8.73: 29–33.
13. Golding and Elliott, 1976; Epstein, 1973.
14. Epstein, 1973: 133.
15. Ibid: 141.
16. Golding and Elliott, 1976: 4/22.

Chapter 4   A stop-watch culture

1.   Wintour, 1972: Ch. 1; Priestland, 1973.
2.   Cf. however, Tuchman, 1969: Ch. 4; Bensman and Lilienfeld, 1971; Park, 1940.
3.   Gurvitch, 1964: 14.
4.   Cottrell, 1939.
5.   Sorokin and Merton, 1937.
6.   Hall, 1959; for a counter-argument see Clark, 1976.
7.   Moore, 1963a: 163.
8.   Marcus, 1960–61; Bohannan, 1953; Evans-Pritchard, 1940: Ch. 3.
9.   Moore, 1963b; Thompson, 1967.
10.   Weber, 1968: 157–8.
11.   Lyman and Scott, 1970.
12.   Williams, 1965: 197.
13.   Berger and Luckmann, 1971: 41.
14.   Day, 1961: 12.
15.   Memorandum from Editor, Television News, to News Staff, 18 June 1972.
16.   Tracey, 1975: 486.
17.   Edwards, 1964: 6, 7; emphasis added.
18.   Cf. Briggs, 1965: 153; Briggs, 1970: 180; Halloran et al., 1970: 185–6 have also noted the particular BBC concern with 'accuracy'.
19.   Cf. Golding and Elliott, 1976; Epstein, 1973.
20.   GAC, 1976: 19–22.
21.   Memorandum, Deputy Editor, Radio News, to News Staff, 31 January 1973.
22.   Slots are products of complex intra-organizational bargaining between the heads of particular departments in the BBC and the Controllers of the channels. As the scheduling of the entire broadcasting day depends on the stability of slots, it is not surprising that they are rarely tampered with. News slots are extended where a special need can be shown: e.g. to cover the shock resignation of Harold Wilson and its immediate implications.
23.   *News Guide*, 1972: 8.
24.   Williams, 1974: Ch. 3.
25.   Tyrrell, 1972: 19.
26.   Swallow, 1966: 83; and cf. Ch. 9 below for further discussion of this point.

Chapter 5   The missing link: 'Professionalism' and the audience

1.   Burns, 1969.
2.   Wright, 1959: 59; McQuail, 1969a: 9; for a general view of producer–consumer relations, and of 'professionalism', see Johnson, 1972.
3.   McQuail, 1969b.
4.   Elliott, 1972; Tracey, 1975.

5.   Breed, 1955; Gieber, 1960; Gieber and Johnson, 1961; Gieber, 1964; Judd, 1961; Tunstall, 1971.
6.   *News Guide*, 1972: 77.
7.   Gans, 180: 10; Cantor, 1971: 165.
8.   Hood, 1967: 38.
9.   Cf. Tunstall, 1971.
10.   *News Guide*, 1972: 14; emphasis added.
11.   Halloran *et al.*, 1970: 149.
12.   Wedell, 1968: 51.
13.   Wheldon, 1971.
14.   Wedell, 1968: 235; cf. also 223–42.
15.   Cf. Burns, 1969: 71–2; Wedell, 1968: 235.
16.   Memorandum, Deputy Editor, Radio News to News Staff, 23 January 1973.
17.   BBC AR, 1957; BBC AR, 1962; BBC AR, 1971; BBC AR, 1973.
18.   Collins, 1976; see his general critique of the audience research.
19.   Tunstall, 1971: 7.
20.   BBC AR, 1971: 10.
21.   Ibid: 10.
22.   Ibid: 11.
23.   BBC AR, 1973: 3.
24.   Crozier, 1958: 129.
25.   BBC AR, 1973: 1, 3.
26.   E.g. Peter Lennon, *The Sunday Times Review*, 11 March 1973; Jonathan Raban, *Radio Times*, 19–25 October 1974. More exceptional in terms of sound and fury are the pieces by Birt and Jay. Why such common-place thinking should receive so much attention is a good question for media sociologists to answer. Cf. below, Chapter 9.
27.   Gans, 1970: 9.
28.   Galtung and Ruge, 1970: 289, have identified this 'law' in their content analysis: 'the lower the rank of the nation, the more negative the news from that nation will be.'
29.   Such images are used in all media organizations. A newsman who had worked for Visnews told me that he wrote for 'the housewife in Hong Kong'. Ed Murrow of CBS told reporters during World War Two that they should 'Talk to be understood by the truck driver while not insulting the professor's intelligence'. Quoted by Smith, 1972c.
30.   *News Guide*, 1972: 7.
31.   Cf. Lang and Lang, 1968: Ch. 8, for a critique.
32.   Whale, 1969: 19.
33.   Cox, 1967: 132–3.
34.   Adam, 1965.
35.   Cox, 1967: 133; emphasis added.
36.   Day, 1970: 79.
37.   Whale, 1969: 24. (The italics are my own.)
38.   Cox, 1967: 135.
39.   BBC AR, 1971: 16.
40.   Elliott, 1972: 151–2.
41.   Johnson, 1972: 41.

Chapter 6   The mediation of control (1) : The editorial system

1.   Breed, 1955: Judd; 1961; Stark, 1962; Matejko, 1970; Warner, 1971; Sigelman, 1973; all take up this theme. In the course of more general studies, so do Cantor, 1971; Epstein, 1973; and Tracey, 1975.
2.   Cf. Briggs, 1965: 369–416; Wedell, 1968: 110–14.
3.   Tracey, 1975: 369–416; quotation from p. 381.
4.   Hill, 1974: 263.
5.   *Principles and Practice*, 1972: 6.
6.   Ibid: p. 20.
7.   Greene, 1969: 82.
8.   Briggs, 1965: 131.
9.   Simon, 1953: 91.
10.   Coatman, 1951: 296.
11.   Grisewood, 1968: 190.
12.   Ibid: 187.
13.   Greene, 1969: 127.
14.   Hill, 1974: Ch. 28.
15.   *Principles and Practice*, 1972: 20–1.
16.   The phrase is that of Wedell, 1969: 145.
17.   Gerth and Mills (eds), 1967: 197.
18.   Wedell, 1968: 176.
19.   Allen, 1971: 186.
20.   Ibid., 187.
21.   Croasdell, 1974.
22.   Friedson, 1971: 48–50.
23.   Cf. Black, 1972b: 73.

Chapter 7   The mediation of control (2) : Corporate ideology

1.   'Commentary: Balance and Impartiality', *Ariel*, BBC Staff Magazine, 23 March 1973: 8.
2.   Cf. Geertz, 1964.
3.   Peterson, in Siebert *et al.*, 1956; Brown in Halmos (ed), 1969.
4.   It is this ultimately positivistic legitimation of the news which seems to have inspired the interest of phenomenologists, Marxists, and radical sociologists alike. The sociological critique of news, not coincidentally, has gathered pace at a time when the sociological critique of sociology is in full swing. Broadcast news in particular has obviously been seen as too good a target to miss. At a time of sharpening ideological struggle the neutrality of the news' representation of reality is bound to be doubted.
5.   Gouldner, 1975: Chs. 1 and 2.
6.   Cf. the discussions in Johnstone *et al.*, 1972–73 and Janowitz, 1975 on journalistic models. Arblaster in Benewick *et al.* (eds), 1973 has relevant comments on 'unattached' social science.
7.   Taylor in Montefiore (ed), 1975: 147.

8. Lang and Lang, 1968: 295.
9. Cf. for example the studies by Halloran *et al.*, 1970; Epstein, 1973; Tuchman, 1972 and 1973.
10. Miliband, 1969: 223–4.
11. Greene, 1965.
12. *Principles and Practice*, 1972: 8.
13. Swallow, 1966: 19–20.
14. Kumar, 1975: 84.
15. Miliband, 1969: 3; for other critiques from the same standpoint cf. Anderson, 1974 and Westergaard and Resler, 1976.
16. Hall, 1972.
17. Curran, 1974a: 782.
18. Cox, 1976: 626-7.
19. BBC GAC, 1976: 10.
20. Harris, 1971: 23.
21. Cf. Murdock in Cohen and Young (eds), 1973; Hall in Rock and MacIntosh, 1974. Some of the most interesting recent work has been in the area of media coverage of 'industrial relations'. John Downing has produced some pioneering work, though as yet regrettably unpublished; see Downing, 1971. Other relevant work taking a similar approach is Morley, 1976 and Glasgow Media Group, 1976.
22. Cf. Hirsch, 1973.
23. Cf. Downing, 1976; and also the works cited in note 15. Murdock and Golding, 1974, have examined the media in relation to such an approach to the political economy of capitalism.
24. Taylor, 1975: 9.
25. Coser, 1965: Chs. 20 and 24.
26. Elliott, 1972: 165.
27. Cf. Mannheim, 1936: Ch. 3 where his position is stated in full. A full account of the social background is to be found in Remmling, 1975; also cf. Coser, 1971: 428–63 and Heeren, 1971.
28. Phrases to be found in GAC 1976 and in Taylor, 1975.
29. An early version occurs in Bloomfield, 1941: 117; as Gans, 1966: 6 notes, the same kind of 'test' is applied in the US news networks.
30. Cf. Epstein, 1973: Ch. 2.
31. Tuchman, 1972.
32. Tracey, 1975: 466.
33. *Principles and Practice*, 1972: 3.
34. *The Jewish Chronicle*, 23 July 1971.
35. *The Listener,* 19 March 1970: 362–3. The correspondence ran every week until 21 May 1970.
36. Litterick, 1976.
37. As *The Sunday Times*, 25 July 1976, put it.
38. Cf. the articles in the NUJ house magazine, *Journalist*, August and September, 1976; also cf. an NUJ press statement on MacShane, dated 6 May 1977.
39. Edwards, 1964: 12.
40. Smith, 1972a.
41. BBC GAC, 1976: 3.

K*

42. Burns, 1972: 302.
43. Goffman, 1971: 231.
44. *Principles and Practice*, 1972: 4.
45. Kumar, 1975: 84.
46. Belfrage, 1951: 107–8.
47. Day, 1961: 50.
48. BBC AR, August 1971: 20–1; February 1971: 4.

Chapter 8   The reporting of Northern Ireland

1.   Beadle, 1963: 23.
2.   Smith, 1972b: 18–19.
3.   Cathcart, 1972: 2.
4.   Smith, 1972b: 19–20.
5.   Elliott, 1976.
6.   Smith, 1972b: 22.
7.   Taylor, 1975: 10.
8.   *Principles and Practice*, 1972: 15.
9.   Ibid, 1972: 15. (The italics are my own.)
10. Hill, 1974: 207.
11. *Private Eye*, No. 258, 5 November 1971: 22–3.
12. *The Guardian*, 2 November 1971; *The Sunday Times*, 7 November 1971.
13. *The Sunday Times*, *The Observer*, 21 November 1971.
14. Hill, 1974: 209.
15. Ibid: 210–211.
16. *The Guardian*, 23 November 1971.
17. *New Statesman*, 31 December 1971: 911–12.
18. *Open Secret*, No. 8, p. 5.
19. Ibid.
20. *News Guide*, 1972: 38.
21. *New Statesman*, 31 December 1971: 911.
22. Taylor, 1975: 13.
23. Hill, 1974: 218.
24. Ibid, 219.
25. Ibid, 221: the entire affair was extensively covered by the British press, beginning with a *Daily Telegraph* report on 24 December 1971. The account draws also on *The Guardian*, *The Sunday Times*, and *The Observer* up to 9 January 1972.
26. Quoted from *The Guardian*, 29 December 1971.
27. Hill, 1974: 224.
28. Taylor, 1975: 13.
29. Crawley, 1976: 166.
30. Curran speaking in an interview on *The World at One*, 13 November 1976.
31. Taylor, 1975: 14.
32. Golding and Elliott, 1976: 3/3–3/11 *passim*; quotation from 3/8.
33. Gardiner, 1975: Ch. 3 para 76.

34. *Irish Times*, 'The Saturday Interview', 15 November 1975.
35. Elliott, 1976.
36. Taylor, 1975: 11.
37. Op. cit., 911.
38. BBC *News Information*, 8 August 1975.
39. Cf. *The Irish Times* interview.
40. Taylor, 1975: 11.
41. Winchester, 1974; Hoggart, 1973, quotation from p. 80; Stephen, 1976.
42. Taylor, 1975: 12.
43. *The Listener*, 20 June 1974.
44. *The Listener*, 18 November 1976.
45. Winchester, 1974: 143–4.
46. Cf. note 44.
47. Memorandum from Chief Assistant to Editor, Television News to Newsroom Staff.
48. Elliott, 1976: 2/4.
49. Ibid: 2/6.
50. *The Listener*, 6 January 1972.
51. *The Listener*, 5 October 1972.
52. Quoted in Taylor, 1975: 10.
53. Ibid.
54. Fisk, 1975: 129.
55. Bell, 1972a.
56. Fisk, 1975: 136.
57. Ibid: 140.
58. Ibid: 137.
59. Quoted in ibid: 127.
60. *The Guardian*, 7 January 1977.
61. During the course of a debate on the Annan committee report on broadcasting, BBC-2, 8.10 p.m., Tuesday, 10 May 1977.
62. Extensive extracts are reprinted in 'Northern Ireland: Francis answers BBC's critics', *Broadcast*, 28 February 1977: 10, 30.
63. See Keith Kyle, 'Bernard O'Connor's story', *The Listener*, 10 March 1977.
64. *The Times*, 14 March 1977; see *The Guardian*, 14 March 1977.
65. *The Sunday Times*, 13 March 1977.
66. 'Insight', *The Sunday Times*, 13 March 1977.
67. *The Guardian*, 15 March 1977; '*Tonight* on Northern Ireland – Sir Charles Curran replies', *The Listener*, 17 March 1977.
68. Annan, 1977: 270.
69. Ibid.
70. It is not only the British government which has put pressure on the BBC and IBA. At a European Broadcasting Union seminar in Dublin on Monday, 23 May 1977, Dr Conor Cruise O'Brien, the Irish Minister for Posts and Telecommunications, 'revealed that he had complained privately to both British networks about interviews with IRA men in the past'. Sir Charles Curran expounded the BBC's familiar line saying 'You can't expect people to understand the political complexities of the situation

unless they understand to some extent what the IRA is up to'. One might doubt that two interviews with the IRA during a period of eight years is a very substantial contribution to enlightenment. Despite all the fuss, this seems to indicate that the state's policy has been pretty effective. See *The Guardian*, 24 May 1977.

Chapter 9   *The limits of change*

1.   Birt and Jay, 1975; and cf. their two subsequent articles of September 1976.
2.   *The Times*, 1 October 1975.
3.   BBC GAC, 1976: 16.
4.   Nordenstreng (ed), 1974: 16, and 17–42 generally; cf. Murdock and Golding, 1974.
5.   Tracey, 1975: 446.
6.   Dearlove, 1974.
7.   Edwards, 1964: 5.
8.   Golding and Elliott, 1976: 2/16.
9.   Gellner, 1970: 115–49.
10.   Burns, 1964: 75–9.
11.   BBC, 1969.
12.   Blumler, 1969: 109; emphasis added.
13.   Tracey, 1975: 237.
14.   Bernstein, 1973: 237–56.
15.   Cf. Robert Dougall, 1973: 305–7.
16.   BBC GAC, 1976: 16.
17.   Bloomfield, 1976.
18.   Ibid: 11.
19.   Lidell, 1972.
20.   McInnes, 1970: 10; emphasis added.
21.   Memorandum, Editor, Radio News, to News Staff, 9 March 1972.
22.   Annan, 1977: 285.
23.   Ibid.
24.   Annan, 1977: 285. The BBC did pre-empt this particular criticism by creating the *Newsnight* programme in Autumn 1976. This is broadcast on weekdays at 7.30 p.m. on BBC-2 – the old *Newsroom* slot. During fieldwork, there was considerable excitement at the prospect of a news team working together with a current affairs team in creating one homogeneous programme. Whether *Newsnight* has been successful in this respect is a matter of opinion. At present, the programme still inhabits the low-audience ghetto, and has something of a show-piece air about it. The test of the BBC's faith in this kind of format will be its emergence on BBC-1.
25.   One may infer this from the commissioning of BBC AR 1973, which was solely concerned with the 'relative standing' of the news services.

Bibliography

Kenneth Adam, 'The BBC's duty to society – II', *The Listener*, 24 June 1965.

Isobel Allen, 'Women in the BBC' in Michael Fogarty, A. J. Allen, Isobel Allen, Patricia Walters, *Women in Top Jobs: Four studies in achievement* (London: George Allen and Unwin) 1971.

David L. Altheide, *Creating reality: How tv news distorts events* (Beverly Hills, London: Sage Publications) 1976.

Charles H. Anderson, *The political economy of social class* (Englewood Cliffs, NJ: Prentice Hall, Inc.) 1974.

Lord Annan (chairman), *Report of the committee on the future of broadcasting*, Cmnd. 6753 (London: HMSO) 1977.

Anon, 'Curran affairs', *Private Eye*, 5 November 1971, pp. 22–3.

Anon, 'The BBC and Northern Ireland', *New Statesman*, 31 December 1971, pp. 911–12.

Anon, 'The rivals' progress: news forced towards a common form', *The Times*, 31 November 1965.

Anthony Arblaster, 'Ideology and intellectuals', in Robert Benewick, R. N. Berki, Bhikku Parekh (eds.) *Knowledge and belief in politics* (London: George Allen and Unwin) 1973.

BBC Audience Research Reports:

The Use of News (Sound only), VR/53/247, 4 June 1953.

News and Newsreel, VR/54/374, 23 July 1954.

The News: A study of news listening and viewing and of the public's attitude towards the BBC News service, LR/57/920, June 1957.

News broadcasting in 1962: a study of news listening and viewing and of the public's attitudes towards news broadcasts, LR/62/1586, October 1962.

News broadcasting and the public in 1970: a study of news bulletin audiences and the public's attitude towards news broadcasts, LR/71/537, August 1971.

The public image of some newsreaders and current affairs presenters, VR/71/15, 22 February 1971.

The relative standing of BBC News and ITN, VR/73/416, July 1973.

BBC, *Broadcasting in the Seventies*, 1969.

BBC General Advisory Council, *The Task of Broadcasting News*, May 1976.

BBC News Information (on the history of BBC News), Alexandra Palace, 20 January 1969.

BBC News Information, 'Political and activist groups in Northern Ireland', Research Unit, Broadcasting House, 8 August 1975.

BBC, *Principles and Practice in News and Current Affairs*, 1971.

BBC Radio News, *News Guide*, revised edition, May 1972.

Erik Barnouw, *The Golden Web: A History of Broadcasting in the United States, 1933–1953* (New York: Oxford University Press) 1968.

Erik Barnouw, *The Image Empire: A History of Broadcasting in the United States from 1953* (New York: Oxford University Press) 1970.

Sir Gerald Beadle, *Television: a critical review* (London: George Allen and Unwin) 1963.

Bruce Belfrage, *One man in his time* (London) 1951.

Martin Bell, 'Views', *The Listener*, 6 January 1972.

Martin Bell, 'Ulster Coverage', *The Listener*, 5 October 1972.

Joseph Bensman and Robert Lilienfeld, 'The journalistic attitude' in Bernard Rosenberg and David Manning White (eds.) *Mass Culture Revisited* (New York: Van Nostrand) 1971.

Peter Berger and Thomas Luckmann, *The Social Construction of Reality* (Harmondsworth: Penguin) 1971.

Basil Bernstein, 'On the classification and framing of educational knowledge' in *Class, Codes and Control* (St Albans: Paladin) 1973.

John Birt, 'Can television news break the understanding barrier?', *The Times*, 22 February 1975.

John Birt and Peter Jay, 'Television journalism: the child of an unhappy marriage between newspapers and film', *The Times*, 30 September 1975.

John Birt and Peter Jay, 'The radical changes needed to remedy TV's bias against understanding', *The Times*, 1 October 1975.

John Birt and Peter Jay, 'How television news can hold the mass audience', *The Times*, 2 September 1976.

John Birt and Peter Jay, 'Why television news is in danger of becoming an anti-social force', *The Times*, 3 September 1976.

Peter Black, (1972a), *The Mirror in the Corner: People's Television* (London: Hutchinson) 1972.

Peter Black (1972b), *The biggest aspidistra in the world* (London: BBC) 1972.

A. J. W. Bloomfield, 'Script report', BBC TV News Internal Memorandum, 11 June 1976.

Paul Bloomfield, BBC (London) 1941.

Jay G. Blumler, 'Producers' attitudes towards television coverage of an election campaign: a case study' in Paul Halmos (ed.) 'The sociology of mass media communicators', *The Sociological Review Monograph 13*, University of Keele, 1969.

Paul Bohannan, 'Concepts of time among the Tiv of Nigeria', *Southwestern Journal of Anthropology*, 1953, pp. 251–61.

Andrew Boyle, *Only the wind will listen: Reith of the BBC* (London: Hutchinson) 1972.

Warren Breed, 'Social Control in the Newsroom: a functional analysis', *Social Forces*, 1955, pp. 326–35.

Asa Briggs, *The Birth of Broadcasting: The History of Broadcasting in the United Kingdom*, Volume 1 (London: Oxford University Press) 1961.

Asa Briggs, *The Golden Age of Wireless: The History of Broadcasting in the United Kingdom*, Volume 2 (London: Oxford University Press) 1965.

Asa Briggs, *The War of Words: The History of Broadcasting in the United Kingdom*, Volume 3 (London: Oxford University Press) 1970.

Roger L. Brown, 'Some aspects of mass media ideologies' in *The Sociological Review Monograph 13*, 1969, pp. 155–67.

Tom Burns, *Cultural bureaucracy: a study of occupational milieux in the BBC* (Department of Sociology: University of Edinburgh) April 1964.

Tom Burns, 'Public service and private world' in *The Sociological Review Monograph 13*, 1969, pp. 53–73.

Tom Burns, 'Commitment and career in the BBC' in Denis McQuail (ed.) *The Sociology of Mass Communications* (Harmondsworth: Penguin) 1972, pp. 281–310.

Michael Burrage, 'Two approaches to the study of mass media', *European Journal of Sociology*, 1969, pp. 238–53.

Michael Burrage, 'Nationalization and the professional ideal', *Sociology*, 1973, pp. 253–72.

Muriel Cantor, *The Hollywood TV Producer: His Work and His Audience* (New York: Basic Books) 1971.

James W. Carey, 'The communications revolution and the professional communicator' in *The Sociological Review Monograph 13*, 1969.

Rex Cathcart, 'The Independent Television Authority as an internal influence on programmes: a case history', Fourth symposium on broadcasting policy, Manchester, 1972.

Roland Cayrol, 'L'ORTF face aux élections de mars 1973: une étude d'observation du service politique de la première chaîne de télévision française', European Consortium for Political Research, Strasbourg, 29 March–April 1974.

Peter Clark, 'The multiplicity of time-reckoning systems in modern western industrial organisations' in R. Stoffle (ed.) *Human Aspects of Industrialisation* (Van Gorcum) 1976.

John Coatman, 'The BBC, Government and Politics', *Public Opinion Quarterly*, 1951, pp. 287–98.

Richard Collins, *Television News*, BFI Television Monograph No. 5 (London) 1976.

Lewis A. Coser, *Men of Ideas: a sociologist's view* (New York: The Free Press; London: Collier-Macmillan) 1965.

Lewis A. Coser, *Masters of Sociological Thought* (New York: Harcourt Brace Jovanovich) 1971.

W. F. Cottrell, 'Of time and the railroader', *American Sociological Review*, 1939, pp. 190–8.

Geoffrey Cox, 'News presentation in Britain' in A. William Bluem and Roger Manvell (eds.) *The Progress of Television: An Anglo-American Survey* (London and New York) 1967, pp. 132–7.

Sir Geoffrey Cox, 'Impartiality is not enough', *The Listener*, 20 May 1976.

Harold Cox, 'The television newsreel' in Paul Rotha (ed.) *Television in the making* (London: The Focal Press) 1956, pp. 88–94.

John Crawley, 'Censorship and the media', *Political Quarterly*, 1976, pp. 160–8.

Celia J. Croasdell, 'Women in the BBC', paper presented to the conference on 'Women and the mass media', BSA mass communications study group, December 1974.

Mary Crozier, *Broadcasting* (*Sound and Television*) (London: Oxford University Press) 1958.

Sir Charles Curran (1974a), 'Broadcasting and public opinion', *The Listener*, 20 June 1974.

Sir Charles Curran (1974b), 'Should we televise our enemies?', *The Listener*, 20 June 1974.

Sir Charles Curran (1976a), 'Reith and the General Strike', *The Listener*, 14 May 1976.

Sir Charles Curran (1976b), 'The BBC's policy on Northern Ireland', *The Listener*, 18 November 1976.

Robin Day, *Television: a personal report* (London: Hutchinson) 1961.

Robin Day, 'Troubled reflections of a TV journalist', *Encounter*, May 1970, pp. 78–89.

John Dearlove, 'The BBC and politicians, *Index*, Spring 1974, pp. 23–33.

Jonathan Dimbleby, *Richard Dimbleby: a biography* (London: Hodder and Stoughton) 1975.

Robert Dougall, *In and out of the box* (London: Collins and Harvill Press) 1973.

John Downing, 'Class and Race in the British News Media', paper delivered to the BSA mass communications study group, December 1971.

John Downing, 'Mass media as ideological state apparatuses', paper delivered to the BSA mass communications study group, March 1976.

Donald Edwards, *BBC News and Current Affairs*, BBC Lunchtime Lectures Series 2, 12 December 1964.

Philip Elliott, *The making of a television series: a case study in the sociology of culture* (London: Constable) 1972.

Philip Elliott, *Reporting Northern Ireland: a study of news in Britain, Ulster, and the Irish Republic* (University of Leicester: Centre for Mass Communication Research) 1976.

Edward Jay Epstein, *News from nowhere: television and the news* (New York: Random House) 1973.

E. E. Evans-Pritchard, *The Nuer* (Oxford) 1940.

Henry Fairlie, 'The BBC', in Hugh Thomas (ed.) *The Establishment* (London: Anthony Blond) 1959.

Robert Fisk, *The Point of No Return* (London: André Deutsch) 1975.

Eliot Friedson, *Profession of Medicine: a study of the sociology of applied knowledge* (New York: Dodd, Mead) 1971.

Johan Galtung and Mari Holmboe Ruge in Jeremy Tunstall (ed.) *Media Sociology: A Reader* (London, Constable) 1970, pp. 259–98.

Herbert J. Gans, 'The shaping of mass media content', expanded version of a paper given to the 1966 meetings of the American Sociological Association.

Herbert J. Gans, 'Broadcaster and audience values in the mass media: the image of man in American television news' in *Transactions of the Sixth World Congress of Sociology*, Evian, 4–11 September 1966 (International Sociological Association) 1970.

Lord Gardiner, *Report of a committee to consider, in the context of civil liberties and human rights, measures to deal with terrorism in Northern Ireland*, Cmnd. 5847 (London: HMSO) 1975.

Clifford Geertz, 'Ideology as a cultural system' in David E. Apter (ed.) *Ideology and Discontent* (New York: Free Press) 1964.

Ernest Gellner, 'Concepts and Society' in Dorothy Emmett and Alasdair MacIntyre (eds.) *Sociological theory and philosophical analysis* (London: Papermac) 1970.

H. H. Gerth and C. Wright Mills (eds.) *From Max Weber: Essays in Sociology* (London: Routledge and Kegan Paul) 1967.

Walter Gieber, 'How the "gatekeepers" view civil liberties news', *Journalism Quarterly*, 1960, pp. 199–205.

Walter Gieber and Walter Johnson, 'The city hall "beat": a study of reporter and source roles', *Journalism Quarterly*, 1961, pp. 289–97.

Walter Gieber, 'News is what newspapermen make it' in Lewis Anthony Dexter and David Manning White (eds) *People, Society and Mass Communications* (New York: The Free Press) 1964, pp. 173–80.

Glasgow University Media Group, *Bad News* volume 1 (London: Routledge and Kegan Paul) 1976.

Erving Goffman, *The presentation of self in everyday life* (Harmondsworth: Penguin) 1971.

Peter Golding and Philip Elliott, *Making the News* (University of Leicester: Centre for Mass Communication Research) 1976.

Maurice Gorham, *Broadcasting and Television since 1900* (London: Andrew Dakers) 1952.

Alvin W. Gouldner, *For Sociology* (Harmondsworth: Penguin) 1975.

Sir Hugh Greene, 'The BBC's duty to society – I'. *The Listener*, 17 June 1965.

Sir Hugh Greene, *The Third Floor Front: a view of broadcasting in the 'Sixties* (London: Bodley Head) 1969.

Harman Grisewood, *One thing at a time* (London: Hutchinson) 1968.

Georges Gurvitch, *The Spectrum of Social Time* (Dordrecht, Holland: D. Reidel) 1964.

Edward T. Hall, *The Silent Language* (New York: Doubleday) 1959.

Stuart Hall, 'The limitations of broadcasting', *The Listener*, 16 March 1972.

Stuart Hall, 'Deviance, politics, and the media' in Paul Rock and Mary McIntosh (eds) *Deviance and Social Control* (London: Tavistock Publications) 1974.

James D. Halloran, Philip Elliott, and Graham Murdock, *Demonstrations and Communication: a case study* (Harmondsworth: Penguin) 1970.

Nigel Harris, *Beliefs in society: the problem of ideology* (Harmondswor' Penguin) 1971.

Philip Harris, 'Authority and dependence: the international news m paper delivered to the BSA mass communications study group October 1976.

John Heeren, 'Karl Mannheim and the intellectual élite', *Briti of Sociology*, 1971, pp. 1–15.

Lord Hill, *Behind the Screen* (London: Sidgwick and Jackso'

Joachim Hirsch, *Wissenschaftlich-technischer Fortschritt System Organisation und Grundlagen administrativer foerderung in der BRD* (Frankfurt am Main: Suhrkar

Simon Hoggart, 'The army PR men of Northern Ireland', *New Society*, 11 October 1973, pp. 79–80.

Stuart Hood, *A Survey of Television* (London: Heinemann) 1967.

Morris Janowitz, 'Professional models in journalism: the gatekeeper and the advocate', *Journalism Quarterly*, 1975, pp. 618–26 and 662.

T. J. Johnson, *Professions and Power* (London and Basingstoke: Macmillan) 1972.

John W. C. Johnstone, Edward J. Slawski and William D. Bowman, 'The professional values of American newsmen', *Public Opinion Quarterly*, 1972–73, pp. 522–40.

Robert P. Judd, 'The newspaper reporter in a suburban city', *Public Opinion Quarterly*, 1961, pp. 35–42.

Krishan Kumar, 'Holding the middle ground: the BBC, the public, and the professional broadcaster', *Sociology*, 1975, pp. 67–88.

Kurt Lang and Gladys Engel Lang, *Politics and Television* (Chicago: Quadrangle Books) 1968.

Alvar Lidell, 'Here is the news', *The Listener*, 2 November 1972.

Tom Litterick, MP, 'The attitude of the BBC to its politically active staff journalists', House of Commons, 1976.

Stanford M. Lyman and Marvin B. Scott, *A sociology of the absurd* (New York: Appleton, Century, Crofts) 1970.

Donald McInnes, 'News by Radio', BBC Copyright, 1970.

F. R. MacKenzie, 'Eden, Suez and the BBC – a reassessment', *The Listener*, 18 December 1969.

F. R. MacKenzie, 'Lobbying', *The Listener*, 19 March 1970.

Joseph MacLeod, *A job at the BBC* (William MacLellan) 1947.

Denis McQuail, 'Uncertainty about the audience and the organization of mass communications' in *The Sociological Review Monograph 13*, 1969, pp. 75–84.

Karl Mannheim, *Ideology and Utopia* (London: Routledge and Kegan Paul) 1936.

John T. Marcus, 'Time and the sense of history: East and West', *Comparative Studies in Society and History*, 1960–61, pp. 123–39.

Aleksander Matejko, 'Newspaper staff as a social system' in Jeremy Tunstall (ed.) *Media Sociology* (London: Constable) 1970, pp. 168–80.

Leonard Miall (ed.) *Richard Dimbleby: broadcaster* (BBC) 1966.

Ralph Miliband, *The state in capitalist society* (London: Weidenfeld and Nicolson) 1969.

Wilbert E. Moore (1963a), 'The temporal structure of organizations' in Edward A. Tiryakian (ed.) *Sociological Theory, Values and Sociocultural Change* (London) 1963.

Wilbert E. Moore (1963b), *Man, Time and Society* (New York and London: John Wiley and Sons Inc.) 1963.

David Morley, 'Industrial conflict and the mass media', *The Sociological Review*, 1976, pp. 245–68.

Graham Murdock, 'Political deviance: the press presentation of a militant mass demonstration' in Stanley Cohen and Jock Young (eds) *The Manufacture of News: deviance, social problems and the mass media* (London: Constable) 1973.

Index

ABC (US), 91
Abercorn, Duke of, 207
ACTT, 214
accuracy, 15, 18, 20, 25, 26, 33, 38, 61, 89–91, 93, 113, 173, 177, 201, 221, 227
'action' film, 41
actuality, 31, 36, 52, 56, 58, 87, 95, 128–9, 164, 172, 200, 209, 262–7
Adam, Kenneth, 129
advertising, 40, 208
Agence France Presse (AFP), 60, 91
Aldershot, bombing at, 67
Alexandra Palace, 36, 39
Amin, Idi, 94–5, 101
Amoore, Derrick, 255, 256, 259
Annan Committee *Report*, *1977*, 241–2, 260, 271
Arabic Service, 24
Army, British, in Northern Ireland, 209, 210, 211–12, 215, 222–7, 240–3
assignments, allocation of, 150–2, 153, 162, 193
Associated Press (AP), 38, 60, 90–1
Associated Television (ATV), 89, 171
Association of Broadcasting Staffs (ABS), 157, 179, 189
audience: class structure, 33–4, 113, 133; grabbing, 41, 42, 103, 110, 208; intellectual level, 122, 133; interest, 116–25, 127, 130–4, 202; political, 171; reactions, 107–8, 114–23, 125, 133–4, 142, 156, 171, 202–3, 209, 223, 235, 236–8, 241, 256, 259, 265, 267; relationship with, 30, 31, 89, 101, 105, 106–34; research, 33, 34, 37, 38, 40, 110,

111–15, 125, 130–1, 133, 202, 255, 257, 259, 267, 271–2; size, 29, 32, 34, 37, 40, 44–5, 103, 111–14, 120, 124, 127, 133, 251, 255–6, 257, 262
Audience Research Department, 111–14, 125–6, 130–1, 255, 256, 262
Auld, Robin, 95, 97
authoritativeness, 41, 92, 156–7, 200, 202, 203, 264
Aviation Week, 93
Aylestone, Lord, 211, 213, 214, 243

background, 105, 121, 122, 245
balance *see* impartiality
Baldwin, Stanley, 16, 17, 18
Ballykinler, 223
Barnouw, Erik, 24, 29, 39
Bartlett, Vernon, 23
Barton, Michael, 188
BBC Club, 145, 194
BBC-1, 48, 57, 76, 95–6, 97, 122, 172, 175, 226, 255, 257, 258, 259
BBC-2, 48, 95–6, 97, 122, 172, 202, 254, 256, 257–8, 259, 264
Beadle, Sir Gerald, 207, 208
Belfast, 52, 214, 215, 219–20, 221, 225–7, 231, 232, 238
Bell, Martin, 232–3, 237
Berger, Peter, 85
Beria, Lavrenti, 93
Bernstein, Basil, 254
Beveridge Committee *Report*, *1952*, 137–8
bias: against understanding, 244; of BBC personnel, 23, 182–7, 195, 202, 204, 221–2; political,

bias – *cont.*
16–19, 143, 163, 165–7, 216, 221–3, 232–3
Birt, John, 244–5, 269
Blott, Eric, 185, 186
Blumler, Jay, 253–4
Board of Deputies of British Jews, 183
Board of Governors, 26, 35, 137–8, 139, 210, 219
Board of Management, 138, 140, 141
Bracken, Brendan, 30
briefings, 65–6, 68
Briggs, Asa, 16–17, 18, 19, 24, 25, 26, 27, 29, 30
Brighton Israel Friendship League, 183, 185
British Gazette, 18
Broadcast, 189
Broadcast over Britain (Reith), 19
Broadcasting Authority Act, 1960 (Eire), 218
Broadcasting House, 11, 36, 37, 38, 39, 47, 48, 51, 69, 70, 75, 76, 82, 190
Broadcasting in the Seventies (BBC), 248, 262, 266
Brookeborough, Lord, 208
'bunching', 104
Burns, Tom, 106, 200, 248
Burrage, Michael, 40
Bush House, 36, 69, 82, 190

CBS (US), 29, 69, 91
Caetano, Dr Marcello, 174, 176
Cahill, Joe, 210
Callaghan, James, 101, 142, 143
cameramen, 36, 41, 52, 64, 66, 67, 102, 160–1, 203
Canterbury, Archbishop of, 17, 35
Caradon, Lord, 215
Cardiff, David, 19, 28
career prospects, 150–2, 154, 155, 157, 181, 195, 197, 200
Carey, James W., 15
Carter, Jimmy, 143
'catchlines', 104, 122, 126

Cathcart, Rex, 208
censorship, 18, 25, 27, 31, 140, 148, 179, 205, 208, 211–13, 216, 218, 219, 231, 239, 241, 242–3
centralism *see* consistency
Chamberlain, Neville, 22, 28
Charter, Royal, 19, 123, 137, 193
Chataway, Christopher, 211–12, 218, 243
Churchill, Winston, 18, 23
Clark, R. T., 26
Coatman, John, 21, 23–4, 26, 139
Collins, Richard, 112
commercial radio, 14, 15, 19, 25, 37, 82, 85, 110, 112, 267
commercial television, 14, 32–3, 34, 39, 40–6, 82, 85, 88–9, 110–14, 202, 208, 248, 256, 260, 269, 272
commercialization, 40
communication, with the audience, 106–34
Communist Party, 166, 171
comprehensibility *see* intelligibility
Compton Committee *Report, 1971,* 223–4
conformity, 135, 149, 150, 161, 162, 180, 192–204, 205;
deviance from, 181–91, 192, 193, 195, 204, 243
consensus politics, 164–70, 205, 206, 211, 229
Conservative Party, 40, 50, 143, 166, 172–3, 176, 177, 187, 191, 215–16, 217, 234, 240
consistency, 32, 53, 66, 76, 140, 147, 149, 201
control, within the BBC, 12, 19, 32, 244, 268; *see also* editorial system, control *and* government, control
Controllers, 21, 31, 32, 86, 193, 195, 208, 210, 211, 214, 219, 221, 222, 231, 232, 238, 239, 257–8
controversy, 23, 43, 139, 169, 173–8, 180, 184, 186, 192, 193, 210, 219, 234

controversy committee, 23, 139
copy-tasters, 60–1, 81, 131, 264
correspondents: political, 154, 222; role and status of, 153–4, 203, 247
Coser, Lewis, 169
Couve de Murville, Maurice, 74
Cox, Harold, 36
Cox, Sir Geoffrey, 45, 128–9, 130, 167
Craigavon, Lord, 207
Crawford Committee *Report*, *1926*, 19
Crawley, John, 210, 217
credibility, 18, 46, 161, 164, 202, 204, 241
credits, 201
crises, role played by news during, 14, 24, 25, 29–30, 35–6, 45, 102, 113, 125, 205–43
criticism: by BBC staff, 267–70; by the press, 115, 261–2
Crozier, Mary, 113
Crystal Palace, 22
culture, national, place of BBC in, 14, 15, 18–20, 28, 31, 33–4, 45, 92, 134, 150, 201, 260
Culture and Society (Williams), 20
Curran, Sir Charles, 167, 189, 214, 216, 217, 228–9, 241
current affairs, 21, 23, 30, 42–6, 70, 72, 74–6, 81, 82, 89, 104, 108, 138–44, 150, 154, 155, 176–7, 179, 181, 191, 195, 200, 201, 203, 210–12, 215, 218, 244, 247–55, 263, 268–72

Daily Audience Barometer, 111
Daily Express, The, 92
Daily Mail, The, 92, 94, 199
Daily Mirror, The, 92, 94, 148
Daily Telegraph, The, 92, 216
Dalai Lama, 38
Day, Robin, 39, 41–2, 88, 129–30, 202
deadlines, 48, 52, 56, 66, 67, 80, 82, 84, 85, 88, 98, 100, 106, 109, 121, 197

Dearlove, J., 246
democracy, BBC commitment to, 163–70, 214, 236, 238, 239
demonstrations, 261
deployment, 51–2, 67, 69, 70, 74, 76–9, 80, 147, 153, 269
Devlin, Lord, 215
Dimbleby, Richard, 21, 22, 24, 30–1, 43
Director-General (DG), 27, 30, 33, 42, 135, 137, 138–44, 147, 148, 162, 165, 167, 181, 209, 210, 211, 212, 216, 228, 231, 236
Director of News and Current Affairs (DNCA), 140
Director of the Spoken Word (DSW), 139–40
disasters, 117, 118, 126
D-notices, 240
documentaries, 104, 107, 200, 211
Dublin, 49, 121, 220, 231, 233, 240, 251
duopoly, 34, 40, 80, 85, 110

Eastern Europe, news services, 92
Eden, Sir Anthony, 35
Editor, News and Current Affairs (ENCA), 138–46, 147, 148, 169, 172, 181, 183, 184, 186, 191, 192, 209, 210, 211, 214, 215, 217, 220, 222, 223, 224, 228, 231, 232, 261
editorial system: assignment allocation, 150–2, 153; control, 48–56, 135–62, 195–204, 205–43, 268; guidance, 50, 135, 137, 141, 144–8, 150, 159, 162, 212, 223, 242; hierarchy, 136, 137–62; inefficiency, 268–70; policies *see* policy; production, 48–82, 127, 171; responsibility, 146–9; sub-editing, 57–9, 61, 150–2, 263, 267, 268
'editorials' and 'editorializing', 17, 23
education, progressive, 95–8
educational role, 19–20, 33–4

Edwards, Donald, 89, 90
Eire, broadcasting, 218
Elliott, Philip, 47, 79, 80, 107,
    108, 133, 169, 209, 218, 230,
    235, 247
Ellis, Terry, 96–8
embargoes, 95, 97, 233, 239
Empire News Department, 22, 24
Entebbe airport raid, 93, 101, 121
entertainment value, 41–2, 116–23,
    249
Epstein, Edward Jay, 79, 80
Europe, 14, 22, 23–4, 27, 30–1, 32
European Commission of Human
    Rights, 223
European Court of Human
    Rights, 240
European Economic Community,
    193
European Parliament, 72
Eurovision, 50, 68–9, 71, 90, 91–2
Evening News, 259
Evening Standard, 95, 96, 97
exclusives, 89, 94, 248, 254
External Services, 69, 71, 78, 141
eye-witness accounts, 16, 20, 21,
    58, 175, 177

factuality, 15, 18, 46, 244, 245,
    249, 252, 253, 256, 271
Fairlie, Henry, 34
Farrell, Michael, 224
Faulkner, Brian, 216
Federation of Broadcasting
    Unions (FBU), 213–14, 243
Fenland Floods 1937, 22
film, 43, 56–8, 61, 66, 68–9, 70,
    80, 88, 90–7, 99, 128–32, 151,
    172, 176–8, 216
Film Department, 43
film industry, competition with, 36
film operations organizer, 66
finance, BBC, 14–15, 19–20, 22, 36,
    44, 69, 71–2, 91, 110, 111, 123,
    124, 147, 257, 262
financial affairs, 76, 78
Financial Times, The, 92
Finland, 245

First Report, 176
Fisk, Robert, 237, 238
'fixing', 70, 71, 82, 86
Forces' Programme, 28, 39, 33
foreign-language broadcasts, 24,
    25
foreign news, lack of interest in,
    117–18, 131
Foreign News Department, 68–9,
    71–5
Foreign Office, 23, 24, 25, 32, 36
Foster, Sir John, 215
France, 22, 27, 30–1, 266
Francis, Richard, 238–41, 242
Franco, General, 24
Free Communications Group,
    213, 268
free-lance work, 91
Frelimo, 74–5, 176
From Our Own Correspondent,
    203, 263
'front-line despatches', 31
Future Events Unit, 70
future planning, 69–75, 86, 102

Gainford, Lord, 17
Gans, Herbert, 115
Gardiner, Charles, 22
Gardiner Committee *Report, 1975*,
    219
Gaumont-British Film Company,
    36
Gellner, Ernest, 247
General Elections: 1966, 253–4;
    1974, 171, 191
general knowledge of newsmen,
    108–9, 161
General News Service (GNS), 60,
    80–2, 93
General Strike 1926, 14, 16–19,
    20, 22, 23, 25, 35, 45, 212, 243
'generic'-broadcasting, 28, 33
Germany, 14, 23, 24, 27, 28, 31
Glasgow, UDA in, 143
Goffman, Erving, 200, 201
Golding, Peter, 47, 79, 80, 218,
    247

good taste, 147, 198, 246, 259, 261, 272
Gorham, Maurice, 16, 26, 29
Gouldner, Alvin W., 164
government: effect of on growth of BBC, 12, 24; information policy, 14, 16, 17, 18, 26, 35 (*see also* propaganda); intelligence gathering, 24; pressures, 12, 15–17, 25–7, 36–6, 46, 91, 138, 178, 201, 205–7, 212, 215–19, 226–7, 229, 234–5, 241–3
Greene, Sir Hugh, 42, 138–9, 140, 165
Grisewood, Harman, 35, 139–40
Guardian, The, 92, 143, 224
Gurvitch, Georges, 83

Haddow, Mr, 96, 97
Haley, William, 33–4
Hall, Stuart, 167
Hardcastle, William, 200
Harris, Nigel, 168
Hastings, Father Adrian, 174–8
headlines, 62, 96, 104, 129
hierarchy, 136, 137–62
Hill, Lord, 138, 210, 212–14, 215–16, 218, 223, 240, 243
Hitler, Adolf, 24, 169
Hoggart, Simon, 224–5
Holden, Allen, 188
Hole, Tahu, 37, 38, 39
Home Service, 24, 26, 28, 33, 44, 113
Hood, Stuart, 39, 40
Howarth, David, 22
human interest stories, 38, 41, 42, 43, 117–23, 131

ideology: corporate, 37, 47, 56, 80, 90, 104–5, 112, 135, 150, 162, 163–204, 213–14, 268; cultural, 20, 33–4, 40, 86–7; political, 17–20, 24, 92, 169, 173
Ideology and Utopia (Mannheim), 169

illegal organizations, 227–31, 241–2
immediacy, 15, 28, 29, 30, 32, 37, 38, 41, 61, 80, 81, 82, 87–98, 100–105, 121, 158, 178, 225, 237, 248, 249, 254, 264
impartiality, 11, 12, 15, 16, 18, 20, 21, 44, 46, 163–204, 205–42, 245, 246, 267; *see also* objectivity
In Britain Now, 203
independence, 16–17, 18, 25, 26–7, 35–6, 45–6, 135–6, 147, 169, 178, 192, 201, 206, 212, 215–19, 242, 243, 245
Independent Broadcasting Authority (IBA), 85, 219, 242
Independent Television (ITV), 207, 217, 218, 244
Independent Television Authority (ITA), 40, 211, 212, 214
Independent Television News (ITN), 39, 41–2, 44, 45, 69, 79, 82, 85, 88–9, 97, 101, 103, 110–14, 124, 128, 129, 167, 176, 198, 201, 202, 245, 256, 260, 267, 272
India, 23
individuality *see* personalities
industrial news, 23, 70, 71, 76, 78, 92, 126, 150, 167
Information, Ministry of, 25, 26, 28, 29, 30, 31, 32
Inner London Education Authority (ILEA), 95, 97
innovation, 244–6, 255–67, 270–2
intelligence gathering, 24
intelligibility, 125–8, 264, 265
interpretation, 46, 47, 165, 213, 225, 226
interviewing, 21, 41, 43, 44, 86, 89, 96, 97, 99, 104, 129, 148, 171, 172, 192, 211, 214, 216, 224, 227–34, 250, 261
Intervision, 92
investigative reporting, 43, 47, 80, 204, 210, 235, 270, 272
Irish Republican Army (IRA), 205–43

Irish Times, 220

Jacob, Sir Ian, 139
Jay, Peter, 244–5, 269
Jay, Tony, 185, 186
Jewish Chronicle, 185
Johnson, T. J., 134

Kennedy, John, 129
Kinchin-Smith, Michael, 185, 186
Kumar, Krishan, 166, 201

Labour Party, 16, 28, 35, 36, 92,
    101, 145, 172–3, 176, 177, 187,
    190, 246
'Land Deals Affair', 148
Lang, Gladys, 164
Lang, Kurt, 164
language, use of, 62, 98, 125–6,
    149, 172, 225, 229–30, 259,
    260–1, 264, 272
lead stories, 57, 93, 99, 101, 110,
    120, 121, 250
legal considerations, 52, 53, 147,
    188, 190
Leicester, shooting incident in, 52
length of programmes *see* time,
    allocations
Levenberg, Dr S., 183
Liberal Party, 172, 187
Libya, 84
licence fees, 14–15, 111, 142, 143
Lidell, Alvar, 262
Light Programme, 30, 33, 44, 113
'light tail-piece', 42
lighting, 52, 64, 66, 70, 80
Lippmann, Walter, 122
Listener, The, 183, 188, 232–3
Litterick, Tom, 187
'live' material, 36, 56, 63, 64, 87,
    88, 128, 129, 262, 264
local stations, 52, 78, 81, 82, 93
logistics, 50–2, 53, 57, 66, 67, 71,
    72, 75, 82, 87, 88, 96
Londonderry, 49, 121, 206, 220,
    237
Luckmann, Thomas, 85
Lyman, Stanford M., 85

Lynch, Jack, 210

McCulloch, Denis, 21
MacDonald, Ramsay, 16, 35
MacGiolla, Tomas, 234
McKenna, Siobhan, 208
MacKenzie, Fergus R., 35–6,
    182–7
McLurg's Law, 117
McQuail, Denis, 106–7
MacShane, Denis, 187–90, 195
MacStiofain, Sean, 218
Maguire, Waldo, 208
Managing-Directors, 16, 17, 110
'mandatory' stories, 124
Mannheim, Karl, 169–70
manpower, 20, 22, 28, 29, 31, 32,
    58, 76, 77, 78–9, 143, 269
Marshall, G. L., 207
Mason, Roy, 238–9, 240, 242, 243
Maudling, Reginald, 188, 212,
    216, 217, 218, 242
Maynard, Joan, 234
Meir, Golda, 182
Midday News, 259
Middle East, 31, 182–7
Midweek, 72, 176–7, 254
Miliband, Ralph, 165
ministerial broadcasts, 35–6, 145
'mirror of reality', 164
monitoring, 93, 108, 111, 112, 124,
    139, 254
Monitoring Service, 24, 60
monopoly, 14–16, 19, 20, 32, 34,
    40, 80
moral values, 165, 212
morale boosting, 25, 26, 241
Morgan, Ken, 189
Morning Star, The, 92
Movietone, 36
Mozambique, 74–5, 173–8
Munich Crisis 1938, 22, 25
Mussolini, Benito, 24

Nasser, President, 38, 60, 93
National Front, 171–3
'national interest', 24, 27, 28, 51,
    166, 205, 216, 228–9, 239, 241

national security, 29–30, 46
National Union of Journalists
 (NUJ), 157, 179, 182, 184–90,
 195, 258, 259, 268
Nationwide, 143, 254
'natural sound', 104, 129, 262
NBC (US), 91
Neave, Airey, 240–1, 243
New Statesman, 213, 214–15, 223
news agencies: competition, 14,
 28; material from, 15, 16, 19,
 20, 21, 28, 38, 45, 52, 57, 60–1,
 67, 70, 72, 80, 82, 90–1, 93, 94,
 95, 160, 172, 177, 214, 221, 234,
 262; professionalism, 15, 38, 46;
 see also specific agencies
News and Newsreel, 37, 38, 43
news angles, 50–1, 104, 109, 135,
 252
News at Ten, 44, 101, 103, 111,
 112, 256
News Chronicle, 23
News Departments, 21, 24, 28,
 49–82, 99, 102, 110–14, 128,
 135, 153, 158, 171, 178, 192,
 232, 244, 246, 248, 253, 254,
 255, 259, 262
news diaries, 50, 52, 53, 56, 57, 66,
 67, 68–70, 80, 102, 153, 253
News Division, 29, 32, 36, 37, 40,
 42–3, 47, 75, 76, 89, 154, 155,
 157, 161, 181, 197, 198, 201,
 254, 258, 268
'news explosion', 43–4, 46
News Extra, 122, 177, 257–8, 272
News Guide (BBC), 79, 90, 98, 107,
 124, 127, 214, 260
news intake, 66–75, 81, 91, 95,
 108
news magazines, 43, 44, 248, 249
news observers, 22, 24, 30–1, 32
news organizers, 66–70, 94, 153,
 172, 225, 227, 237, 253, 254, 269
News Section, 21
News Service, 25
'news talks' *see* 'talks'
news values, 36–8, 41–2, 45, 51,
 56, 57, 60–1, 64, 68, 70, 72, 74,

83, 88, 91, 98–100, 109, 111,
 116–34, 135, 157–8, 165, 176–7,
 195, 206, 220, 233, 234, 246,
 252, 266, 270, 271
Newsbeat, 154, 252, 269
newsbreaks, 64, 82, 85, 94, 100,
 159
newscasters, 41, 101, 156; *see also*
 newsreaders
Newsday, 151, 257
newsdays, 48–56, 66, 85, 87, 98,
 102, 104, 121, 132, 252, 253,
 259
Newsdesk, 252, 269
newsflashes, 82, 101
news-gathering, 15, 16, 19, 21, 29,
 30, 41, 43, 53, 56, 57–8, 66, 67,
 70, 75–82, 93, 155
Newsnight, 257
newsreaders, 56, 58, 61–2, 64,
 103–4, 159, 200, 255–6, 259;
 anonymity of, 29–30, 37, 262;
 delivery and timing, 98–9, 270;
 impartiality of, 201;
 personalization of, 30, 37, 39,
 41, 44, 116, 202; role of, 29, 63,
 127, 202, 262–3, 265; women as,
 156–7
newsreels, 21, 36, 38–9, 41
Newsroom, 256, 264
newsworthiness *see* news values
Nigeria, civil war, 181
Nine O'Clock News (radio), 29,
 32, 44
Nine O'Clock News (tv), 44, 48,
 64, 97, 101, 104, 111, 156, 173,
 202, 255–7, 258, 259
Nixon, Richard, 72; *see also*
 Watergate
Normanbrook, Lord, 138
North Africa campaign, 27
Northern Ireland, 12, 35, 46, 49,
 52, 59, 91, 102, 121, 123–4, 126,
 132, 140, 143, 147, 150, 167,
 192, 205–43, 268

objectivity, 15, 164, 165, 171, 204,
 235, 249; *see also* impartiality

Observer, The, 224
O'Connell, David, 228, 233
official secrets, 150
Ogilvie, F. W., 27
Olympic Games 1976, 51
on-location filming, 43
on-the-spot reporting, 22, 30, 44,
    56, 87, 91, 225, 264
Open Secret, 213
Oppenheim, Sally, 143
outside broadcasts (ob's), 22, 31,
    36, 63, 67, 70, 87, 141, 159,
    254
Overseas Service, 22, 27, 29, 30,
    36
oversetting, 64

pace, 103–4
Palestine, 182–7
Panorama, 43, 72, 209, 253
parliamentary proceedings, 19,
    142
party conferences, 152
paternalism, 19–20, 106, 199
Paulu, Burton, 22, 37–8, 42, 45
People's Democracy, 224
PEP report, 1971, 155, 156
personal commitment, and
    impartiality, 191–204, 205
personalities, 30, 37, 39, 41, 43,
    81, 97, 149, 152, 154
phone-ins, 188–9
pictorial values, 36–9, 42, 71, 91,
    127, 128–32, 270
Pilkington Committee *Report,
    1962*, 43
Platform, 188
PM, 251
police, 64, 142, 193, 225, 240, 241
Police Federation of Northern
    Ireland, 241
policy, 16–17, 20, 28–34, 45, 49,
    76, 90, 93, 135, 138, 140, 141,
    146, 148, 206–43, 270
political correspondents, 154
Political Warfare Executive, 26
politics: extremist, 166, 208–43;
    party, 152, 167–8, 171–8, 181,

187, 191; party political
    broadcasts, 23, 191; political
    conduct of newsmen, 178–204,
    221–2, 246; *see also* audience,
    political; bias, political;
    consensus politics; government;
    ideology, political;
    parliamentary proceedings;
    satire, political *and* time,
    allocation to political parties
populism, 28, 31, 34, 41, 44, 45, 46
Portugal, 74–5, 91, 152, 173–8
post-mortems *see* retrospective
    reviews
Post Office, licence to broadcast,
    14–15, 19
predictability of news, 69, 70, 79,
    80, 87, 102
presentation, 41–2, 45, 46, 103,
    132–3, 135, 201
press: censorship, 27; competition,
    14, 15, 16, 25, 28–9, 31, 32, 38,
    85, 98, 112; criticisms, 115,
    261–2; ideology, 163; material,
    57, 60, 61, 67, 70, 80, 85, 87,
    90–8, 108–9, 121, 126, 127, 129,
    155, 172, 177, 240; newsmen,
    197, 199; restrictions on news
    programmes, 15, 16, 20, 21, 22,
    25, 28, 45; role, 167; *see also*
    specific newspapers
Press Association (PA), 52, 60, 67,
    82, 91, 95, 97, 98, 172, 177
pressure groups, 44, 51, 143, 182
*Principles and Practice in News
    and Current Affairs* (BBC), 141–2,
    165, 200, 203, 209–10
Private Eye, 145, 210, 224
problem stories, 52–3, 131, 133,
    143, 147, 150
producers, 32, 53, 98, 107, 127, 128
Production Operations Assistants
    (POA's), 157–8
professionalism, 82, 86, 88, 89,
    105, 150–2, 157, 164, 178, 180,
    204, 221, 229, 263, 264, 266, 267;
    and the audience, 106–34;
    deviance from, 181–93, 195, 204

promotion, 150–2, 154, 155, 157, 181, 195, 197, 200, 263, 265, 266

propaganda, 18, 24–8, 72, 92, 211, 219, 223, 228–9, 232, 234, 237, 239, 240

public interest *see* 'national interest'

public order, 209, 222–43

public relations (PR), 25–7, 67, 70, 210, 224, 225–7, 260, 261

public service role of news, 107, 110, 123–5, 197, 204, 245

Question of Ulster, The, 206, 215–19, 239, 242, 243

racial matters, 51, 53, 142, 143, 150, 165, 166, 172, 173, 182–7, 188–9

Radio London, 187, 188, 269

radio news, development of, 14–34, 43–4

Radio Newsreel, 30, 263

Radio 1, 48, 122

Radio 2, 48, 122

Radio 3, 48, 122, 265

Radio 4, 48, 57, 75–6, 114, 122, 248, 262

Radio Telefis Eireann (RTE), 218–19, 229

Radio Times, 98, 115

ratings, 33, 40, 110, 111, 257

rationalization, staff, 76

recordings, 21, 29, 31, 53, 56, 58, 59, 62, 64, 69, 71, 148, 158, 172, 214, 228, 231, 233; *see also* videotape

Rees, Merlyn, 238

regional newsrooms, 71, 81, 82, 93, 207

rehearsals, 62, 63, 86

Reid, Jimmy, 59

Reith, John, 16, 17–18, 19–20, 21, 25, 28, 33, 34, 40, 45, 46, 137, 138, 140, 146, 197, 212, 260

Relative Standing of the BBC News and ITN, 1973, 113

reliability, 25, 89–93, 113, 147, 150–2, 155, 162, 194, 202–3

religious affairs, 23, 76, 78, 163, 208

reporters, role and status of, 153–4

'representative newsroom theory', 196

responsibility, 15, 25, 26, 123–5, 129, 137, 146–9, 158, 163, 179, 203, 212, 213, 218, 223, 234–42, 261, 270

Restricted and unrestricted staff, 179–80

retrospective reviews, 141, 147–8, 162, 173, 226

Reuter, 60, 90, 91

revenue, 14–15, 111

Review of the Year 1930 (BBC), 21

Rippon, Angela, 156

role of the BBC, 14, 19–20, 24, 25, 26, 28, 33–4, 45, 110, 123, 163–70, 178–204

Royal Family, 16, 37, 67, 76, 109, 118–19, 142, 155, 261

Royal Ulster Constabulary (RUC), 240, 241

running order, 57, 59, 60, 61, 63, 64, 65, 67, 99, 111, 149, 159; *see also* sequences

running stories, 102

running times *see* time, allocations

Ryan, A. P., 27, 31, 32

Rydbeck, Erik, 143

satellites, communication, 43, 50, 68, 69, 71, 72, 124

satire, political, 246, 272

Scannell, Paddy, 19, 27–8

Scarman Committee *Report, 1972*, 237

schedules, 110

scoops, 29, 37, 38, 80, 88, 177

Scott, Marvin B., 85

script-writing, 58, 64, 96

Second Front, 22, 27, 30–1, 32
Second World War, 14, 21–32,
 35, 45, 202
'selling' stories, 71, 72
sensationalism, 20, 91
sequences, 100, 101, 103–4, 126–7,
 132–3, 159, 251, 252; *see also*
 running order
'seven-o'clock rule', 15, 16, 20
Simon of Wythenshawe, Lord, 33
 34, 40, 41, 139
Sinn Fein, 229, 234
'six-o'clock rule', 20, 28
Smith, Anthony, 43, 207–8, 209
Smith, Ian, 138
Soares, Dr, 174
social order, BBC commitment to,
 163–70, 246
'soft stories', 155
sound reproduction, 52, 66, 104,
 129, 158, 159, 160, 262, 266
South of the Border, 211
Spain, 24, 91
Spectator, 182–6
Spector, David, 183, 185
'speculation' stories, 94–5
sport, 16, 21, 67, 70, 78, 125, 252
'spot news', 72, 80, 101–2
staff regulations, 179, 182–7
Standing, Michael, 31
Stansted Airport, 93–5
state *see* government
status, 153–6, 199, 254, 263
Stephen, Andrew, 224
stills, 38, 39, 56, 61, 65, 69, 96, 97,
 130, 172
strikes, 17–18, 124–5, 126, 166,
 238; BBC, 187, 189–90; *see also*
 General Strike
'stringers', 75, 78, 91
Stuart, Douglas, 38, 39
studio directors, 51, 62, 63, 64, 65,
 99, 159, 160, 201
sub-editors *see* editorial system,
 sub-editors
Suez crisis 1956, 35–6, 38, 46, 113,
 217
Sun, The, 92

Sunday Times, 241
Swallow, Norman, 44, 165–6
Swann, Sir Michael, 138, 238–9
Sweden, 15, 79
Sykes Committee *Report, 1923*,
 15–16, 23

'talking heads', 129–30
'talks', 22, 23, 30, 139, 251
Talks Departments, 21, 42–3
tape recordings *see* recordings
Task of Broadcasting News, The
 (GAC), 92
Tass, 60
Taylor, Charles, 164
Taylor, Desmond, 183, 184, 209,
 215, 217, 220–1, 224, 228, 236
technical factors, 22, 29, 30, 31,
 37, 43, 51–2, 62, 63–4, 65, 70,
 71, 80, 130
technical staff, 157–61, 162
telecine machines, 62, 159
telephone system, 22, 53, 67
teleprinters, 53, 60, 82
Television Act, 1954, 40, 110, 208
Television Centre, 11, 47, 48, 62,
 65, 70, 75, 82, 111, 189, 253,
 258
Television Film Department, 36
television news, development of,
 32–4, 36–42
Television Talks Department, 42–3
Ten O'Clock, 44
terrorism, 205, 211, 212, 219, 223,
 229–30, 234, 239, 240, 241, 243
Thatcher, Margaret, 50, 143, 172
Third Programme, 33
Thurrock by-election, 171–3
time: allocation on radio, 14–16,
 20–2, 25, 48, 248–50; allocation
 on television, 37, 48, 63, 64,
 255, 258; allocation to political
 parties, 23, 143, 171–3; factors
 in production, 83–106, 121, 126,
 148, 158, 159, 227; *see also*
 deadlines *and* immediacy
Times, The, 44, 45, 92, 173–4, 190

time-slots, 58, 87, 90, 96, 98–100, 101, 103, 249, 269–70
time-values, 98–100, 101
Tindall, David, 97
'tip-offs', 57, 70, 82, 88, 91, 93, 94–5
Today, 44
Today in Parliament, 34
Today Programme, 143, 248
Todd, Andrew, 255, 258–62
Tonight, 43, 208, 240–1, 257
topicality, 15, 249, 254
Tracey, Dick, 187
Tracey, Michael, 17, 18, 43, 89, 107, 138, 171, 246, 254
trades unions, 17, 187–8, 195, 213–14; *see also* National Union of Journalists
Trades Unions Congress (TUC), 17, 35, 70, 76
transmission, 63–6
24 Hours, 89, 124, 138, 210–11, 253, 254
TV Times, 98
'two agency rule', 90

UDA, 143, 228, 231, 233
UFF, 228
Ullswater Committee *Report, 1935*, 22, 24
Ulster Television (UTV), 207, 208
Ulster Workers' Council (UWC), 238, 239, 242–3
Underhill, Reg, 172
United Press International (UPI), 60, 90–1
United States: broadcasting, 29, 31, 69, 91; commercial radio, 15, 25, 37; correspondents in, 77, 78–9; Mrs Thatcher in, 50; news agencies, 38, 60, 90–1; press, 15, 29, 93–4; television, 39–40, 44, 79, 80, 103, 115, 131, 165–6; *see also* Watergate
up-dating, 59–61, 67, 87
UVF, 210–11, 228, 231

value-freedom *see* impartiality
videotape (vt), 56, 58, 59, 65, 68, 69, 71, 128, 159, 254
Vietnam, 69, 117, 151, 235, 266
violence, 44, 142, 147, 205–39
Visnews, 69, 91
visual material, 56, 58, 62, 65, 67, 103, 160, 260–1; *see also* pictorial values
voice reports, 69, 262–7, 270

War Office, 31
War Report, 32, 263
War Reporting Unit, 31, 33
Watergate, 72, 74, 101, 102, 104, 118, 124, 254
Watson, Alan, 187
Weber, Max, 84, 146
Wedell, E. G., 138, 147
Westminster, political staff at, 63, 154
Wheldon, Huw, 110
Whitelaw, William, 187, 226, 228
William Tyndale School, 95–8, 105
Williamo, massacre at, 173–8
Williams, Marcia (Lady Falkender), 148
Williams, Raymond, 19, 20, 85
Wilson, H. H., 40
Wilson, Harold, 101, 138, 145, 148
Winchester, Simon, 224
women staff, 154–7
Woon, Peter, 182, 262–7
World at One, The, 44, 210, 248, 250–1, 252, 263, 269
World in Action, 211
World Service, 30, 109
World this Weekend, The, 74
World Tonight, The, 248, 249, 250
World War II *see* Second World War
Wright, Alan, 241
Wyndham-Goldie, Grace, 42–3

Yesterday's Men, 246

191 Dud Lam